THE EMPIRE
of
GOD

PART II

THE EMPIRE

of

GOD

The Imperial Anointing

Part II

THE HIGHEST ANOINTING IN THE KINGDOM

DAVID E. TAYLOR

JOSHUA MEDIA MINISTRIES INTERNATIONAL
PO Box 1270 Florissant, MO 63031

For more information on ordering products (books, CDs, DVDs, etc.) from David E. Taylor, and for information on the next Miracles in America Crusades happening around the world, call 877-843-4567.

Or visit on the Internet: www.joshuamediaministries.org

ISBN 13: 978-1-940657-66-0

ISBN 10: 1-940657-66-0

For Worldwide Distribution, Printed in the U.S.A.

Dedication

To Jesus, my Best Friend
who is the very reason for my being,
who has stood with me through
the darkest times of my life.
To the person of the Holy Spirit,
Who is also my Friend and closest companion.

Table of Contents

CHAPTER 6
Seven Divine Emperors

CHAPTER 6
Seven Divine Emperors

The Office of the Emperor

Now I must share with you more about the office of the emperor. The emperor is an office just as the king is an office. The emperor far outranks the king because where the king rules over a kingdom and principalities, the emperor rules over entire worlds and all kingdoms! The words of an emperor are much more powerful than the words of a king.

Signs of an Empire

The Lord revealed to me seven divine emperors in the Bible that walked in the office of the emperor. These were not just natural kings they were divine eternal kings with spiritual power to impact and influence the whole world! You must also understand the difference between natural and divine emperors. Natural kings and emperors only operate in the natural realm of the Earth and do not have any power that extends beyond this realm. To recognize these spiritual and divine emperors, these are nine signs you need to look for:

1. **Divine Emperors Have Direct Dealings with God the Father Himself** God has face to face contact with them. As a result, their

lives affect and influence the whole world! This means that they have a direct covenant and working relationship with the Godhead. Divine emperors are also pontiffs that have power to bring God down on the Earth, whether presently or in the future!

2. **Divine Emperors are Princes with God and Sons of God** They are not just kings unto God, they are princes with God. Princes with God are even more powerful than kings of kings. Jesus, for example, is called in Revelation 1, the *"Prince of the Kings of the Earth."*

3. **Divine Emperors Have *"The Power of One"*** When a man attains this status, God swears by them! God deals with the whole world through them. Anything that affects them affects the whole world! When God gives you the power of one, He is prepared to destroy everything and everyone and start all over with you!

4. **Divine Emperors are Given World Assignments** Divine emperors have global mandates from the Father. They are a blessing to the whole world! Their life and ministry affects all people, nations, and languages. They are therefore multicultural in perspective. Whenever God wants to do something around the whole world, He connects with a divine emperor to do it.

5. **Divine Emperors are Established as Eternal Authorities with Worlds to Rule Over for All of Eternity** Many of the kings God appointed on the Earth never made it into the eternal kingdom realm. For example, God rejected Saul from entering this realm because he could not obey Him. David, on the other hand, and the apostles of Christ were made eternal kings.

6. **Divine Emperors Have Powers from Above to Rule the Earth** Divine emperors walk in great power with God to execute His will on the Earth with miracles signs and wonders.

7. **Divine Emperors are Birther of Kings** Kings give birth to princes, and emperors give birth to kings. Consequently, kings are given power over prince demons, and emperors have power over king demons! God established these royal identities so that you can outrank overcome and break demonic ranks in Satan's kingdom! As a king, God gives you royal assignments to take out demonic princes. But to take out demonic kings you need the rank and office of the emperor!

8. **Divine Emperors Reign Over All the Kings of the Earth** They are high kings who are exalted higher than all the kings of the Earth!

9. **Divine Emperors Have Divine Power and Authority to Kill** Like "Double 007" of the James Bond movies, divine emperors have license from God to kill. Divine emperors have so much weight and power that God will destroy everything and everyone for them

These are the seven divine emperors the Bible talks about: Adam, Noah, Abraham, Moses, David, Jesus, and Peter.

The First Divine Emperor: Adam

*"And God said, Let us make man in our image, after our likeness: **and let them have dominion** over the fish of the sea, and over the fowl of the air, and over the cattle, and over all the earth, and over every creeping thing that creepeth upon the earth"* (Genesis 1:26).

Adam, the first man God created in our civilization, is the first divine emperor. When God made Adam, He made him a prince, and that is why He crowned him with glory and honor and put all his works under Adam's dominion. Adam was the prince of the whole world. God gave him dominion over all the Earth. All creation was subject to him. Many do not realize this, but Adam had a spiritual crown given to him as the emperor of the world. The Bible says, *"... and hast crowned him with glory and honour."* Adam was God's crown on the Earth. *"Thou shalt also be a crown of glory in the hand of the LORD, and a royal diadem in the hand of thy God"* (Isaiah 62:3). God put a spiritual crown on Adam's head. The Bible speaks of this in Psalms,

> *"For thou hast made him a little lower than the angels, and **hast crowned him with glory** and honour. **Thou madest him to have dominion** over the works of thy hands; thou hast put all things under his feet"* (Psalm 8:5-6).

These verses are speaking of Adam. Adam had a crown. He was crowned with glory and honor. You've got to understand that Adam reigned and ruled over the whole Earth. Adam had dominion over everything God created on the Earth! His dominion was not limited to the Earth only. Adam's dominion stretched from the sun, moon, and stars in the Heavens, all the way down to the Earth! (Psalm 8:3-8). All of that was under Adam's dominion. That word dominion is a Kingdom word. This means God crowned Adam as emperor or the king over all other kings of the whole Earth. The crown God gave Adam represents reigning power and has glory and honor in it. The glory in the crown is the glory of the kingdoms. It is what he reigns over. And this was not just the crown of a King, the Adamic crown was really the crown of an emperor!

When you see the crown of an emperor, you are not just talking about one crown, it is really a crown of many crowns because the emperor rules over all kings and their kingdoms! That is why John saw Jesus in Revelation 19 with many crowns on his head. There is a level of glory in those crowns, and you got to know what is in the crown to know what you have power to rule over! Psalm 8 reveals the reigning power in the Adamic crown.

> *"When I consider thy heavens, the work of thy fingers, the moon and the stars, which thou hast ordained; **Thou madest him to have dominion over the works of thy hands;** thou hast put all things under his feet. All sheep and oxen, yea, and the beasts of the field; The fowl of the air, and the fish of the sea, and whatsoever passeth through the paths of the seas"* (Psalm 8:3, 6-8).

In that Adamic crown was dominion over the *"heavens, the work of thy fingers, the moon and the stars."* In that crown was also dominion over all the beast of the Earth and the birds of the air. That is why all divine emperors have great power over creation. The animals came to Adam to be named, the animals came to Noah to be placed in the ark, Moses performed powerful miracles with frogs, locusts, and flies, Abraham had huge flocks of animals, animals in the forest fought for David against Absalom, and the fish gave Jesus money to pay His taxes! The glory in the crown was to command animals and all the works of God's hands! Creation is waiting for these divine emperors and sons of God to rise up again to command it.

"For the earnest expectation of the creature waiteth for the manifestation of the sons of God" (Romans 8:19).

Adam was a Prince with God

Adam had so much power and dominion that we see all the animals lining up to him to be named. This is because as a Prince you get named by God himself, and you also have power to name or to give identity and function to everything in your domain. A prince with God is actually an emperor who rules over worlds! We see this also with Jacob. After Jacob wrestled all night with the angel of God he finally got blessed when the angel said to him, *"… Thy name shall be called no more Jacob, but Israel: **for as a prince hast thou power with God** and with men, and hast prevailed"* (Genesis 32:28). Jacob as a prince got a new name and had power to work with God! Jacob was renamed Israel because he was now a prince to God. In this realm of dominion, when you become a prince with God you get named and you also get the authority to name!

Adam was therefore the prince of the World. Jesus also had power to name because he was a prince with God, as the last Adam. In this capacity, Jesus renamed Simon, James, and John. In Luke 6 we see Jesus walking in this realm.

*"And it came to pass in those days, that he went out into a mountain to pray, and continued all night in prayer to God. And when it was day, he called unto him his disciples: and of them he chose twelve, **whom also he named apostles**; Simon, (**whom he also named Peter,**) and Andrew his brother, James and John, Philip and Bartholomew"* (Luke 6:12-14).

After praying all night, Jesus selected twelve of His disciples *"whom also he named apostles."* He gave them a title and commissioned them in that title to represent him all over Israel. He also renamed Simon, *"whom he also named Peter."* Jesus gave new surnames to James and John as the Bible says, *"And James the son of Zebedee, and John the brother of James; **and he surnamed them Boanerges**, which is, The sons of thunder"* (Mark 3:17) In other words, Jesus gave new names. When you know your princeship you have authority to name.

Adam, a Birther of Kings

Adam was the Father of all living and kings were to come out of him just like how God told Abraham, *"And I will make thee exceeding fruitful, and I will make nations of thee, **and kings shall come out of thee"** (Genesis 17:6). God said this to Abraham, but you see God was really just re-establishing the original covenant he made with Adam. God made this original covenant with Adam as the Bible says,

*"And God blessed them, and God said unto them, **Be fruitful, and multiply**, and replenish the earth, and subdue it: and have dominion over the fish of the sea, and over the fowl of the air, and over every living thing that moveth upon the earth"* (Genesis 1:28).

Adam was to populate and fill up the Earth with his seed. As a divine emperor, he was to replenish the Earth and birth multiple kings that would rule over the kingdoms of the world. This is one powerful grace that divine emperors walk in. All God needs to populate a world is just one divine emperor! God takes just one man and fills the Earth with that person. God told Adam he was to be fruitful and multiply and replenish or repopulate the whole Earth. God did the same with Noah. God told Noah he was to multiply and fill the Earth after He destroyed every living person on Earth.

Adam's Direct Dealings with God

Adam as a divine emperor had direct dealings with God the Father himself! God would come down in the cool of the day, every morning, to visit him and work with him. *"What is man ... **that thou shouldest visit him every morning...**"* (Job 7:17-18). You see, Adam as a son of God worked directly with the Father. Jesus explains this father-son relationship when He said, *"Verily, verily, I say unto you, **The Son can do nothing of himself, but what he seeth the Father do:** for what things soever he doeth, these also doeth the Son likewise"* (John 5:19). You see the Father working closely with His son even in the naming of the animals.

*"And out of the ground the LORD God formed every beast of the field, and every fowl of the air; **and brought them unto Adam to see what he would call them:** and whatsoever Adam called every living creature, that was the name thereof. **And Adam gave names to all cattle, and to the fowl of the air, and to every beast of the field;** but for Adam there was not found an help meet for him"*
(Genesis 2:19-20).

Do you see how God worked with his son Adam? Adam was God's crown on the Earth! When Adam was in his rightful position, the animals came to him to be named. He did not go calling them. He did not put out a summoning for the animals. The animals knew to come to Him. They recognized the crown on his head! Creation recognizes sons of God as the Bible says, *"For the earnest expectation of the creature waiteth for the manifestation of the sons of God"* (Romans 8:19). That is why the animals came to Adam to be named.

When God made Adam, He did not make him a baby, He created Adam as a full grown man, a full son. The creation loves that. They love when sons of God come into manifestation. However, because a lot of us

17

do not come into our sonship, we can hardly get the beasts of the Earth to obey us. We can't make a tiger sit down. Well, they will sit down if you know sonship! In the next book in the Kingdom Series, I teach on the office of Sonship. After you master this revelation about your identity as an emperor, you need to get that next, because that will take your emperorship to the next dimension!

The Contest of Kings: Adam vs. Satan

Adam was given dominion over all the Earth. As a Prince with God, he had a global mandate to reign and rule over the Earth. He had the crown to rule over the whole Earth. He was to dress and keep it. Now Satan wanted that Adamic crown. That is why Jesus commands us, *"Behold, I come quickly: hold that fast which thou hast, that no man take thy crown"* (Revelation 3:11). Satan wants your crown! You need to know what to do to keep it and not lose it. You must understand that there is a major controversy over your kingship. Satan dreads you ever coming into your kingship! He knows that is the only realm that can effectively confront and break him! It takes a king to confront a king. And you have to understand how Satan used the serpent to win the crown from Adam. Satan used the wisdom of the serpent to win this contest of kings!

"Now the serpent was more subtil than any beast of the field which the LORD God had made. And he said unto the woman, Yea, hath God said, Ye shall not eat of every tree of the garden?" (Genesis 3:1).

You first have to understand that the snake was not an evil animal in the beginning. God made him the wisest beast in the garden. Satan chose the serpent because he understood the power of wisdom! The Bible records that Satan was full of wisdom. *"...Thou sealest up the sum, **full of wisdom,** and perfect in beauty"* (Ezekiel 28:12). Satan knew that the best strategic point to get man to sin was to outflank him by deceiving the woman through the wisest beast - the serpent. The snake was wiser than all the beasts of the field which made him the best candidate for Satan's wicked plan.

Satan knew that to win the contest of kings battle with Adam he had to use wisdom. The Bible says, *"Wisdom strengtheneth the wise more than ten mighty men which are in the city"* (Ecclesiastes 7:19). Being full of wisdom himself, Satan knew it takes wisdom to take a city. The Bible talks about a poor wise man in the Bible who through wisdom delivered a city.

*"There was a little city, and few men within it; and there came a great king against it, and besieged it, and built great bulwarks against it: Now there was found in it a poor wise man, **and he by his wisdom delivered the city;** yet no man remembered that same poor man"* (Ecclesiastes 9:14-15)

You take cities by wisdom. *"A wise man scaleth the city of the mighty, and casteth down the strength of the confidence thereof"* (Proverbs 21:22). It takes a wise person to break a city and take it over! All it took to deliver the city from a great king was a *"poor wise man."* Deliverance does not just take place by laying hands and seeing green stuff come out of people. Deliverance is also accomplished through strategic points of wisdom. Satan gained the whole world through a strategic point of wisdom. That is why the Bible says that wisdom is the principal thing!

Adam Loses the Crown to the Serpent

Satan possessed the serpent and through subtlety seduced Eve and convinced her to disobey God. The word "subtle" is prefixed by the Latin word "Sub" meaning *under.* The word "subtle" gives you the idea of operating from underneath or from below. The snake can always see and sense you before you can sense it. This is because the serpent's wisdom is to stay low to the ground so he can see everything around you. The wisdom of the serpent is termed "subtlety" which is a form of humility. We are high walking above on the ground and snakes are low on the ground and as a result they can see us before we see them.

You know how the story goes. Eve ate the fruit, and if you notice the eyes of Adam and Eve were not opened until Adam also ate the fruit. The moment Adam ate the fruit, their eyes were opened. At that very moment Adam yielded his dominion to Satan and started serving another kingdom, Satan's kingdom. Satan was now his master. That is why the Bible says,

*"Know ye not, **that to whom ye yield yourselves servants to obey, his servants ye are to whom ye obey;** whether of sin unto death, or of obedience unto righteousness?"* (Romans 6:16).

*"And the devil, taking him up into an high mountain, shewed unto him **all the kingdoms of the world** in a moment of time. And the devil said unto him, All this power will I give thee, and the glory of them: **for that is delivered unto me;** and to whomsoever I will I give it"* (Luke 4:5-6)

By eating the fruit, Adam was unwittingly obeying and submitting to Satan's voice. That was very tragic because a divine emperor has the Power of One. Everything a divine emperor does, affects all mankind. When Adam started submitting to Satan, his dominion and everything he reigned over was delivered to the devil. That is why Satan told Jesus in Luke 4 that all the kingdoms had been delivered over to him. And from that moment Satan's kingdom began to take over and fill up what was Adam's dominion. Paul reveals what happened in Romans 5:

*"Wherefore, **as by one man sin entered into the world**, and death by sin; and so death passed upon all men, for that all have sinned: Nevertheless **death reigned from Adam to Moses**, even over them that had not sinned after the similitude of Adam's transgression, who is the figure of him that was to come"*
(Romans 5:12,14).

Because Adam sinned, all had sinned! This is the Power of One. Whatever happens to a divine emperor affects the whole Earth. From that moment, the whole creation was under a curse, and death began to reign over all of men. Death began to reign because God had warned Adam, *"But of the tree of the knowledge of good and evil, thou shalt not eat of it: for in the day that thou eatest thereof **thou shalt surely die"** (Genesis 2:17). Satan was now in control. He now had the Adamic crown because the moment Adam sinned, the crown God gave him fell off his head and Satan picked it up! That is why the Bible says, ***"The crown is fallen from our head:*** *woe unto us, that we have sinned!"* (Lamentations 5:16).

Satan Becomes the Prince and God of the World

Now that Adam was submitted to Satan's kingdom, all his dominion and titles were assumed by Satan! Satan put on his own head the Adamic crown and from that moment he officially became the prince and god of this world. Adam had those titles at the beginning, but because he disobeyed the voice of God and listened to Satan's voice, he lost them. When Jesus came on the scene four thousand years later, he did not say to Satan, "Oh you slew foot devil." No, He addressed Satan by his official title, *"Prince of the World,"* because He saw the crown, the same crown that God gave to Adam now resting on Satan's head! Satan had acquired the crown lawfully, but in the wrong way. Even now, until the time of the reformation, Satan still has the titles, *Prince and god of this World.* But this is the world that is disobedient to God and in allegiance with the devil.

"Hereafter I will not talk much with you: ***for the prince of this world*** *cometh, and hath nothing in me"* (John 14:30).

"In whom ***the god of this world*** *hath blinded the minds of them which believe not, lest the light of the glorious gospel of Christ, who is the image of God, should shine unto them"* (2 Corinthians 4:4).

"Wherein in time past ye walked according to the course of this world, according to the ***prince of the power of the air,*** *the spirit that now worketh in the children of disobedience"* (Ephesians 2:2).

Adam lost his dominion, and the whole empire of the world, because he disobeyed God and yielded to the devil. Now Satan, as the god and emperor of the world starts reigning and uses death as the tool of his stronghold. Death became Satan's main agent to reign with because Satan knew that once man died he had to come under his control. That is why every man who died, including David and all the patriarchs, had to go to Hell because they were subject to the devil because of Adam's sin.

21

Paul talks about this, *"Wherefore, **as by one man sin entered into the world, and death by sin; and so death passed upon all men, for that all have sinned"*** (Romans 5:12).

Do you see how powerful divine emperors are? They have the Power of One. Adam sinning meant all men had sinned! And in much the same way, Jesus came back and reversed what Adam did. Jesus came four thousand years later to recover the crown. He submitted to the righteousness of God and gained back the crown lawfully! Just as he told John the Baptist, it is important for all righteousness to be fulfilled. Jesus strove lawfully and righteously for the crown. The Bible says, *"And if a man also strive for masteries, **yet is he not crowned, except he strive lawfully"*** (2 Timothy 2:5). Jesus came back to the Earth in the same lineage of Adam and gained back the crown with the wisdom of the serpent, the same way Satan got the crown from Adam.

The Second Divine Emperor: Noah

*"And God blessed Noah and his sons, and said unto them, Be fruitful, and multiply, and replenish the earth. And the fear of you and the dread of you shall be upon every beast of the earth, and upon every fowl of the air, upon all that moveth upon the earth, and upon all the fishes of the sea; **into your hand are they delivered"*** (Genesis 9:1-2).

After Adam's sin, the whole Earth was plunged into a debilitating curse of hardship. *"And unto Adam he said, Because thou hast hearkened unto the voice of thy wife, and hast eaten of the tree, of which I commanded thee, saying, Thou shalt not eat of it: **cursed is the ground for thy sake; in sorrow shalt thou eat of it all the days of thy life"*** (Genesis 3:17). Man could not get much out of the ground after Adam was cast out of the Garden of Eden. But God in His mercy set up another divine emperor to reverse the curse. That man was Noah. Man had become increasingly corrupt and God had to destroy all of mankind, especially when angels started coming to the Earth to copulate with the daughters of men. This caused a strange race of giants to fill up and take over the whole Earth. God had to intervene because the whole Earth had become corrupt. Only Noah maintained his integrity in that perverse generation! The Bible says,

*"And the LORD said, I will destroy man whom I have created from the face of the earth; both man, and beast, and the creeping thing, and the fowls of the air; for it repenteth me that I have made them. **But Noah found grace in the eyes of the LORD.** These are the generations of Noah: **Noah was a just man and perfect in his generations**, and Noah walked with God"* (Genesis 6:7-9).

God had found another person to work with as a divine emperor! God decided to destroy all mankind and repopulate the world with another man - Noah. You see, when God has a divine emperor on the Earth, He is prepared to kill and destroy everything and everyone and start all over with that person. That is why you have to be very careful not to mess around with anyone who occupies the rank and office of a divine emperor. It is very dangerous to do so. Divine emperors have direct dealings with God the Father himself, and God guards that relationship jealously. He will even kill to preserve the right level of reverence for his divine emperors!

Noah Receives Adamic Dominion

God killed every living being and left only Noah and his family alive. For forty days and nights, God drowned the whole Earth in water. The highest mountains were covered with water up to fifteen cubits. At the same time, God preserved the life of Noah in an ark. God commanded Noah to build this ark and fill it up with some of the animals of the Earth. These animals came by themselves to Noah and got in the ark! Noah had dominion over all the beasts and fowls of the Earth because he was a divine emperor. Just like Adam, Noah was given dominion over all the animals and birds. Later on, when Noah came out of the ark, God made a covenant with him and gave him the same kind of blessing he gave Adam, in a lesser measure.

*"And God blessed Noah and his sons, and said unto them, **Be fruitful, and multiply, and replenish the earth**. And the fear of you and the dread of you shall*

*be upon every beast of the earth, and upon every fowl of the air, upon all that moveth upon the earth, and upon all the fishes of the sea; **into your hand are they delivered"** (Genesis 9:1-2).*

Now Noah was to repopulate and replenish the Earth just like Adam. God gave Noah dominion over the Earth. I want you to see how similar Noah's dominion was to Adam's dominion. The Bible says,

"And God blessed them, and God said unto them, Be fruitful, and multiply, and replenish the earth, and subdue it: and have dominion over the fish of the sea, and over the fowl of the air, and over every living thing that moveth upon the earth"
(Genesis 1:28).

Do you see how God gave both Adam and Noah dominion over every beast of the Earth, every fowl of the air and over every fish of the sea? When divine emperors are raised, they have great power over the Earth. Creation recognizes their sonship and submits to their authority and dominion. Can you imagine how powerful you are going to be when you receive and walk in this truth I am sharing? God has called you to this office. Will you accept the call? I pray you do. You can walk in this realm of power!

God Enters into Covenant with Noah

God dealt with the whole Earth through Noah. He knew man was rebellious, but because there was a divine emperor on the Earth, He could still restore the Earth. Out of that direct dealing God had with Noah, He made a powerful covenant with Noah that is still operating today! Because of Noah, God lifted the curse off the Earth and restored times and seasons to mankind.

*"And the LORD smelled a sweet savour; and the LORD said in his heart, **I will not again curse the ground any more for man's sake;** for the imagination of man's heart is evil from his youth; **neither will I again smite any more every thing living, as I have done.** While the earth remaineth, seedtime and harvest,*

and cold and heat, and summer and winter, and day and night shall not cease"
(Genesis 8:21-22).

A divine emperor has power to work with God to restore blessing to the Earth. God can save entire nations, continents, and even the whole Earth through that one person. Because Noah occupied that office, he had power with God to restore the Earth to its former condition. Because of him, the curse was broken, and a command was issued to preserve the Earth even in spite of man's continual evil imagination. The office of the emperor is a powerful counterweight in the judicial system of God. God can bless the whole Earth through that one person! God entered into a powerful eternal covenant with Noah. This is the covenant that God made with Noah,

*"And God spake unto Noah, and to his sons with him, saying, And I, behold, I establish my covenant with you, and with your seed after you; **And with every living creature that is with you, of the fowl, of the cattle, and of every beast of the earth with you; from all that go out of the ark, to every beast of the earth.** And I will establish my covenant with you; neither shall all flesh be cut off any more by the waters of a flood; neither shall there any more be a flood to destroy the earth. And God said, This is the token of the covenant which I make between me and you and every living creature that is with you, for perpetual generations: **I do set my bow in the cloud, and it shall be for a token of a covenant between me and the earth.** And it shall come to pass, when I bring a cloud over the earth, **that the bow shall be seen in the cloud: And I will remember my covenant,** which is between me and you and every living creature of all flesh; and the waters shall no more become a flood to destroy all flesh* (Genesis 9:8-15).

Being a divine emperor, this covenant affected all the earth. In other words, God told Noah that this covenant will affect not only he and his family but also all the birds and animals with him and all the Earth! Every time you see the rainbow in the sky after a rainstorm remember that Noah's covenant is still working! Divine emperors have dealings with God that even transcends their generation. Their dealings with God affects not only their generation but also generations after them. As a divine emperor,

Noah had a global mandate that affected all the Earth. That is why God could say to him,

*"This is the token of the covenant which **I make between me and you and every living creature that is with you, for perpetual generations:** I do set my bow in the cloud, and it shall be for a token of a covenant between **me and the earth"***
(Genesis 9:12-13).

The rainbow is the token of the covenant God made with Noah. Because Noah was a divine emperor, when God spoke to him, He was actually speaking to the whole Earth at one time for *"perpetual generations."* You must see how powerful that is. God took the bow that is around his throne and set it up in the clouds to be a sign for Noah! Ezekiel and John bear witness that the rainbow that God calls *"my bow"* is truly a manifestation around his throne.

*"And I saw as the colour of amber, as the appearance of fire round about within it, from the appearance of his loins even upward, and from the appearance of his loins even downward, I saw as it were the appearance of fire, and it had brightness round about. **As the appearance of the bow that is in the cloud in the day of rain,** so was the appearance of the brightness round about. **This was the appearance of the likeness of the glory of the LORD.** And when I saw it, I fell upon my face, and I heard a voice of one that spake"* (Ezekiel 1:27-28).

*"And immediately I was in the spirit: and, behold, a throne was set in heaven, and one sat on the throne. And he that sat was to look upon like a jasper and a sardine stone: **and there was a rainbow round about the throne,** in sight like unto an emerald"* (Revelation 4:2-3).

John saw the rainbow around God's throne! The Lord revealed to me that the rainbow around God's throne is really the light of God reflecting off the different stones on God's body! The rainbow is a manifestation of God's glory! That bow you see in the clouds after a rain is not a natural phenomenon, it is supernatural. It is a heavenly sign on Earth! In these last days as divine emperors are raised up, you will see signs in Heaven and on Earth in the sight of all men!

"And I will shew wonders in the heavens and in the earth, blood, and fire, and pillars of smoke" (Joel 2:30).

When I started coming more fully into this realm God's face started appearing in clouds over cities and nations that he sent me to. This first happened in June 2006 in Spokane, Washington. I was ministering in that region when God appeared in a rainbow of fire visibly in the clouds above Spokane, Washington. This was captured by the news media for a whole hour! Even National Geographic carried that image in their magazine. We still have that picture. God's face showed up tangibly in a rainbow of fire. There were bright clouds of rainbow colors. That is a manifestation of the office of a divine emperor! Divine emperors have power to bring God down on the Earth to execute global mandates! This happened after God appeared to me in a dream and told me He was coming down on the Earth visibly. After I prophesied this it happened! That is how God works with divine emperors.

Noah had Nations and Kings in His Loins

*"Now these are the **generations of the sons of Noah**, Shem, Ham, and Japheth: and unto them were sons born after the flood. These are the families of the sons of Noah, after their generations, in their nations: **and by these were the nations divided in the earth after the flood"** (Genesis 10:1-2).

As a divine emperor, Noah had all nations in his loins. In Genesis 10, we see what Bible scholars call the Table of Nations. In that passage, seventy nations and kingdoms came out of Noah's loins and filled the whole Earth! These were the direct seed of Noah and they became the people, nations, and languages of the Earth. From just one seed, many different races and nations were birthed! As a divine emperor, Noah had a powerful blessing to be fruitful, multiply and replenish the Earth. God gave him this blessing. God can fill up a whole world with just one divine emperor!

*"And God blessed Noah and his sons, and said unto them, **Be fruitful, and multiply, and replenish the earth"** (Genesis 9:1).

Noah fulfilled this global mandate to replenish the Earth. His three boys Shem, Ham and Japheth multiplied to fill the Earth with Arabs, Asians, Caucasians, Africans, Hispanics and all the other nations of the Earth! A divine emperor has multiple nations in his loins. That is why the Bible says,

*"And hath made **of one blood all nations of men for to dwell on all the face of the earth**, and hath determined the times before appointed, and the bounds of their habitation"* (Act 17:26).

As a divine emperor, Noah became the progenitor and ruler over all nations, cultures, and peoples! As you receive this revelation, you must understand that you cannot walk in this imperial grace if you are racist or prejudiced against other nations and races. You will stay only in the realm of your kingship, and your sphere of dominion will never expand beyond one nation or culture of people until you break every hold of racism on your life. You must love all nations and all people to be a divine emperor!

The Third Divine Emperor: **Abraham**

*"As for me, behold, my covenant is with thee, and thou shalt be **a father of many nations**. Neither shall thy name any more be called Abram, but thy name shall be Abraham; for **a father of many nations** have I made thee. And I will make thee exceeding fruitful, **and I will make nations of thee, and kings shall come out of thee"** (Genesis 17:4-6).*

After Noah, the next person God raised up to be a divine emperor was Abraham. God skipped over many generations before He could find another divine emperor to work with. Divine emperors are also pontiffs that have power to bring God down on the Earth whether presently or in the future. Their lives affect generations to come. For generations to come God works through the covenants He made with them to bless mankind! **Like a king, an emperor has to pay the heavy price of leaving all to follow God.** When God found His next divine emperor, He told him to leave everything and come after him. The Bible says,

*"Now the LORD had said unto Abram, **Get thee out of thy country, and from thy kindred, and from thy father's house,** unto a land that I will shew thee: And I will make of thee a great nation, and I will bless thee, and make thy name great; and thou shalt be a blessing: And I will bless them that bless thee, and curse him that curseth thee: and in thee shall all families of the earth be blessed"* (Genesis 12:1-3).

God had to separate him from his country, relatives, and father's house because he was going to make Abram a Father of all Nations. God has to break your allegiance to your race or nation before you can walk in the office, power, and authority of the emperor! God promised Abraham that through him *"all families of the earth"* will be blessed. That is a global mandate! When God said to Abraham, *"...for a father of many nations have I made thee"* (Genesis 17:5) he was setting up Abraham to be a divine emperor!

Abraham was raised up by God to be a divine emperor with a global mandate! In the present, and even in the future after he was long dead and gone, Abraham was still going to be a blessing to all the nations of the Earth. Today, all those who receive Jesus are called the seed of Abraham and therefore heirs of the promise God made to him. As the Bible says, *"And if ye be Christ's, then are ye Abraham's seed, and heirs according to the promise"* (Galatians 3:29).

Abraham's License to Kill

*"And I will bless them that bless thee, and curse him that curseth thee: **and in thee shall all families of the earth be blessed"*** (Genesis 12:3).

When anyone enters the realm of the divine emperor, God is prepared to kill and destroy everything and everyone for that person's sake! Anyone that comes against Abraham would attract God's wrath! That is why God said He would *"curse him that curseth thee."* This is because the Kingdom of God is not based on majority or quantity, it is based on quality. And so wherever Abraham went in his journeys, God preserved his life by coming against kings that were a hindrance to Abraham. In Egypt when Pharaoh took Abraham's wife Sarah, God severely punished Pharaoh.

*"And the **LORD plagued Pharaoh and his house with great plagues** because of Sarai Abram's wife."* (Genesis 12:17) *"He suffered no man to do them wrong: yea, **he reproved kings for their sakes"*** (Psalm 105:14).

Another king, Abimelech, also took Abraham's wife Sarah. Big mistake! God came to Abimelech in a dream and warned him to give back Sarah otherwise He would have to kill him. The Bible says, *"But God came to Abimelech in a dream by night, and said to him, Behold, thou art but a dead man, for the woman which thou hast taken; for she is a man's wife. But Abimelech had not come near her: and he said, Lord, **wilt thou slay also a righteous nation?"*** (Genesis 20:3-4).

Abimelech the king, knowing the ways of royalty, understood the divine death sentence on his life would destroy his entire kingdom. This is because a king represents all the people in his domain. Any judgment on a king is judgment also on the people he rules over. Everyone in his dominion was at risk of the judgment. That is why he asked God, *"Wilt thou slay also a righteous nation?"* The entire nation he ruled over was in danger of being wiped out by God because he had taken Abraham's wife Sarah! God gave him another chance because of his heart of integrity.

When Abimelech woke up in great fear that morning, he immediately made amends! He reimbursed Abraham for taking his wife and restored Sarah to him. Then he gave Abraham full and unfettered access to his land! *"And Abimelech took sheep, and oxen, and menservants, and womenservants, and gave them unto Abraham, **and restored him Sarah his wife.** And Abimelech said, Behold, my land is before thee: dwell where it pleaseth thee"* (Genesis 20:14-15). That is imperial power! How I wish our generation would understand this mystery!

Moreover, for Abraham's sake, all the nations occupying the land of Canaan were doomed by a divine death sentence. God made a covenant with Abraham in which he promised to remove all the nations and people living in the Promised Land. *"And he said unto him, I am the LORD that brought thee out of Ur of the Chaldees, **to give thee this land to inherit it"*** (Genesis 15:7). The word *"inherit"* in the Hebrew is "yârash yârêsh" which means, *to occupy by driving out previous tenants, and possessing in their place* (Strong's Concordance H3423). Many years after Abraham's death, Moses brought the Israelites to the border of the Promised Land and God instructed Moses,

*"But of the cities of these people, which the LORD thy God doth give thee for an inheritance, thou **shalt save alive nothing that breatheth: But thou shalt utterly destroy** them; namely, the Hittites, and the Amorites, the Canaanites, and the Perizzites, the Hivites, and the Jebusites; as the LORD thy God hath commanded thee"* (Deuteronomy 20:16-17).

For the sake of the divine emperor, Abraham, God destroyed entire nations! He told Moses, *"Thou shalt save alive nothing that breatheth: But thou shalt utterly destroy them."* This is a great mystery about the office of the emperor. The weight of that office is so heavy and the rank so high that God is prepared to kill everyone and then repopulate the Earth with that one person He has chosen to be the emperor. All divine emperors have this power.

How Abraham Operated in the Power of One

As a divine emperor, Abraham was God's crown on the Earth! Before God could do anything major on the Earth, He had to consult his friend Abraham. That is a great characteristic of a divine emperor! God funnels His will and plans through His divine emperors. So, when God had to destroy Sodom and Gomorrah, He had to consult with Abraham.

*"And the men rose up from thence, and looked toward Sodom: and Abraham went with them to bring them on the way. **And the LORD said, Shall I hide from Abraham that thing which I do;** Seeing that Abraham shall surely become*

*a great and mighty nation, and **all the nations of the earth shall be blessed in him?"** (Genesis 18:16-18).*

God had come into the domain he gave Abraham. Abraham as the heir of the world could not be kept in the dark in things pertaining to his realm. God had to tell Abraham His plan to destroy Sodom and Gomorrah (Genesis 18:20-21). And in Genesis 18 you see Abraham interceding with God for Sodom and Gomorrah. He said to God, *"...Wilt thou also destroy the righteous with the wicked?"* (Genesis 18:23). Abraham pleaded for the two doomed cities and finally got God to agree to not to destroy those cities if ten righteous people were found in them.

The angels of God did not find ten righteous people in the city so God rained fire down on them. However, God delivered Lot because he was the only one found righteous! *"For that **righteous man** dwelling among them, in seeing and hearing, **vexed his righteous soul** from day to day with their unlawful deeds"* (2 Peter 2:8). Lot was delivered for Abraham's sake! *"And it came to pass, when God destroyed the cities of the plain, that **God remembered Abraham, and sent Lot out of the midst of the overthrow,** when he overthrew the cities in the which Lot dwelt"* (Genesis 19:29).

Power of One: Father of us All

*"Therefore it is of faith, that it might be by grace; to the end the promise might be sure to all the seed; not to that only which is of the law, but to that also which is of the faith of Abraham; who **is the father of us all,** (As it is written, I have made thee a father of many nations,) before him whom he believed, even God, who quickeneth the dead, and calleth those things which be not as though they were"* (Romans 4:16-17).

Through Abraham, all the nations of the Earth were to be blessed. God made him the *"father of us all."* Abraham is the Father of both the Jews and Gentiles. We are all blessed with him through the principle of the Power of One. *"So then they which be of faith are blessed with faithful Abraham"* (Galatians 3:9). Every believer is blessed in Abraham! That is why in

Galatians 3, Paul revealed that Jesus has redeemed us all from the curse of the law so, *"That the blessing of Abraham might come on the Gentiles through Jesus Christ; that we might receive the promise of the Spirit through faith"* (Galatians 3:14). The blessing of Abraham belongs to you! His blessing is your blessing through Christ Jesus!

We are able to receive and walk in all the covenants and blessings God gave Abraham because of the Power of One principle. God is able to deal with the whole world through the covenant he made with Abraham! That is why God said to Abraham,

*"And I will establish my covenant between me and thee and thy seed after thee in their generations for an everlasting covenant, **to be a God unto thee, and to thy seed after thee"*** (Genesis 17:7).

God can be a God to us today in our generation because of this powerful promise He made to Abraham, *"... to be a God unto thee, and to thy seed after thee."* And do you know that you are the seed of Abraham? If you belong to Jesus Christ then you are! *"And if ye be Christ's, then are ye Abraham's seed, and heirs according to the promise"* (Galatians 3:29). Do you see that? You are Abraham's seed and you are an heir according to the promise. What does it mean when we say you are an heir? Let's find out!

Abraham the Heir of the World

*"For the promise, that **he should be the heir of the world**, was not to Abraham, or to his seed, through the law, but through the righteousness of faith"* (Romans 4:13).

*"And if ye be Christ's, then are ye Abraham's seed, **and heirs according to the promise"*** (Galatians 3:29).

To answer the question, "What does it mean to be an heir?" we must first understand that Abraham was the divine emperor and father of all nations is also the *"heir of the world."* As the heir of the world, he was to have dominion over all the nations of the world. This is why Abraham is

33

a divine emperor. This is the heritage you have as the seed of Abraham! Since you are the seed of Abraham then you are also an Heir! *"And if ye be Christ's, then are ye Abraham's seed, **and heirs according to the promise"*** (Galatians 3:29).

You are not just Abraham's seed, you are an heir according to the promise! Whatever God promised Abraham he promised you! You need to go through the Bible and pull up every promise made by covenant to Abraham and you can have it as you walk in his footsteps! *"And the father of… **who also walk in the steps** of that faith of our father Abraham, which he had being yet uncircumcised"* (Romans 4:12). I did that and today I walk in the immutable covenant God made with Abraham. That is how I made sure in my life all the promises God gave me. As you walk in the footsteps of Abraham may you begin to inherit what God promised him, the world!

That heirship is what you read about in Galatians 4:1, *"Now I say, That the heir, as long as he is a child, differeth nothing from a servant, though he be lord of all."* You are an heir to a throne! And when you mature into full sonship you come fully into that inheritance as a son of God! Abraham's dealings with God, as a divine emperor, affected his generation and all generations to come. That is why he is the father of us all.

Abraham: A Birther of Kings

*"And I will make thee exceeding fruitful, and I will make nations of thee, **and kings shall come out of thee"*** (Genesis 17:6).

As a divine emperor, Abraham could only give birth to kings. That is why God said to Abraham, *"And kings shall come out of thee."* Emperors give birth to kings, and kings give birth to princes! God made Abraham the emperor of the world when He said to him, *"Kings shall come of thee!"* So, if you are the seed of Abraham what does that make you? A king! That is what it means for you to be an heir. Abraham as the heir of the world was chosen by God to be an emperor, a high king. God only sets up emperors when He wants to start a world. He then uses their seed, kings, to fill up the world. Princes fill up a kingdom while kingdoms fill up an empire. And so God tells him, *"Kings shall come out of thee."* God was saying, *"Abraham I am starting with you. You will be a Father of many nations."*

All God's spiritual kings have Abraham as their father. God established this imperial promise with Isaac and Jacob also! God said to Jacob, the grandson of Abraham, *"Kings shall come out of thy loins"* (Genesis 35:11). This imperial promise extended all the way down to Jesus. Jesus Himself had to come as the seed of Abraham and became the first divine emperor in the New Testament to fulfill the promise made to Abraham. Jesus, as the seed of Abraham, could legitimately inherit the whole world. That is how Jesus became the heir of the world. In the New Testament, Jesus is called the seed of Abraham,

*"For verily he took not on him the nature of angels; **but he took on him the seed of Abraham"** (Hebrews 2:16).*

Some of you might ask, "How can this be?" Well, when God deals with a divine emperor, He is also dealing with the person's seed after him for many generations to come! This is confirmed in Matthew 1:1, *"The book of the generation of Jesus Christ, the son of David, **the son of Abraham."*** Jesus is called "the son of Abraham!" Now you can understand how that Jesus having come into the earth legally through the canal of a woman could be the heir of the world. It is in this capacity that Jesus was *"appointed heir of all things"* and was given the whole earth as an inheritance.

*"Hath in these last days spoken unto us by his Son, **whom he hath appointed heir of all things,** by whom also he made the worlds"* (Hebrews 1:2).

*"Ask of me, and **I shall give thee the heathen for thine inheritance,** and the uttermost parts of the earth for thy possession"* (Psalms 2:8).

*"And there was given him dominion, and glory, and a kingdom, **that all people, nations, and languages,** should serve him: his dominion is an everlasting dominion, which shall not pass away, and his kingdom that which shall not be destroyed"* (Daniel 7:14).

Jesus inherited the whole world, including all peoples, nations, and languages because God promised Abraham that his seed would possess the gates of his enemies and *"In thy seed shall all the nations of the earth be blessed; because thou hast obeyed my voice"* (Genesis 22:18). Jesus was that seed, and in Christ Jesus, you are that seed! I believe that now you are getting a better understanding of your spiritual heritage! You have the DNA of an emperor in your blood! You come from a lineup of divine kings and emperors! You are royalty! You are not just the seed of Abraham; you are also an heir according to the promise!

The Fourth Divine Emperor: **Moses**

Four-hundred years after Abraham, God raised Moses to be the next divine emperor. To establish the imperial mandate and DNA of Moses, God connected him to the fathers and the divine emperor before him by appearing to him as the God of the Fathers. When God appeared to Moses on Mount Sinai, He identified himself as the God of the Fathers before Moses that is, Abraham, Isaac, and Jacob.

*"Moreover he said, I am the **God of thy father, the God of Abraham**, the God of Isaac, and the God of Jacob. And Moses hid his face; for he was afraid to look upon God ...And God said moreover unto Moses, Thus shalt thou say unto the children of Israel, **The LORD God of your fathers, the God of Abraham**, the God of Isaac, and the God of Jacob, hath sent me unto you: this is my name for ever, and this is my memorial unto all generations. Go, and gather the elders of Israel together, and say unto them, **The LORD God of your fathers, the God of Abraham, of Isaac, and of Jacob**, appeared unto me, saying, I have surely visited you, and seen that which is done to you in Egypt"* (Exodus 3:6, 15-16).

I have noticed that usually when God is raising a divine emperor, He connects them to the divine emperor before them. The divine emperor before Moses was Abraham, so when God first appeared to Moses He told him, *"I am the God of thy Father, the God of Abraham ..."* Do you see that? For Moses to be a divine emperor, he had to be connected to the fathers and divine emperors before him!

Four times in that same encounter in Exodus 3 and 4, God identified Himself to Moses as the God of his Fathers! *"That they may believe that the LORD God of their fathers, the God of Abraham, the God of Isaac, and the God of Jacob, hath appeared unto thee"* (Exodus 4:5). As God is raising up kings in our generation to walk in imperial anointing, it is imperative that you understand how God worked with the divine emperors He raised up before us. This helps you to understand how he will work in our generation with the divine emperor he raises and this develops the right kind of honor for this powerful office and anointing. You can learn a lot about the imperial realm and imperial power by studying the divine emperors in the Bible.

God's Direct Dealings with Moses

*"And there arose not a **prophet since in Israel like unto Moses, whom the LORD knew face to face,** In all the signs and the wonders, which the LORD sent him to do in the land of Egypt to Pharaoh, and to all his servants, and to all his land, And in all that mighty hand, and in all the great terror which Moses shewed in the sight of all Israel"* (Deuteronomy 34:10-12).

Moses was one of the most powerful divine emperors. God appeared to him and worked directly with him face to face to fulfill his imperial mandate. Each divine emperor has direct dealings with God the Father. They are princes with God and have special one on one relationship with God that blesses the whole world. God would come to Adam in the cool of the day to visit with him every day! God revealed himself to Noah face to face by the disclosure of words and gave him very detailed instructions about the ark he was to build. After He brought Noah and his family out of the ark, God appeared to Noah again to establish him as the first divine emperor after the flood to repopulate and fill up the Earth again. God appeared to Abraham ten times in Genesis and at one time He physically appeared to him at his home and ate with him (Genesis 18).

But Moses, particularly, more than the other divine emperors, had an awesome face to face direct working relationship with God. God spoke

37

to him face to face as a man speaks to his friend (Exodus 33:11). This special working relationship between Moses and God resulted in the most amazing signs and wonders ever manifested in the Old Testament. That is why the Bible says, *"And there arose not a **prophet since in Israel like unto Moses, whom the LORD knew face to face,** In all the signs and the wonders..."* This is the kind of special relationship divine emperors have with God. God has face to face contact with them! God establishes covenants between Himself and divine emperors and works directly with them to fulfill global mandates! Divine emperors have the unique ability to bring God from Heaven down to the Earth. Generations privileged to have these divine emperors, experience more of God than other generations.

With each divine emperor, God progressively reveals more and more of His identity. God said to Moses, *"And I appeared unto Abraham, unto Isaac, and unto Jacob, by the **name of God Almighty, but by my name JEHOVAH was I not known to them"** (Exodus 6:3). When God appeared to Abraham, Isaac, and Jacob He introduced Himself to them as "God Almighty" that is "El Shaddai." In that capacity, God protected and provided abundantly for the patriarchs. All the patriarchs walked in great prosperity and abundance because they had God in their life as El-Shaddai. But now, God was raising Moses to perform another imperial assignment. He was raising Moses to go and execute deliverance for the children of Israel. Moses had to go and confront another nation and bring out Israel from the Egyptian oppression. Moses would have to go to war with Egypt! For Moses to fulfill that mandate, God had to appear to him as Jehovah the Man of War!

*"The LORD (Jehovah) **is a man of war:** the LORD is his name"*
(Exodus 15:3).

*"Or hath God assayed to go and take him a nation from the midst of another nation, by temptations, by signs, and by wonders, **and by war,** and by a mighty hand, and by a stretched out arm, and by great terrors, according to all that the LORD your God did for you in Egypt before your eyes?"* (Deuteronomy 4:34).

38

When Moses went to Pharaoh and told him, *"Let my people Go!"* that was a declaration of war! God fought with Pharaoh and used the elements to subdue him and bend him to His will. That is why Deuteronomy 4:34 reveals that it took a war to bring Israel out of Egypt. On the day of Passover, God himself descended into Egypt to judge the gods of Egypt and the firstborn of the Egyptians!

"For I will pass through the land of Egypt this night, and will smite all the firstborn in the land of Egypt, both man and beast; and against all the gods of Egypt I will execute judgment: I am the LORD" (Exodus 12:12).

The Dreadful Consequence of Coming Against a Divine Emperor

Pharaoh discovered too late how dangerous it is to come against a divine emperor. In just one night, all the firstborn of Egypt were killed and the gods of Egypt broken and destroyed. He still did not learn his lesson because after allowing Moses to lead Israel out of Egypt he pursued them to the Red Sea. At the Red Sea, he saw Moses dividing the sea and then taking the Israelites through the dry pathway in the sea. In his madness, he commanded all his men to pursue the Israelites through the Red Sea. That was a bad mistake.

*"And Moses stretched forth his hand over the sea, and the sea returned to his strength when the morning appeared; and the Egyptians fled against it; and the LORD overthrew the Egyptians in the midst of the sea. And the waters returned, and covered the chariots, and the horsemen, **and all the host of Pharaoh that came into the sea after them; there remained not so much as one of them"***
(Exodus 14:27-28).

Every Egyptian that pursued Moses and the Children of Israel died, *"... there remained no so much as one of them."* This is because divine emperors have God-given power and authority to kill. God is prepared, if necessary, to destroy everything and everyone for the sake of His divine emperors. God could judge Egypt in this way and manifest great signs and wonders because He was working with a divine emperor. Later on in the wilderness, God severely judged and killed many of those that came against Moses. Even Miriam, the sister of Moses, was struck with leprosy because she dared to come against Moses. Many times when the Israelites ganged up on Moses, God would appear in the pillar of cloud to protect and defend His divine emperor. Let me detail here just some of the times God fought against those that opposed Moses.

Egyptian Army Drowned at the Red Sea

At the Red Sea, God killed Pharaoh and all the Egyptians who pursued after Israel.

> *"And Moses stretched forth his hand over the sea, and the sea returned to his strength when the morning appeared; and the Egyptians fled against it; and the LORD overthrew the Egyptians in the midst of the sea. And the waters returned, and covered the chariots, and the horsemen, and all the host of Pharaoh that came into the sea after them; there remained not so much as one of them"*
> (Exodus 14:27-28).

When God was establishing me in the office of the emperor, He gave me a powerful night vision. In this dream, He took me back into the past to the time of Moses. In the dream, I saw myself deep in a sea and I was not drowning, somehow I could still breathe. Suddenly, I brushed up against the corpse of a dead Egyptian! I recoiled in fear and revulsion at the dead corpse. Then I woke up. As I pondered on that dream the Lord said to me, *"This is what I will do to all those who come against you!"* This is what I need you to understand it is a dreadful thing to come against these emperors.

Fire Consumes Murmurers at Taberah

"And when the people complained, it displeased the LORD: and the LORD heard it; and his anger was kindled; and the fire of the LORD burnt among them, and consumed them that were in the uttermost parts of the camp. And the people cried

unto Moses; and when Moses prayed unto the LORD, the fire was quenched"
(Numbers 11:1-2).

The Fiery Serpents

*"**And the people spake against God, and against Moses,** Wherefore have ye brought us up out of Egypt to die in the wilderness? for there is no bread, neither is there any water; and our soul loatheth this light bread. **And the LORD sent fiery serpents** among the people, and they bit the people; **and much people of Israel died"** (Numbers 21:5-6).*

Rebels Swallowed by the Earth

*"And the sons of Eliab; Nemuel, and Dathan, and Abiram. This is that Dathan and Abiram, which were famous in the congregation, **who strove against Moses** and against Aaron in the company of Korah, when they strove against the LORD: **And the earth opened her mouth, and swallowed them up together with Korah, when that company died,** what time the fire devoured two hundred and fifty men: and they became a sign"* (Numbers 26:9-10).

Korah had somehow convinced the whole congregation to come against Moses. This was a major insurrection in the camp of Israel. Their main complaint was that Moses had lifted himself up over the congregation who were as good as he was. He was trying to equalize with Moses and bring him down to the level and rank. *"And they gathered themselves together against Moses and against Aaron, and said unto them, **Ye take too much upon you,** seeing **all the congregation are holy,** every one of them, and the LORD is among them: wherefore then lift ye up yourselves above the congregation of the LORD?"* (Numbers 16:3).

They were basically telling Moses, *"You are acting in pride, you are just like us and you are acting as if you are greater in rank than all of us! God is also with us –Hhe is with all of us! How can you claim to be the only person God works with?"* But it was not Moses that took on that responsibility, it was God himself that chose Moses to be the deliverer and spoke to him openly in the sight of all Israel. Divine emperors often have to deal with people undermining their authority and equalizing with them. This is a major offense in God's Empire. God deals severely with those who rebel against his divine emperors. So, when Korah and the other rebels came against Moses in Numbers 16, God rushed to the scene ready to destroy all the Israelites! The Bible says,

> *"And Korah gathered all the congregation against them unto the door of the tabernacle of the congregation: **and the glory of the LORD appeared unto all the congregation.** And the LORD spake unto Moses and unto Aaron, saying, Separate yourselves from among this congregation, that I may consume them in a moment"* (Number 16:20-21).

God was about to kill all of them! Moses had to pray and intercede to save the nation of Israel from being wiped out. *"And they fell upon their faces, and said, O God, the God of the spirits of all flesh, shall one man sin, and wilt thou be wroth with all the congregation?"* (Numbers 16:22). God heard Moses and agreed not to destroy the whole congregation but singled out the main rebels for judgment. He said to Moses, *"Speak unto the congregation, saying, Get you up from about the tabernacle of Korah, Dathan, and Abiram"* (Numbers 16:24). My dear friend, do not get mixed up with those who rebel against divine authorities. It is a very dangerous thing to do. It took the intercession of Moses to save the rest of the Israelites from being destroyed with the leaders of the insurrection. After the Israelites moved away from Korah and his colleagues, Moses moved in his office as a divine emperor and said,

> *"... Hereby ye shall know that the LORD hath sent me to do all these works; for I have not done them of mine own mind. **If these men die the common death of all men, or if they be visited after the visitation of all men; then the LORD hath not sent me.** But if the LORD make a new thing, and the earth open her mouth, and swallow them up, with all that appertain unto them, and they go down quick into the pit; then ye shall understand that these men have provoked the LORD. And it came to pass, **as he had made an end of speaking all these words, that the ground clave asunder that was under them:** And the earth opened her mouth, and swallowed them up, and their houses, and all the men that*

appertained unto Korah, and all their goods. They, and all that appertained to them, went down alive into the pit, **and the earth closed upon them: and they perished from among the congregation***" (Numbers 16:28-33).

Do you see that? That is imperial power in manifestation! With God's face looking down at the congregation from the clouds, Moses stepped into his office as an emperor and son of God and commanded the Earth to swallow up the rebels and it did! He could do that because he was a divine emperor. Divine emperors have that kind of power. They have power to kill.

I Will Make You a Great Nation

As God is restoring the office of the emperor in our generation, it is important that we understand how this office operates. Emperors rule worlds, so God is able to use them to fill up worlds. When God destroyed the Earth by water, He raised up a divine emperor, Noah, to fill the whole Earth up again. Anytime God is replenishing the Earth, He chooses an emperor to start an empire. Emperors do not birth princes, they birth kings. It takes kingdoms to fill up an empire and principalities to fill up a kingdom. So to fill up a world, God raises an emperor!

I had to share that to help you understand why on two different occasions God was ready to destroy the whole nation of Israel and start all over with Moses. Since Moses was a divine emperor, God could use him to fill up a world again! On the first occasion, Israel had just gone apostate worshipping the golden calf. This was right after God told them not to make any gods before Him. In His wrath, God told Moses, *"Now therefore let me alone, that my wrath may wax hot against them, and that I may consume them: and **I will make of thee a great nation.***" God was going to make a great nation out of Moses just as He did with Abraham! This is the same thing He told Abraham! *"And I will make of thee a great nation ..."* (Genesis 12:2).

Some may wonder how God making you a great nation makes you an emperor. Well, it takes a great nation to be able to bless all the nations of the Earth! *"... and in thee shall all families of the earth be blessed"* (Genesis

12:3). When God says to someone, *"I will make thee a great nation,"* He is basically saying, *"I am setting you up to be an emperor ruling over an empire. Your nation will rule over the whole world, just as Rome ruled the Roman Empire!"* God was prepared to do that with Moses, but Moses stood in the gap and asked Him not to put aside the covenant he made with Abraham! God listened to Moses and did not destroy Israel.

On the second occasion, Moses had finally led Israel to the borders of the Promised Land at Kadesh Barnea. Now was the time to go over and possess the land, but the elders insisted on spies being sent over to survey the land to be sure it was as good as God promised. These twelve spies returned after forty days with an evil report. In Numbers 13, when they returned, they reported that the land was as good as God said it would be, but that it was full of massive giants that made them seem like grasshoppers. The Israelites hearing this cried all night and the next day they decided chose another leader and go back to Egypt. At that point, they were even ready to stone Moses. *"But all the congregation bade stone them with stones. And the glory of the LORD appeared in the tabernacle of the congregation before all the children of Israel"* (Numbers 14:10).

The Israelites were about to stone and kill God's divine emperor, Moses! God had to appear before the whole nation to stop that foolish plan. It was on this occasion that God said to Moses,

*"… How long will this people provoke me? and how long will it be ere they believe me, for all the signs which I have shewed among them? I will smite them with the pestilence, and disinherit them, **and will make of thee a greater nation and mightier than they**"* (Numbers 14:11-12).

Again God offered to destroy the nation of Israel and make of Moses, *"… a greater nation and mightier than they."* And God would have done that, but for the intercession of Moses! God would have wiped out the whole nation of Israel and started all over again with Moses, just as God destroyed the whole world with a flood and started all over with Noah! God can fill up a whole world with just one emperor! One of God's prime objectives is to raise emperors, high kings, who will rule over entire worlds in the next age! Selah! Will you be one of those high kings?

The Global Mandate of Moses

Moses as a divine emperor had global mandates from God Himself. His life affected the whole Earth because of the office he carried. Now that God had another divine emperor on the Earth, He could come down in the sight of man. There are some things God would like to do on a global scale, but He can only accomplish those global plans through a divine emperor. He must work with a divine emperor on Earth to fulfill global mandates. If He works with a king He can only affect a king, but when he works with an emperor the whole world would be impacted! Working with Moses, God elevated the nation of Israel into imperial status with Him.

*"Now therefore, if ye will obey my voice indeed, and keep my covenant, then ye shall be a peculiar treasure unto me **above all people: for all the earth is mine:** And ye shall be unto me a **kingdom of priests,** and an holy nation. These are the words which thou shalt speak unto the children of Israel"* (Exodus 19:5-6).

You see God saying to Israel through Moses that He wants to lift them above all the nations of the Earth. He made Israel the imperial power over all the Earth! This was God's purpose for the nation of Israel. God could do that because He had a divine emperor working with Him. This is also why the Bible says, *"... the LORD thy God will set thee on high above all nations of the earth"* (Deuteronomy 28:1). In Exodus 19, after Moses brought the whole nation of Israel to meet with God, God said to them, *"... ye shall be unto me a Kingdom of Priests..."* It was at this point that God gave the Kingdom or His Empire to Israel! In the days of Solomon Israel fulfilled that mandate. All the kings of the Earth came to Solomon to hear his wisdom! (2 Chronicles 9:22-23).

God's Name is Declared Throughout All the Earth

*"And in very deed for this cause have I raised thee up, for to shew in thee my power; and that **my name may be declared throughout all the earth**"*
(Exodus 9:16).

In the days of Moses, God wanted to reveal Himself to the whole world. He needed a divine emperor to work with to accomplish this. Egypt was the imperial power on the Earth at this time and so anything that happened in Egypt would affect the whole known world. God raised Moses and gave him imperial power as an emperor to confront and break Pharaoh. Actually, because Pharaoh also had imperial power, God had to give Moses another rank even higher than a divine emperor. He had to make Moses a god to Pharaoh. *"... See, I have made thee a god to Pharaoh..."* (Exodus 7:1).

A fully developed divine emperor is also a prince with God and a son of God! I share more on this in the next book in the Kingdom Series, *Sonship*. Moses was not just a divine emperor, he was a god! God made him a god with imperial power to break Egypt! That is why Moses displayed such power with creation to bend Pharaoh. Moses displayed more power than most of the other divine emperors God raised. He had great power and dominion over all the five elements when he released miracles of judgment on Egypt. Through these miracles and devastating plagues, God's name gained fame and renown all over the world. Up to this point in time, there was very little known about God's identity.

God used this situation to announce and unveil His identity. When Moses first confronted Pharaoh and told him God wants him to let his people go, Pharaoh said, *"... **Who is the LORD,** that I should obey his voice to let Israel go? **I know not the LORD,** neither will I let Israel go"* (Exodus 5:2). The world did not know the true identity of God! Pharaoh did not know God! Even though God created the Earth, the world did not know him. They were worshiping other gods in total oblivion of God's true identity. God used a divine emperor, Moses, to announce and reveal His name, Jehovah, to the entire world. Through the miracles, signs, and wonders

God did through Moses, Pharaoh and the whole world became aware of who God is.

*"For the scripture saith unto Pharaoh, Even for this same purpose have I raised thee up, that I might shew my power in thee, and that **my name might be declared throughout all the earth"** (Romans 9:17).*

As God plagued Egypt, Pharaoh grew to know who He was. After the plague of hail Pharaoh said, *"... I have sinned this time: **the LORD is righteous**, and I and my people are wicked"* (Exodus 9:27). As the plagues multiplied in Egypt, Pharoah discovered that God was the Lord of the Earth. *"... thou mayest know that I am the LORD in the midst of the earth"* (Exodus 8:22). Pharaoh also learned that there was no other God like Jehovah. *"... that thou mayest know that there is none like me in all the earth"* (Exodus 9:14). He finally realized that the whole Earth belonged to God. *"... neither shall there be any more hail; **that thou mayest know how that the earth is the LORD'S"*** (Exodus 9:29).

Apart from using the plagues to free up Israel from Egypt, God was using the plagues to educate Pharaoh on his identity so that his name and identity would be *"declared throughout all the earth."* He could do this because he had an emperor working with him. All these miracles of judgment God did in Egypt had never been seen before. They were unprecedented and become immortalized and memorialized for all generations! To this day, the world still marvels at how God used Moses to bring Israel out of Egypt. Several movies about Moses have been produced by both believers and the secular world. God fulfilled this major global mandate to make His name known throughout the entire world through Moses!

The Covenant of Marvels

*"And he said, Behold, I make a covenant: **before all thy people I will do marvels, such as have not been done in all the earth,** nor in any nation: and all*

the people among which thou art shall see the work of the LORD: for it is a
terrible thing that I will do with thee" (Exodus 34:10).

Later on, God made a covenant with Moses to ensure that this global mandate of proclaiming His name over all the Earth would never be lost. In this covenant of marvels, God promised that He would continue to do with Moses the unprecedented miracles, signs, and wonders He did with him. In a trip to Heaven in the late nineties, God gave me a major revelation of a mystery called "The Inheritance of the Fathers." He revealed to me that the inheritance in the saints Paul talks about in Ephesians are released through two major lineages, Moses and Elijah. This is why both Moses and Elijah appeared to Jesus on the Mount of Transfiguration. (Learn more about this mystery in my book, *Inheritance by Lineage*).

The covenant God made with Moses in Exodus 34:10 is a covenant for all ages. When God makes a covenant with a divine emperor it is to benefit the whole world for all time. God made a covenant with Noah to stop storms from destroying the whole Earth. He made a covenant with Abraham to multiply him and make him a blessing to all nations. God also made the Sure Mercies of David covenant with David. All these are divine emperors. Because they had direct dealings with God, their lives and the covenants God made with them continue to affect the whole world.

Today all believers can tap into this covenant to manifest the type of miracles Moses walked in. In this same trip to Heaven, the Lord Jesus revealed to me that I am in the Mosaic lineage. After I learned that I began to walk in amazing miracles. I began to glow as Moses glowed when he came down the mountain. God made me the healing shepherd over America just as he used Moses to heal an entire nation. Just as God came down physically and openly in the sight of all Israel, God has come down in our generation in many cities where He sent me, because I am in the Mosaic lineage!

Do you see how powerful a divine emperor is? That covenant God made with Moses is for us today! As God is getting ready to bring in the greatest harvest of all time be ready to experience what he said to Moses, *"before all thy people I will do marvels, such as have not been done in all the earth, nor in any nation: and all the people among which thou art shall see the work of the LORD: for it is a terrible thing that I will do with thee."* Jesus also came in this same lineage and he talked about doing marvels! *"For the Father loveth the Son, and sheweth him all things that himself doeth: and he will shew him greater works than these, that ye may marvel"* (John 5:20).

The Fifth Divine Emperor: David

The next divine emperor after Moses is David! God accomplished different things with each divine emperor. They all had some common characteristics but each one of them was used differently to fulfill a major piece of God's global agendas. God chose David, in particular, to foreshadow and formulate the kingship and emperorship of the Lord Jesus Christ. God raised David to be a divine emperor through whom He would establish His throne and empire on Earth, and also through whom He would establish a kingdom dynasty forever! David had other Divine Imperial characteristics such as the Power of One, Direct Dealings with God, Power to Kill, and being a Birther of Kings. But God used him particularly to forge his Empire on Earth. The Empire of God is established on the throne of David!

> *"Of the increase of his government and peace there shall be no end, upon the throne of David, and upon his kingdom, to order it, and to establish it with judgment and with justice from henceforth even for ever. The zeal of the LORD of hosts will perform this"* (Isaiah 9:7).

The Throne of David

When the angel Gabriel came to Mary to announce to her that she had been chosen as the vessel through whom God would birth His Son into the Earth realm, he said to her concerning Jesus, *"He shall be great, and shall be called the Son of the Highest: and the Lord God shall give unto him the* **throne of his father David"** (Luke 1:32). Just as was prophesied in Isaiah 9:7, the Empire of God that Jesus brought from Heaven was established on the *"Throne of David."* This is because the divine royal lineage through which Jesus, God's King and Emperor, was born, was channeled through the house and lineage of David!

"And Joseph also went up from Galilee, out of the city of Nazareth, into Judaea, unto the city of David, which is called Bethlehem; (because he was of the **house and lineage of David:)"** (Luke 2:4).

This is so important to understand! Jesus was birthed in Bethlehem because *"he was of the* **house and lineage of David!"** David, the divine emperor before Jesus, had to foreshadow and establish a covenant with God for the imperial dynasty to be established! What most do not even understand is that even though Jesus is known as the seed or son of David, He is also his root! He predates him and also came through him. That is why Jesus called himself the root and offspring of David,

"I Jesus have sent mine angel to testify unto you these things in the churches. I am the **root and the offspring of David**, *and the bright and morning star"*
(Revelations 22:16).

I am sharing this with you to help you understand why David is a divine emperor. He was chosen to foreshadow Jesus in his kingship. Today we can learn a lot about our kingship identity by just studying David. A lot of what Jesus did in His kingship was mirrored on the life of David because He was the seed and son of David.

"Concerning his Son Jesus Christ our Lord, **which was made of the seed of David** *according to the flesh"* (Romans 1:3).

"The book of the generation of Jesus Christ, **the son of David,** *the son of Abraham"* (Matthew 1:1).

*"And the multitudes that went before, and that followed, cried, saying, **Hosanna to the Son of David:** Blessed is he that cometh in the name of the Lord; Hosanna in the highest"* (Matthew 21:9).

*"Saying, What think ye of Christ? whose son is he? They say unto him, The **Son of David"** (Matthew 22:42).*

*"And when he heard that it was Jesus of Nazareth, he began to cry out, and say, **Jesus, thou Son of David,** have mercy on me"* (Mark 10:47).

"I Have Found David, a Man After My Heart!"

As we have seen, Jesus was *"of the house and lineage of David."* David, the divine emperor before Jesus had to foreshadow and establish a Covenant with God for the imperial dynasty to be established! God, through His direct dealings with David, established a covenant with him to ensure that His throne, kingdom, and house (lineage) would be established forever. To do this, God entered into a covenant of salt with David, called the *Sure Mercies of David*. This is the covenant that protects God's divine kings and emperors.

God could have established this covenant with Saul, the King before David, but you must understand that the throne must be established in righteousness. Saul could not obey the commands of God and that caused him to be rejected from being an eternal king. You see, you can be a king, but are you an eternal king? Many were birthed into their kingship but lost that realm in the course of their life through disobedience. That is why Jesus said to the church, *"Behold, I come quickly: hold that fast which thou hast, **that no man take thy crown"*** (Revelation 3:11). You can lose your crown!

*"And Samuel said to Saul, Thou hast done foolishly: **thou hast not kept the commandment of the LORD thy God,** which he commanded thee: **for now would the LORD have established thy kingdom upon Israel for ever. But now thy kingdom shall not continue:** the LORD hath sought him a **man after his***

51

own heart, and the LORD hath commanded him to be captain over his people, because thou hast not kept that which the LORD commanded thee"
(1 Samuel 13:13-14).

*"And Samuel said, Hath the LORD as great delight in burnt offerings and sacrifices, as in obeying the voice of the LORD? Behold, to obey is better than sacrifice, and to hearken than the fat of rams. For rebellion is as the sin of witchcraft, and stubbornness is as iniquity and idolatry. Because thou hast rejected the word of the LORD, **he hath also rejected thee from being king"** (1 Samuel 15:22-23).*

Two times God commanded Saul, and two times Saul rejected God's command. That is why God rejected Saul from being king. It was God that directed Samuel to anoint Saul to be king over Israel. One would have thought that should have established Saul forever, yet his continual disobedience to God's commands disqualified Saul for being established as an eternal king. The Bible says, *"It repenteth me that I have set up Saul to be king: for he is turned back from following me, and hath not performed my commandments"* (1 Samuel 15:11). The crown is held by obedience to the throne. That is also why Adam lost dominion over the Earth. When he betrayed God and yielded to Satan, he lost his crown! That is why the Bible says, *"The crown is fallen from our head: woe unto us, that we have sinned!"* (Lamentations 5:16).

There is a realm in God where you can establish your throne and crown forever. In David's generation, God wanted to establish a kingdom dynasty that would never lose its place with Him. He needed a royal lineage that could never be destroyed, and through which He could release his son, Jesus! And for that, he needed to enter into covenant with a king on Earth who could obey Him. David fit the bill! God found His own man, David. Saul, on the other hand, was a man of the people, a man pleaser. David was a God pleaser. He was a man after God's heart!

*"And when he had removed him, he raised up unto them David to be their king; to whom also he gave testimony, and said, **I have found David the son of Jesse, a man after mine own heart, which shall fulfil all my will"** (Acts 13:22).*

You need to pay particular attention to God's reports and testimonies of men. God said a similar thing concerning another divine emperor, Abraham, *"And the LORD said, Shall I hide from Abraham that thing which I do ...* **For I know him,** *that he will command his children and his household after him, and they shall keep the way of the LORD, to do justice and judgment;* **that the LORD may bring upon Abraham** *that which he hath spoken of him"* (Gen 18:17,19). God said concerning Abraham, *"For I know him."* And now he is saying about David, another divine emperor, *"I have found David ... a man after mine own heart."* He knew that David would fulfill all His will. God had finally found a man through whom He could forge His Kingdom and Empire on Earth.

Samuel Anoints David to be King

"I have found David my servant; with my holy oil have I anointed him" (Psalm 89:20).

God had found a man that He could work with. The first time God rejected Saul, God said to him through Samuel, *"But now thy kingdom shall not continue: the LORD hath sought him a man after his own heart, and the LORD hath commanded him to be captain over his people, because thou hast not kept that which the LORD commanded thee"* (1 Samuel 13:14). God carefully searched and found a man *"after his own heart"* that is, a man whose only desire was to please Him. Now it was time to prepare David to be king. For this purpose, God sent Samuel on a secret mission to Bethlehem to go anoint him.

"And the LORD said unto Samuel, How long wilt thou mourn for Saul, seeing I have rejected him from reigning over Israel? fill thine horn with oil, and go, I will send thee to Jesse the Bethlehemite: **for I have provided me a king among his sons.** *And Samuel said, How can I go? if Saul hear it, he will kill me. And the LORD said,* **Take an heifer with thee, and say, I am come to sacrifice to the LORD.** *And call Jesse to the sacrifice, and I will shew thee what thou shalt do: and thou shalt anoint unto me him whom I name unto thee"* (1 Samuel 16:1-3).

This was a very dangerous mission for Samuel because he was going to anoint someone to be king while Saul was still king. That is why Samuel told God, *"If Saul hear it, he will kill me."* You see there is always great controversy surrounding the birthing of a king. When Jesus was born in Bethlehem, it caused a great stir in Jerusalem when they got wind of it in Herod's royal court. Herod wanted to kill him. Moreover, when Moses was born, Satan got wind of it and he moved Pharaoh to release an edict to kill the male born Israelite children.

God instructed Samuel to say to people when they asked about his mission, *"… I am come to sacrifice to the Lord."* Now some would say that, "Oh God is lying." No, God does not lie, but He uses subtlety to outwit the enemy. God had to instruct Samuel to say that because every time God raises a new king there is a great upheaval in the Earth. All of Hell is stirred up to try to stop God's kings from coming out. So, God had to activate David's kingship in a subtle way. He had to shroud the whole process in a mystery.

The Kingdom of God is a mystery, so even David's kingship, which is part of the reign of Christ, had to be shrouded in mystery when Samuel had to go anoint him to be king. God did not even tell Samuel beforehand which of Jesse's sons was His choice. God had to do this because the devil was in Saul. The devil does not want God's kings in the Earth. He always tries to kill them before they can ever be a threat to him. This is because it takes a kingdom to confront another kingdom. He knows that God's kings are a threat to his kingdom. It was important the real purpose of Samuel going to Jesse's house be hidden from Saul.

Samuel obeyed God and anointed David to be king. *"Then Samuel took the horn of oil, and anointed him in the midst of his brethren: and the Spirit of the LORD came upon David from that day forward. So Samuel rose up, and went to Ramah. But the Spirit of the LORD departed from Saul, and an evil spirit from the LORD troubled him"* (1 Samuel 16:13-14). David was anointed very early, but it took another twenty years before he finally became king over all of Israel. He had to go through the process to become a king and an emperor. After thirteen years, he was anointed to be king over the tribe of

Judah and then seven years later he was anointed again to be king over all of Israel. From that point the Bible says,

> *"And David went on, and grew great, and the LORD God of hosts was with him"* (2 Samuel 5:10).

In a face to face appearance, the Lord revealed to me that God was not with David in that way until he had fulfilled the process he had to go through to be made a king. The moment God started working with him as the "Lord God of Hosts" that signified a major turning point in David's life. He was now not just a king, but a prince with God. That made him a divine emperor. Later on in Psalm 89, it was revealed to Ethan that God made David higher than the kings of the Earth.

> *"Also I will make him my firstborn, higher than the kings of the earth"* (Psalm 89:27).

David entered the realm of sonship where God could now more directly work with him to fulfill global mandates. David called God his Father! *"He shall cry unto me, Thou art my father, my God, and the rock of my salvation"* (Psalm 89:26). It was later on that Jesus made God's title as "Father" the most common identity of God in the New Testament. David foreshadowed Jesus in this respect.

The Sure Mercies of David

> *"... Also the LORD telleth thee that **he will make thee an house.** And when thy days be fulfilled, and thou shalt sleep with thy fathers, **I will set up thy seed after thee, which shall proceed out of thy bowels, and I will establish his kingdom.** He shall build an house for my name, and I will stablish the throne of his kingdom for ever. **I will be his father, and he shall be my son.** If he commit iniquity, **I will chasten him with the rod of men,** and with the stripes of the children of men: **But my mercy shall not depart away from him, as I took it from Saul,** whom I put away before thee. And thine house and thy kingdom shall be established for ever before thee: **thy throne shall be established for ever"***
> (1 Samuel 7:11-16).

Now that God had found His man, he entered into a covenant with David, to establish him as an eternal king and emperor. This was after David was anointed king over all Israel. To establish David's throne forever, God had to enter into covenant with him. You can learn more about this in my messages on *"The Sure Mercies of David."* In 2 Samuel 7 and Psalm 89, this covenant is detailed. In this covenant, God promised to make him a house. That is a kingdom dynasty. David would never fail to have a lamp in Jerusalem (2 Kings 8:19). In this vein, God told David, *"I will set up thy seed after thee, which shall proceed out of thy bowels, and I will establish his kingdom."* That was not just Solomon God was referring to, this scripture refers ultimately to Jesus, the seed of David. Through this covenant, God would establish an eternal kingdom and He promised never to reject David from being king as He did to Saul.

*"**But my mercy shall not depart away from him, as I took it from Saul,** whom I put away before thee. And thine house and thy kingdom shall be established for ever before thee: thy throne shall be established for ever"* (2 Samuel 7:15-16).

David had already paid the price to walk in this covenant when he served Saul and when he had to run from Saul. During his days as a fugitive, David had two opportunities to kill his enemy Saul, but he decided not to. He understood that even though Saul was rejected by God, the crown that God gave him was still on his head. The Lord said to me in a face to face appearance, *"Do you know that when David was running from Saul he was really running from me? He was running from the crown that we gave Saul. It was our crown that was pursuing David."*

David was smart! He knew that even though the king was wrong and rejected by God, he still carried the crown. He was still the *"anointed of the Lord."* He therefore refused to kill Saul. He had mercy on his enemy! David said to his men when he had Saul at his mercy in a cave, *"... The LORD forbid that I should do this thing unto **my master, the LORD'S anointed,** to stretch forth mine hand against him, seeing he is the anointed of the LORD"* (1 Samuel 24:6). David understood the Mystery of Authority, that one should never touch God's divine authorities. Saul was still God's anointed even though he was a rejected king. It was God that eventually cut off Saul (2

Samuel 7:9). David did not have to take on God's offense with Saul! On another occasion, David said to Abishai, one of his men who were about to kill Saul,

*"… Destroy him not: for who can stretch forth his hand **against the LORD'S anointed,** and be guiltless?"* (1 Samuel 26:9).

Two times David refused to kill Saul, who was pursuing him to kill him. That is why God could establish the Sure Mercies of David with him because as the word says, *"Blessed are the merciful: for **they shall obtain mercy"** (Matthew 5:7). That is how David paid the price to enter into the eternal covenant. He was merciful to Saul. Now God could make sure His covenant of Sure Mercies with David! *"I have made a covenant with my chosen, **I have sworn unto David my servant,** Thy seed will I establish for ever, and build up thy throne to all generations. Selah"* (Psalm 89:3-4). Because David had mercy on Saul, God said concerning David,

*"**My mercy** will I keep for him for evermore, and my covenant shall stand fast with him"* (Psalm 89:28).

Today you, too, can enter into this covenant. In Isaiah 55:3, God offers to enter this covenant with you! *"Incline your ear, and come unto me: hear, and your soul shall live; and **I will make an everlasting covenant with you,** even the sure mercies of David"* (Isaiah 55:3). I hear the Lord saying to you right now, *"I want to make this everlasting covenant of the Sure Mercies of David with you!"* May you walk in this covenant!

God established an eternal covenant with David that protects all His spiritual kings for all of time, including you! Jesus rose from the dead because God had made this covenant of salt with his father David!

*"And as **concerning that he raised him up from the dead,** now no more to return to corruption, he said on this wise, **I will give you the sure mercies of David"*** (Acts 13:34).

As you mature in your kingship, you will enter into many battles with the kingdom of darkness. That is how God strengthens your kingship! The Spirit of God will lead you into battle, as He led Jesus to be tempted by the devil. *"Then was Jesus **led up of the Spirit** into the wilderness to be tempted of the devil"* (Matthew 4:1). That was a contest of kings! Satan, the prince of the world, tried to subdue the Prince of Life, Jesus, for forty days. Jesus won that contest as He dismissed the devil from His presence after forty days of fasting and prayer. The Bible says, *"Then saith Jesus unto him, **Get thee hence, Satan:** ... **Then the devil leaveth him** and, behold, angels came and ministered unto him"* (Matthew 4:10-11). After that battle, Jesus returned with power!

*"**And Jesus returned in the power of the Spirit into Galilee:** and there went out a fame of him through all the region round about"* (Luke 4:14).

The more battles you win, the stronger you get in your kingship! More power is released in you every time you return from a battle! In your kingship, you will enter into the contest of kings where the devil will try to do everything in his power to take your crown away from you. God in his foreknowledge secured your victory with the covenant he made with David, so that no matter what happens you will still come out unscathed! Jesus was crucified and then buried in the grave, but because of the Sure Mercies of David, He rose from the dead!

The Sure Mercies of David is what protects and secures your kingship from being destroyed! No matter what you go through, no matter what battles you face in life, I decree as a divine emperor that you will not lose your crown, you will not lose any battle! Even if you seem to have been defeated and destroyed, by the Sure Mercies of David I command you to be resurrected from your grave! By the Sure Mercies of David, the Lord will not allow you to see corruption in your kingship!

David Made Higher Than the Kings of the Earth

"I have found David my servant; with my holy oil have I anointed him: With whom my hand shall be established: mine arm also shall strengthen him. He shall

cry unto me, Thou art my father, my God, and the rock of my salvation. Also I
*will make him **my firstborn, higher than the kings of the earth***"
(Psalm 89:20-21, 26-27).

One major revelation about divine emperors is that God establishes His divine will and plans through them. They become a pattern for ages to come. God made David a divine emperor! You cannot just make yourself an emperor, you have to be made one! Jesus, by His death, burial, and resurrection, has already made you a king. Now you have to fulfill the call on your life to be an emperor. In this passage in Psalm 89, you see how God Himself inaugurated David into the imperial realm. He said concerning David, *"I will make him my firstborn, higher than the kings of the earth."* By making David higher than the kings of the Earth, God was basically making him the emperor of the whole world! This foreshadowed the coronation of Jesus as the prince of the kings of the Earth.

"And from Jesus Christ, who is the faithful witness, and the first begotten of the
*dead, **and the prince of the kings of the earth...***" (Revelation 1:5)

God called David, *"my firstborn,"* and Jesus is also called *"the first begotten of the dead..."* Jesus is also called the firstborn of all creation. *"Who is the image of the invisible God, **the firstborn** of every creature"* (Colossians 1:15). That is what made Jesus the *"Prince of the Kings of the Earth."* The word "prince" in Greek is "archōn" which according to the strong concordance means, *first in rank or power.* When God calls you "my firstborn," He is calling you a prince. A prince with God is much higher than a king with Jesus. A prince with God is an emperor! God made David an emperor, His firstborn, higher than the kings of the Earth! David foreshadowed Jesus in His identity as the "Prince of the Kings of the Earth!"

This is why David never lost a battle against any king that came against him. The kings that came against him did not realize that he had been made head over the kings of the Earth by God himself. As a divine emperor, David far outranked any earthly king. He could never lose a battle against a king. He was virtually indestructible in battle! This is what happens when you understand the imperial power you have in your joint seating with Jesus on the imperial right-hand seat.

David did not start out being this powerful. He had to be made a divine emperor. There was a time in his life where God had to deliver him from enemies that were too strong for him, *"He delivered me from my strong enemy, and from them which hated me: for they were too strong for me"* (Psalm 18:17). In the course of his life, God began to strengthen his kingship through battle. *"He teacheth my hands to war, so that a bow of steel is broken by mine arms. Thou hast also given me the shield of thy salvation: and thy right hand hath holden me up, **and thy gentleness hath made me great"*** (Psalm 18:34-35). This is how greatness is forged. God taught David warfare and made him great!

As David walked with God, he progressively became greater and greater until God made him the head of the heathen! *"Thou hast delivered me from the strivings of the people; and **thou hast made me the head of the heathen:** a people whom I have not known shall serve me"* (Psalm 18:43). The heathen are the nations of the world! Divine emperors rule over all the kings of the Earth. David did not just suddenly become a divine emperor with God. The process of time matured David into the imperial realm! *"And David went on, and grew great, and the LORD God of hosts was with him"* (2 Samuel 5:10).

David's Divine Power to Kill and Win Battles

God said to David when He was establishing the Sure Mercies Covenant with him, *"And I was with thee whithersoever thou wentest, **and have cut off all thine enemies out of thy sight,** and have made thee a great name, like unto the name of the great men that are in the earth"* (2 Samuel 7:9). God cut off or killed everyone that rose up against David! As I have shared with you, this is one of the things very unique to a divine emperor. God will kill everyone for the sake of a divine emperor.

When David's son Absalom, for example, mobilized all the tribes of Israel against David, he still lost! David was outnumbered by Absalom's massive army, but he still won because he was a divine emperor! When David heard about his son Absalom coming against him with a huge army, he strategically retreated from Jerusalem into the woods to strengthen himself. Absalom pursued his father into the woods where he was destroyed. During that battle, even the wood and animals fought for David against Absalom.

*"So the people went out into the field against Israel: and the battle was in the wood of Ephraim; Where the people of Israel were slain before the servants of David, and there was there a great slaughter that day of twenty thousand men. For the battle was there scattered over the face of all the country: **and the wood devoured more people that day than the sword devoured"** (2 Samuel 18:6-8).*

You see, divine emperors are also sons of God with powers over creation. Divine emperors have great power with God and are endowed with dominion and mastery over the elements. Therefore, as Absalom fought David's army, the forest and the wild beasts also fought for David against Absalom! *"The wood devoured more people that day than the sword devoured!"* A tree actually arrested Absalom as he tried to flee the battle!

*"And Absalom met the servants of David. And Absalom rode upon a mule, and the mule went under the thick boughs of a great oak, **and his head caught hold of the oak, and he was taken up between the heaven and the earth;** and the mule that was under him went away. And a certain man saw it, and told Joab, and said, Behold, I saw Absalom hanged in an oak"* (2 Samuel 18:9-10).

Absalom realized too late how foolhardy he was to rise against his father, David. An oak tree caught him and lifted him clear off the ground into the air! The oak tree lifted him between *"Heaven and Earth."* This is because creation is groaning and praying earnestly for divine emperors, sons of God, to manifest. David was such a person. Creation assisted David in his battle against Absalom.

As a divine emperor with God, David was supernaturally endowed to win battles. He fought many wars to consolidate his kingship. He never ever lost a battle! In his teenage years, he killed Goliath, a Philistine giant that everyone else was scared off. Several times the Philistines came against David and they lost every time. All those that ever rose up against him died. This is because God is prepared to kill everyone to protect and preserve his divine emperor.

David did not have the greatest character. He made mistakes. He made mistakes that would have destroyed any other person, but because of his covenant with God, he was preserved. Many tried to use his mistakes against him and they all died. In fact, after his greatest mistake, when he killed Uriah and married Bathsheba, Uriah's wife, David went to war and won! This was right after the prophet Nathan told him the sword would never leave his house because of the sin of adultery and murder David committed. Despite all that, David still never lost a war. He went to the nation of Ammon and won a great battle there. He took off the king's crown and put it on his own head and violently subdued that nation.

*"And he took their king's crown from off his head, the weight whereof was a talent of gold with the precious stones: and it was set on David's head. And he brought forth the spoil of the city in great abundance. And he brought forth the people that were therein, and **put them under saws, and under harrows of iron, and under axes of iron, and made them pass through the brickkiln:** and thus did he unto all the cities of the children of Ammon. So David and all the people returned unto Jerusalem"* (2 Samuel 12:30-31).

David fought many nations and would subdue violently with great slaughter. David was a very bloody and violent warrior! In fact, God could not allow David to build the temple because of the bloody wars he was engaged in. God called David a man of war who had made great wars! God said concerning David, *"Behold, I have given him for a witness to the people, a leader and commander to the people"* (Isaiah 55:4). God appointed David to be a "commander" to His people Israel. That means that David was a general, a warrior king. God raised him up to wage war against the enemies of Israel to establish the nation and kingdom of Israel. His son

Solomon was a different kind of king. He was a man of peace. I have detailed below scriptures describing the bloody nature of David's reign.

"And David said to Solomon, My son, as for me, it was in my mind to build an house unto the name of the LORD my God: But the word of the LORD came to me, saying, **Thou hast shed blood abundantly, and hast made great wars:** *thou shalt not build an house unto my name, because thou hast shed much blood upon the earth in my sight."* (1 Chronicles 22:7-8) *"But God said unto me, Thou shalt not build an house for my name, because* **thou hast been a man of war, and hast shed blood"** (1 Chronicles 28:3).

"And Solomon sent to Hiram, saying, Thou knowest how that David my father could not build an house unto the name of the LORD his God **for the wars which were about him on every side, until the LORD put them under the soles of his feet"** (1 Kings 5:2-3).

David Had Great Revelations of God as a King and Emperor

Divine emperors have face to face contact with God. They have direct dealings with the Lord God. *"Seek the LORD, and his strength: seek his face evermore"* (Psalm 105:4). Since God was forging his eternal empire on Earth through David, He had to give David several face to face visions, revelations and trips to Heaven to help him understand his Kingdom. David was being used by God to release Kingdom of Heaven on Earth. David was a great king because he knew God in his identity as a king and an emperor.

God allowed David to have several face to face encounters with him so that he could imprint his imperial identity on his life. That is why David's psalms were full of references to the imperial nature and Empire of God. God formulated His imperial likeness and DNA on David through face to face contact (1 John 3:2 and 2 Colossians 3:18). David said, *"As for me, I will behold thy face in righteousness: I shall be satisfied, when I awake,* **with thy likeness"** (Psalm 17:15). Every time David would wake up from these powerful dreams, he had the likeness of God on him! David knew the face of God because he sought the face of God continually! *"Seek the LORD and his strength, seek his face continually"* (1 Chronicles 16:11). David sought God's face diligently because God commanded him to do so!

"When thou saidst, Seek ye my face; **my heart said unto thee, Thy face, LORD,** *will I seek"* (Psalm 27:8).

Now you understand why David was a man after God's heart. David also said, *"I have set the LORD always before me: because he is at my right hand, I shall not be moved"* (Psalm 16:8). You may ask why I am belaboring this point. You see, God raised David to be the divine emperor who would reveal through his life, through his kingship, and through the revelations he gave him, the nature and identity of God's Empire. Just as God had to show Moses the heavenly tabernacle, God showed David His Empire in Heaven. He had to see Heaven to be able to accurately project God's Empire on the Earth! David had the some of the greatest revelations of God as a king. David, in particular, made more references to God as a king than any other person! These are just a few examples:

"The LORD is King for ever and ever..." (Psalm 10:16).

"Thy throne, O God, *is for ever and ever: the sceptre of thy kingdom is a right sceptre"* (Psalm 45:6).

"For the LORD most high is terrible; **he is a great King over all the earth"** (Psalm 47:2).

"For **God is my King of old,** *working salvation in the midst of the earth"* (Psalm 74:12).

"For the LORD is a great God, and **a great King** *above all gods"* (Psalm 95:3).

"The LORD hath **prepared his throne in the heavens; and his kingdom** *ruleth over all"* (Psalm 103:19).

You see, when God wants to release something on Earth, He must first get a man through whom He would channel that plan. David saw Jesus being crowned as a king in Psalm 2. *"Yet have I set my king upon my holy hill of Zion. I will declare the decree: the LORD hath said unto me, Thou art my Son; this day have I begotten thee"* (Psalm 2:6-7). David prophesied many details about the kingship of Jesus! He prophesied concerning Jesus, *"Thy throne, O God, is for ever and ever: the **sceptre of thy kingdom is a right sceptre. Thou** lovest righteousness, and hatest wickedness: therefore God, thy God, **hath anointed thee with the oil of gladness** above thy fellows"* (Psalm 45:6-7).

He saw Jesus being crucified in Psalm 22. *"... My God, my God, why hast thou forsaken me? ... they pierced my hands and my feet ... They part my garments among them, and cast lots upon my vesture"* (Psalm 22:1, 16, 18). He even saw the chief priests who were mocking Jesus as he hung on the cross, *"All they that see me laugh me to scorn: they shoot out the lip, they shake the head, saying, **He trusted on the LORD that he would deliver him:** let him deliver him, seeing he delighted in him"* (Psalm 22:7-8). He saw them give Jesus the vinegar when He cried out in thirst! *"They gave me also gall for my meat; **and in my thirst they gave me vinegar to drink"*** (Psalm 69:21).

David also saw that God would not leave Jesus in Hell but would resurrect Him. He revealed this in Psalm 16, ***"For thou wilt not leave my soul in hell;** neither wilt thou suffer thine Holy One to see corruption"* (Psalm 16:10). He actually prophesied the ascension of Jesus when he said, *"Thou hast ascended on high, thou hast led captivity captive: thou hast received gifts for men; yea, for the rebellious also, that the LORD God might dwell among them"* (Psalm 68:18). Do you know that David also saw Jesus being invited by God the Father to sit on His right hand after He ascended into Heaven? David saw this ceremony and talks about it in Psalm 110,

*"A Psalm of David. **The LORD said unto my Lord, Sit thou at my right hand,** until I make thine enemies thy footstool. The LORD shall send the rod of thy strength out of Zion: rule thou in the midst of thine enemies"* (Psalm 110:1-2).

God took David into the future to see this! He heard the Father speak to the Son, Jesus Christ! Jesus, many centuries later, refers to this incident in Matthew 22:42-45. God truly established and ordered His Kingdom or Empire on the throne of David! *"Of the increase of his government and peace there shall be no end, **upon the throne of David, and upon his kingdom, to order it, and to establish** it with judgment and with justice from henceforth even for ever. The zeal of the LORD of hosts will perform this"* (Isaiah 9:7). Do you see how connected all of this is? Now let us move on to study the premier divine emperor, Jesus Christ!

The Sixth Divine Emperor: **Jesus Christ**

"And Jesus came and spake unto them, saying, All power is given unto me in heaven and in earth" (Matthew 28:18).

*"And from Jesus Christ, who is the faithful witness, and the first begotten of the dead, **and the prince of the kings of the earth.** Unto him that loved us, and washed us from our sins in his own blood, **And hath made us kings and priests** unto God and his Father; to him be glory and dominion for ever and ever. Amen"* (Revelation 1:5-6).

*"And out of his mouth goeth a sharp sword, that with it he should smite the nations: and he shall rule them with a rod of iron: and he treadeth the winepress of the fierceness and wrath of Almighty God. And he hath on his vesture and on his thigh a name written, **KING OF KINGS, AND LORD OF LORDS"*** (Revelation 19:15-16).

Jesus is the next divine emperor. In fact, He is the penultimate divine emperor. All the divine emperors before Him were foreshadowing his imperialship. They were all types and shadows of him. He was the substance they foreshadowed! Their lives prophesied about him! Each divine emperor fulfilled a particular worldwide assignment or global mandate God wanted to execute on the Earth. God executed His worldwide plans progressively through all the divine emperors.

Adam was given dominion over all the works of God's hands to replenish the Earth. Noah was raised to replenish the Earth after God flooded it and destroyed all mankind except Noah and his family. God established a covenant with Noah to ensure that the Earth would not be destroyed in that way again. God then established a covenant with Abraham to make him the father of all nations and a birther of kings. Later on, Moses was raised as the divine emperor to execute the word God gave Abraham to deliver Israel from the oppression of Egypt and lead them to the Promised Land. David was then raised by God to start the process to forge His Empire on Earth! God sealed that mandate with the Sure Mercies of David Covenant.

Jesus was the ultimate fulfillment of all those dealings God had with the first five divine emperors! The assignment of Jesus was to seek and save man and reconcile us back to the Father through His death on the cross. His assignment was also to bring the Kingdom of Heaven to Earth and recover the Adamic crown from Satan. What you must understand is that with each divine emperor, God had a specific global agenda to fulfill. Jesus is the fulfillment of the lives the earlier emperors. He came to complete, fulfill, and substantiate with His life all the preceding global mandates. *"Think not that I am come to destroy the law, or the prophets: I am not come to destroy, but to fulfil"* (Matthew 5:17).

Jesus Recovers the Adamic Imperial Crown

"And so it is written, The first man Adam was made a living soul; the last Adam was made a quickening spirit" (1 Corinthians 15:45).

God gave the first man, Adam, dominion over the whole Earth and everything that He made with His hands, including the sun, moon, and stars. As we have seen, Adam lost all of that to the devil. Satan then filled that entire realm with his own kingdom. But the Father had a backup plan.

*"And all that dwell upon the earth shall worship him, whose names are not written in the book of life of **the Lamb slain from the foundation of the world**"* (Revelation 13:8).

67

God had a plan all along to ensure that the crown would be recovered from the devil and Jesus was God's plan! Jesus had to die for all of mankind because Adam's disobedience caused death to reign over all men. *"Wherefore, as by one man sin entered into the world, and death by sin; and so death passed upon all men, for that all have sinned"* (Roman 5:12). That is why every man who died including Abraham, David, Jeremiah, and all the saints, had to go to Hell because they were subject to death. Jesus had to come in the flesh and give His life as a ransom for all of mankind.

*"Forasmuch then as the children are partakers of flesh and blood, **he also himself likewise took part of the same; that through death he might destroy him that had the power of death, that is, the devil; And deliver them who through fear of death were all their lifetime subject to bondage.** For verily he took not on him the nature of angels; but he took on him the seed of Abraham"*
(Hebrews 2:14-16).

Jesus had to strive lawfully to recover the crown. *"And if a man also strive for masteries, **yet is he not crowned, except he strive lawfully"** (2 Timothy 2:5). Even though He is a member of the Godhead, He did come down to the Earth in the form of God or angels to take back the crown. He had to strive lawfully as a man on Earth to gain mastery over the Adamic crown. In other words, He could not come as a divine person, not even as an angel, to get back the crown. He had to come in the flesh as the Son of Man. This is because it is illegal to fight wrong in the kingdom.

That is also why Jesus told John the Baptist *"... Suffer it to be so now: for thus it becometh us to fulfil all righteousness"* (Matthew 3:15). All righteousness had to be fulfilled otherwise any attempt to regain the crown would be invalidated. Jesus had to be born that way to legally restore the crown to us. His whole purpose for being born and dying on the cross was to be a king. He told Pilate this as it is written, *"Pilate therefore said unto him, Art thou a king then? Jesus answered, **Thou sayest that I am a king. To this end was I born, and for this cause came I into the world,** that I should bear witness unto the truth. Every one that is of the truth heareth my voice"* (John 18:37).

Jesus the Last Adam

If Jesus did not come into the Earth through the womb of the woman, as the seed of the woman, our position would not have been restored. He came as the last Adam to restore the dominion and crown that Adam had at the beginning. Jesus said to Pilate, *"To this end was I born, and for this cause came I into the world."* His purpose for coming to the Earth was to recover and restore the crown we had when God gave Adam dominion over all the Earth and over all the works of his hands.

Jesus had to come to the Earth in the same Adamic Lineage as the last Adam. That is why Jesus is called the ast Adam! *"And so it is written, The first man Adam was made a living soul; the last Adam was made a quickening spirit"* (1 Corinthians 15:45). He came to the Earth in the form of man. And as a man, He was tempted on all points. He went through every temptation man goes through and aced the test! Jesus was *"… in all points tempted like as we are, yet without sin"* (Hebrews 4:15).

Jesus became flesh and that is the great mystery of God! *"And without controversy great is the mystery of godliness: God was manifest in the flesh"* (1 Timothy 3:16). Jesus came to the Earth legally through the womb of a woman, Mary the virgin. When He became full grown and received God's stamp of approval into sonship, Jesus started re-establishing the Kingdom of Heaven on Earth. He preached saying, *"… Repent: for the kingdom of heaven is at hand"* (Matthew 4:17). Then He mobilized up discipleship teams and sent them out two by two to also preach the Gospel of the Kingdom and heal the sick.

Wise as a Serpent

"And as Moses lifted up the serpent in the wilderness, even so must the Son of man be lifted up" (John 3:14).

Satan used the wisdom of the serpent to take the crown from Adam. God recovered the crown the same way it was lost, through the wisdom of the serpent. So, Jesus began to restore and salvage the wisdom of the serpent when He sent out the disciples. As He sent out the disciples, He said, *"Behold, I send you forth as sheep in the midst of wolves: **be ye therefore wise as serpents,** and harmless as doves"* (Matthew 10:16). He instructed them to employ the wisdom of the serpent in preaching the Kingdom of God. *"Be ye therefore wise as serpents!"*

God is always ahead of the devil, and that is why Jesus was slain from the foundation of the world. Jesus was crucified before anything good or evil happened. God hid this divine plan from the devil and his dark kingdom in the hidden wisdom realm!

*"But we speak the wisdom of God in a mystery, **even the hidden wisdom,** which God ordained before the world unto our glory. **Which none of the princes of this world knew: for had they known it, they would not have crucified the Lord of glory"** (1 Corinthians 2:7-8).*

God hid this plan deep inside Himself in the realm called *"the hidden wisdom."* Satan, when He was Lucifer, according to Ezekiel 28, was full of wisdom. However, that fullness did not include the hidden wisdom sovereign realm of God. That is why Satan was deceived by the meekness and humility of Jesus. So, when the devil got into Judas Iscariot to betray Jesus and got all of Israel to cry out for Jesus to be crucified, He was serving the purpose of God. Through the subtlety of the serpent, Jesus made it look as if He was losing by yielding to death. Jesus was being wise as a serpent all throughout that ordeal, and the moment the devil fulfilled the Will of God by crucifying Jesus, the crown fell off his head!

Death had been reigning from Adam until Moses, and now God through Jesus was fighting to get back the world with the wisdom of a snake. Jesus prophesied to Nicodemus that just as Moses lifted up the serpent in the wilderness so must He be lifted up. You must understand that the cross was a serpent strategy. The whole cross strategy was the wisdom of the serpent in manifestation. It was a Kingdom move to recover the Adamic crown from the devil! The cross was really a warfare move of the Kingdom of God that devastated the kingdom of Satan. That is why

Jesus could use the cross to triumph over the principalities and powers of Satan.

Satan thought he had Jesus when he killed Him on the cross, but what he did not understand is that it actually pleased God to bruise Jesus. *"Yet it pleased the LORD to bruise him…"* (Isaiah 53:10). The Father was not weeping when Jesus was crucified, He was happy. He knew what he was doing. He was taking back the whole world from the devil. That is great power! That is the strategy of an emperor. An emperor does not just win kingdoms, he wins worlds!

The Kingdom Strategy of the Cross

It was the Will of God for Jesus to die on the cross. This plan was affirmed on the Mount of Transfiguration, when Moses and Elijah appeared in glory and spoke to Jesus about how He was to die. From that time, Jesus began to privately tell the disciples how He would be crucified and be resurrected after three days. To safeguard this highly classified information, Jesus went into stealth mode right before the hour of darkness descended. He said to the disciples,

"Hereafter I will not talk much with you: for the prince of this world cometh, and hath nothing in me" (John 14:30).

In the Garden of Gethsemane, as Jesus prayed, the Father made it clear that it was His will that Jesus dies on the cross. At Gethsemane, Jesus yielded His will totally to the Father when He said, *"O my Father, if this cup may not pass away from me, except I drink it, **thy will be done"*** (Matthew 26:42). The death of Jesus on the cross was the Father's perfect will! Satan did not realize that. If He knew that, He would not have crucified Jesus. He had no idea that Jesus was employing the serpent strategy of wisdom through subtlety to get back the Adamic crown. When Satan had Jesus crucified, he was yielding to the will of God! The moment he crucified Jesus, the devil became subject to Jesus because of this powerful spiritual law of royalty,

"Know ye not, that to whom ye yield yourselves servants to obey, his servants ye are to whom ye obey; whether of sin unto death, or of obedience unto righteousness?" (Romans 6:16).

In the same way the first Adam lost the crown, Jesus recovered the crown, through the wisdom of the serpent! The cross was a strategic point of wisdom - the serpent's wisdom. That is why the Bible says, *"And as Moses lifted up the serpent in the wilderness, even so must the Son of man be lifted up"* (John 3:14). God encoded this awesome plan in Numbers 21 when fiery serpents were biting and killing the Israelites for speaking against Moses and God. To heal those dying from the deadly bites of the fiery serpents, God commanded Moses,

"Make thee a fiery serpent, and set it upon a pole: and it shall come to pass, that every one that is bitten, when he looketh upon it, shall live" (Numbers 21:8).

We think Jesus dying on the cross was just fulfilling what Moses did when he raised up the brazen serpent in the wilderness. It is so much deeper than that. That incident in Numbers 21 was just a type and shadow of how Jesus would later on use the wisdom of the serpent to outwit and outmaneuver the devil, and fool him into obeying the will of God. Once Satan did that he became a servant of Jesus! He was subject to the Lord. He lost the crown and Jesus took it back!

Jesus Casts out the Prince of the Whole World

Satan ruled the world from the time of Adam until Jesus came preaching the Gospel of the Kingdom and saying, *"Repent, for the Kingdom of Heaven is at hand"* (Matthew 4:17). Jesus did not preach a church message. He had to preach a kingdom message because he was not fighting a church devil who sang in the choir in Heaven. He was fighting a devil who was a royal power having his own kingdom. That is why Jesus said,

*"And if Satan cast out Satan, he is divided against himself; how shall then **his kingdom** stand?"* (Matthew 12:26).

Jesus said Satan had a kingdom! Jesus came to destroy that kingdom by casting out the devil. That is why He preached and manifested the Kingdom of God. He said, *"But if I cast out devils by the Spirit of God, then the kingdom of God is come unto you"* (Matthew 12:28). It takes a kingdom to displace another kingdom. Jesus brought the Kingdom of Heaven to cast out Satan. Casting out devils is a key manifestation of the Kingdom of God! Now, Jesus did not come to just deal with little demons, He came to dislodge the prince over the whole world! Jesus had to work with the Father to cast out the Prince of the World. This is recorded in John as follows,

"Father, glorify thy name. Then came there a voice from heaven, saying, I have both glorified it, and will glorify it again. The people therefore, that stood by, and heard it, said that it thundered: others said, An angel spake to him. Jesus answered and said, This voice came not because of me, but for your sakes. Now is the judgment of this world: **now shall the prince of this world be cast out.** *And I, if I be lifted up from the earth, will draw all men unto me. This he said, signifying what death he should die"* (John 12:28-33).

In this passage, you see how God as an emperor displaced Satan by just speaking openly out of Heaven. Just His voice speaking out of Heaven, **"I have both glorified it, and will glorify it again"** totally displaced the Prince of the World. That is why Jesus said, "Now shall the prince of the world be cast out." God's voice displaced Satan's power! Now, when a prince demon is knocked off his throne and his crown falls off his head, somebody has to pick it up. Somebody has to get his scepter. Somebody has to take over his throne.

Jesus was basically saying in that John passage, *"I cannot be lifted up in the air with a prince demon over there. When the prince is cast out, I will then be lifted up from the Earth up into the air to take over his dominion. Once the mind blinding power of the prince is broken off the minds of the men under his control, they will then be free to make a decision to serve another king. And now, all the men who were under the control of the prince will be drawn unto me when I am lifted up."*

This is exactly what Jesus meant when He said, *"No man can enter into a strong man's house, and spoil his goods, except he will first bind the strong man; and then he will spoil his house"* (Mark 3:27).

Satan, as the Prince of the World, was the strong man holding captive all the souls of men. Once the prince was broken, Jesus could spoil his goods, including the souls of men. That is exactly what Jesus did through the power of the cross. Jesus delivered all the souls held bondage by death and hell and brought them all out of the grave! He took captivity captive! He spoiled the principalities and powers of the devil in Hell and took possession of the keys of Hell and death! *"And having spoiled principalities and powers, he made a shew of them openly, triumphing over them in it"* (Colossians 2:15). He rose from the grave victorious having conquered devil and his entire kingdom!

The Adamic Crown is Restored with Greater Majesty

So, when Jesus rose from the dead, He proclaimed victoriously, *"...All power is given unto me in heaven and in earth"* (Matthew 28:18). Before the crucifixion, Jesus was not the Prince of the World, but after his resurrection he became the Prince of the all the Kings of the Earth. Jesus is now the potentate of God! *"Which in his times he shall shew, who is the blessed and **only** Potentate, the King of kings, and Lord of lords"* (1 Timothy 6:15). He has been given dominion over all of Heaven and Earth! Jesus recovered the crown Adam lost to the devil! Jesus is now the Prince of the Kings of the Earth, which makes him the emperor of the whole Earth!

*"And from Jesus Christ, who is the faithful witness, and the first begotten of the dead, and **the prince of the kings of the earth.** Unto him that loved us, and washed us from our sins in his own blood, And hath made us kings and priests unto God and his Father; to him be glory and dominion for ever and ever. Amen"*
(Revelation 1:5-6).

When Jesus rose from the dead, He did not just make us princes, he made us kings! That is why it is written, *"And hath made us kings and priests unto God"* (Revelation 1:6). And you've got to understand that when Jesus rose from the dead, He did not just recover the crown Adam lost, He got back so much more. This is because in the Kingdom when God restores you it is never Him just giving you back what you lost, He gives you multiples of what you lost! That is why the Bible says, "

*"If the theft be certainly found in his hand alive, whether it be ox, or ass, or sheep; **he shall restore double"*** (Exodus 22:4).

*"But if he be found, **he shall restore sevenfold;** he shall give all the substance of his house"* (Proverbs 6:31).

*"The thief cometh not, but for to steal, and to kill, and to destroy: I am come that they might have life, **and that they might have it more abundantly"*** (John 10:10).

Jesus does not just make you a prince, He makes you a king. And He does even better than that, Jesus, in other words, says, *"I will raise you up to sit with me in heavenly places."* You are no longer like the first Adam on Earth with a crown as a prince over the whole Earth realm. You now have power in two worlds! You have the power and authority of a king in God's World and Empire! You sit with Jesus in the heavenly places, and as a king in God's Kingdom, you are to use the powers of the world to come in this world down here on Earth!

Now, this is the point you must understand. When Jesus resurrected from the grave after recovering the crown, He did not just give us back the Adamic crown. He gave us so much more. He gave us His crown too! The Adamic crown that Jesus has as the last Adam is invested with infinitely so much more glory and power and dominion than Adam's crown ever had. This is as a result of the divine principle of restoration. So, in the first Adam we were made a little lower than angels, but in the restoration, we were raised together with Jesus above the angels! Hebrews sheds more light on this mystery.

"Who being the brightness of his glory, and the express image of his person, and upholding all things by the word of his power, when he had by himself purged our sins, sat down on the right hand of the Majesty on high; **Being made so much better than the angels, as he hath by inheritance obtained a more excellent name than they.** *For unto which of the angels said he at any time, Thou art my Son, this day have I begotten thee? And again, I will be to him a Father, and he shall be to me a Son? And again, when he bringeth in the firstbegotten into the world, he saith,* **And let all the angels of God worship him"** (Hebrews 1:3-6).

The first shall be last and the last shall be first. So, the last crown ranks so much higher than the first crown. In the restoration, Jesus, together with us, was exalted and raised above the angels to sit on the right hand of the majesty on high. The last Adam was made *"so much better than the angels."* The last Adam also has *"a more excellent name"* than the angels. And the Father has issued a decree saying, *"Let all the angels of God worship him."*

And this is the deal, we are sitting in the same seat that Jesus is sitting on! *"And hath* **raised us up together, and** *made* **us sit together in heavenly places in Christ Jesus"** (Ephesians 2:6). We have been raised up together and we sit together with the Lord in the heavenly places. We share the imperial status of the right-hand seat when we walk in the imperial anointing!

And so, by the power of the Holy Ghost, we can command angelic powers. We can command angels who rule other worlds because the imperial crown that Jesus wears deals with worlds! We have power and the ability not just only to control the air, sea, and land in this world, God has now made us sit in the same seat with His son and to have the same power as His son to command these angels!

"But to **which of the angels** *said he at any time, Sit on my right hand, until I make thine enemies thy footstool?* **Are they not all ministering spirits, sent forth to minister** *for them who shall be heirs of salvation?"* (Hebrews 1:13-14).

We were first made lower than the angels, but now the angels have now been commissioned to serve us. We are the heirs that scripture is talking about. We are heirs to God's throne! *"And if children, then heirs; heirs of God, and joint-heirs with Christ..."* (Romans 8:17). We are not just joint heirs with Christ, we are also heirs of God, and that is why the angels now serve us. This is also why angels come to our services to hear what the Holy Spirit in us is saying, as the Bible says,

"Unto whom it was revealed, that not unto themselves, but unto us they did minister the things, which are now reported unto you by them that have preached the gospel unto you with the Holy Ghost sent down from heaven; which things the angels desire to look into" (1 Peter 1:12).

You see, the angels come to our services because when we minister God actually dwells in us and speaks through us! They come to listen to the God in us. This happens when you allow the Holy Spirit to speak through you.

The Global Mandate of Jesus

*"His eyes were as a flame of fire, **and on his head were many crowns**; and he had a name written, that no man knew, but he himself"* (Revelations 19:12).

Now, as the Emperor of all of Heaven and Earth, and in His position as God's potentate, Jesus has the mandate to see to it that all the dominions of the world are subdued at his feet. When that mandate is fulfilled, He will then hand over the whole Empire back to the Father.

*"Then cometh the end, when he shall have **delivered up the kingdom to God,** even the Father; when he shall have put down all rule and all authority and power"* (1 Corinthians 15:24).

Following the resurrection and ascension of Jesus, in just twenty years, the apostles turned the whole world upside down. They were able to do this because the prince who controlled the whole world had lost his place. Jesus broke and spoiled him with the cross. But since then, Satan has down through the dark ages gained a foothold in the world. For many centuries both the message and ministry of the Kingdom has been lost because the church did not occupy what Jesus gained at the cross. But this is the good news: we still have the same authority of the kingdom and resurrection power of the Lord! Jesus does not have to come down to the Earth and die all over again. We are still kings and emperors and we can take over the world just like the Apostles did with the Kingdom message that Jesus has restored in our generation!

At the end of time, God will send His Son back to the Earth to subdue kingdom of darkness and wage war until all the kingdoms of the world are subdued under His feet. This is also why John sees Jesus wearing many crowns on His head. *"His eyes were as a flame of fire, and on his head were many crowns; and he had a name written, that no man knew, but he himself"* (Revelation 19:12). These crowns on the head of Jesus represent all the kingdoms and dominions of the world! John revealed this in the book of Revelation,

> *"And the seventh angel sounded; and there were great voices in heaven, saying,* ***The kingdoms of this world are become the kingdoms of our Lord,*** *and of his Christ; and he shall reign for ever and ever"* (Revelation 11:15).

This is happening right now! The end times are upon us. One of my callings is to be an end-time general. And the Lord God has commissioned me to mobilize and deploy the Joel End-Time Army to fulfill this royal commission. You are going to see the Kingdom of God invade all the nations of the world because Jesus the potentate, the Emperor of the World, has been dispatched to subdue all rebellion in God's Empire on the Earth! This is why Jesus is appearing face to face to multitudes all over the world!

Jesus Has the Power of One as a Divine Emperor

> *"And not as it was* ***by one*** *that sinned, so is the gift: for the judgment was* ***by one*** *to condemnation, but the free gift is of many offences unto justification.* ***For if by one man's offence death reigned by one;*** *much more they which receive*

*abundance of grace and of the gift of righteousness shall reign **in life by one, Jesus Christ.** Therefore as by the **offence of one judgment came upon all men** to condemnation; **even so by the righteousness of one the free gift came upon all men** unto justification of life. For as by **one man's disobedience many** were made sinners, so by the obedience of **one shall many be made righteous"***
(Romans 5:16-19).

In Romans 5, we see how the Power of One was employed by Jesus to save the whole world and reverse every evil thing Adam's sin introduced into the world. By one man, sin came into the world and affected all men, as it is written, *"Wherefore, as by one man sin entered into the world, and death by sin; and so death passed upon all men, for that all have sinned"* (Romans 5:12). Because Adam had the Power of One as a divine emperor, his offense brought judgment *"upon all men to condemnation."* Jesus, on the other hand, by His righteousness and obedience, made many righteous with the Power of One.

Whereas Adam's sin caused death to reign over all men, Jesus' obedience and righteousness causes us much more to *"reign in life by one, Jesus Christ."* Adam's sin enslaved all mankind, but Jesus' death, burial, and resurrection caused all who believe to be redeemed and delivered from the power of darkness! Jesus redeemed and washed us in His own blood to make us kings and priests who will *"reign in life by one, Jesus Christ."* This is the Power of One!

Everything Jesus did was leveraged by the Father to include all the saints! For example, in Daniel 7, when Jesus received dominion, glory, and a kingdom, we see that what He received was given to the *"saints of the most high."* Jesus got the kingdom back and all saints together with Him inherited this kingdom!

*"I saw in the night visions, and, behold, one like the Son of man came with the clouds of heaven, and came to the Ancient of days, and they brought him near before him. And **there was given him dominion, and glory, and a kingdom, that all people, nations, and languages, should serve him:** his dominion is an*

everlasting dominion, which shall not pass away, and his kingdom that which shall not be destroyed" (Daniel 7:13-14).

*"And the kingdom and dominion, and the greatness of the kingdom under the whole heaven, **shall be given to the people of the saints of the most High**, whose kingdom is an everlasting kingdom, and all dominions shall serve and obey him"* (Daniel 7:27).

In the first passage, you see how Jesus as the *"Son of Man"* was led into the presence of the Father, the Ancient of Days, who gave Him *"... Dominion, and glory and a kingdom, that all people, nations, and languages should serve him."* Daniel had this vision in a trip to Heaven, and during that vision, He asked a guide to interpret or explain the vision of the Son of Man to him. The guide interpreted the vision by explaining that what he saw given to the Son of Man was also given to the saints of the Most High! That is why in Daniel 7:27 the guide tells Daniel, *"And the kingdom and dominion and the greatness of the kingdom under the whole heaven **shall be given to the people of the saints of the most High.**"*

The crown is now on Jesus' head. But here's the thing, He did not just get the crown, He gave it to us! He gave dominion over the Earth back to us! That is why Jesus, by His blood washed us and made us kings and priests unto God. Now, you understand why Jesus can also appoint to you a kingdom. That is why and how the Apostles turned the world upside down. Before then it was not possible because a strongman, the devil, had the whole world in his grip. But through the cross, Jesus displaced the devil. Jesus triumphed over the devil with the cross through the wisdom and subtlety of the serpent. He achieved all this through the Power of One as a divine emperor!

As a Divine Emperor, He Has the License to Kill

*"Having yet therefore one son, his wellbeloved, he sent him also last unto them, saying, **They will reverence my son.** But those husbandmen said among themselves, This is the heir; come, let us kill him, and the inheritance shall be ours. And they took him, and killed him, and cast him out of the vineyard. What*

*shall therefore the lord of the vineyard do? **he will come and destroy the husbandmen,** and will give the vineyard unto others"* (Mark 12:6-9).

The Father is prepared to destroy everyone who rejects His Son Jesus Christ because Jesus is an Emperor! Jesus is the Prince of the Kings of the Earth. That is why Jesus began to cry when He looked over the City of Jerusalem. He saw how the Father was going to judge all of Israel for rejecting Him.

*"And when he was come near, he beheld the city, and wept over it, Saying, If thou hadst known, even thou, at least in this thy day, the things which belong unto thy peace! but now they are hid from thine eyes. For the days shall come upon thee, that thine enemies shall cast a trench about thee, and compass thee round, and keep thee in on every side, **And shall lay thee even with the ground, and thy children within thee; and they shall not leave in thee one stone upon another; because thou knewest not the time of thy visitation"*** (Luke 19:41-44).

And at the end of times during the white throne judgment, the punishment for not receiving Jesus is even more terrifying! *"And whosoever was not found written in the book of life was cast into the lake of fire"* (Revelation 20:15). Because Jesus is a divine emperor, anyone who rejects Him cannot inherit the Kingdom of God. In fact, when Israel rejected Jesus, God disinherited the whole nation! Anyone who does not believe in Jesus is forever undone! *"And this is the record, that God hath given to us eternal life, **and this life is in his Son.** He that hath the Son hath life; **and he that hath not the Son of God hath not life"*** (1 John 5:11-12). There has to be great reverence for Jesus as the divine emperor over the Earth. That is why David prophesied in the second Psalm, ***"Kiss the Son, lest he be angry, and ye perish*** *from the way, when his wrath is kindled but a little"* (Psalm 2:12).

Jesus Judges Capernaum

Jesus personally exercised this license to kill over Capernaum when He decreed over that city, *"And thou, Capernaum, **which art exalted unto heaven, shalt be brought down to hell...***"* (Matthew 11:23). Jesus judged

Capernaum because they did not repent after seeing all the miracles He did. *"Then began he to upbraid the cities wherein most of his mighty works were done, because they repented not"* (Matthew 11:20).

Capernaum was the city where Jesus did most of His miracles, but getting to the end of His earthly ministry the people of Capernaum began to lapse into unbelief. In John 6, we see how the people of Capernaum began to challenge Jesus and question His ministry even after all the miracles signs and wonders He had performed in that city. They began to murmur when He spoke about them eating His flesh and drinking His blood.

*"The Jews then murmured at him, because he said, I am the bread which came down from heaven. **And they said, Is not this Jesus, the son of Joseph**, whose father and mother we know? how is it then that he saith, I came down from heaven?"* (John 6:41-42).

The people of Capernaum had great honor for Jesus at first, unlike the people of Nazareth. But after three years, they began to devalue and dishonor Him by equalizing His ministry. Now they were parroting what the people of Nazareth said three years earlier about Jesus, *"Is not this the carpenter's son? ..."* (Matthew 13:55). The people of Capernaum were now also saying, *"... Is not this Jesus, the son of Joseph?"* (John 6:42). They no longer had honor for Jesus. No wonder Jesus cast them down from Heaven to Hell. He virtually consigned that whole city to Hell, which is much worse than killing them physically. They were forever undone.

Jesus Judges the Jewish Religious Leaders

Jesus also judged the Jewish religious leaders before He finished His earthly ministry. He looked them in the eye and said, *"I said therefore unto you, **that ye shall die in your sins**: for if ye believe not that I am he, ye shall die in your sins"* (John 8:24). Anyone who does not believe on Jesus Christ is forever undone.

*"He that believeth and is baptized shall be saved; but **he that believeth not shall be damned"** (Mark 16:16).*

*"He that believeth on him is not condemned: but **he that believeth not is condemned already,** because he hath not believed in the name of the only begotten Son of God"* (John 3:18).

This is because as a divine emperor, Jesus has the license to kill. His death sentence is infinitely more extensive in scope than that of any other earthly divine emperor, because His death sentence is an eternal one! Jesus did not exercise this license to kill people physically while He was alive on the Earth, but He exercised the license to kill by issuing pre-emptive judgments on those that opposed Him. They would live on the Earth but in the next age they would have to face Jesus.

But in other cases when He was opposed, Jesus chose to walk in mercy. At one time, Jesus tried to pass through a Samaritan village and the people of that village refused Him passage. This infuriated His disciples who tried to get permission from Jesus to call down fire from Heaven to consume them. But Jesus rebuked them saying, *"… Ye know not what manner of spirit ye are of. **For the Son of man is not come to destroy men's lives, but to save them** …"* (Luke 9:55-56). Jesus did not come to the Earth to kill or destroy men, He came to save lives. As a divine emperor, He had the authority and power to destroy that village, but He chose not to do so because that was not His assignment. His assignment was to save lives!

The Father, on the other hand, as the Emperor of All Emperors, has the ultimate license to kill. His powers to kill cover both this present time and the time to come. Jesus warned His disciples about this immense power His Father has.

*"And fear not them which kill the body, but are not able to kill the soul: but rather fear him which is **able to destroy both soul and body in hell"***

(Matthew 10:28).

*"And I say unto you my friends, Be not afraid of them that kill the body, **and after that have no more that they can do.** But I will forewarn you whom ye shall fear: Fear him, which **after he hath killed hath power to cast into hell;** yea, I say unto you, Fear him"* (Luke 12:4-5).

You see how Jesus limited this license to kill to the eternal realm. This is because the mission of Jesus on the Earth was to save the lives of men not to destroy them. But the Father, who has the greater rank, has an unlimited use of this power to destroy both *"soul and body in Hell."* The Father, the highest emperor, has the power to kill and to cast into Hell!

He Rules Over All Nations

As a divine emperor, Jesus rules over all the people, nations, and languages. God gave Him a blank check when He told him, *"Ask of me, and I shall give thee the heathen for thine inheritance, and the uttermost parts of the earth for thy possession"* (Psalm 2:8). Well, Jesus asked for and received dominion over all the kingdoms of the world! He died on the cross for all mankind and redeemed all nations by His blood. All nations were redeemed by Him and are now subject to Him.

"And they sung a new song, saying, Thou art worthy to take the book, and to open the seals thereof: for thou wast slain, and hast redeemed us to God by thy blood out of every kindred, and tongue, and people, and nation; And hast made us unto our God kings and priests: and we shall reign on the earth" (Revelations 5:9-10).

That is why He is the Prince of all the Kings of the Earth. And in the fullness of time, all the kingdoms of the world shall be subject to Him! *"And the seventh angel sounded; and there were great voices in heaven, saying, The kingdoms of this world are become the kingdoms of our Lord, and of his Christ; and he shall reign for ever and ever"* (Revelation 11:15).

Eternal Kingdom

"And there was given him dominion, and glory, and a kingdom, that all people, nations, and languages, should serve him: his dominion is an everlasting dominion, which shall not pass away, and his kingdom that which shall not be destroyed" (Daniel 7:14).

Jesus has an eternal empire and His dominion is an everlasting dominion. He paid a heavy price for this eternal dominion. The Bible says He learned obedience by the things He suffered. He pleased God by His obedience to every one of His Father's commands. Before Jesus became the emperor of the world, many empires and emperors were raised up who had total world dominion. But since Jesus rose from the dead and sat on the right hand of God, no other emperor has risen on the Earth with total world dominion. Many tried and failed. Napoleon and Hitler for example tried and failed to rule the whole world. Jesus is the Prince of the Kings of the Earth!

Jesus is a Birther of Kings

*"Ye are they which have continued with me in my temptations. **And I appoint unto you a kingdom,** as my Father hath appointed unto me; That ye may eat and drink at my table in my kingdom, and sit on thrones judging the twelve tribes of Israel"* (Luke 22:28-30)

*"And from Jesus Christ, who is the faithful witness, and the first begotten of the dead, **and the prince of the kings of the earth.** Unto him that loved us, and washed us from our sins in his own blood, **And hath made us kings and priests unto God** and his Father; to him be glory and dominion for ever and ever. Amen"* (Revelations 1:5-6).

Jesus, as a divine emperor, is a birther of kings. According to Revelation 1, Jesus died for us and washed us in His own blood and has made us kings and priests unto God. As an emperor, He is a birther of kings! That is why He could appoint a throne and a kingdom to each of

His apostles. He did that in his office and authority as a divine emperor. And so when He was raised up we were raised up too! We are seated together with Him in heavenly places. In His function as a birther of kings, He is called the King of Kings and the Lord of Lords.

> *"And he hath on his vesture and on his thigh a name written, **KING OF KINGS, AND LORD OF LORDS"** (Revelation 19:16).*

We were born into His Kingdom and made kings when we receive Him and believe on Him! The title *King of Kings* is another imperial title Jesus has as a divine emperor. He is the "King" and we are the "kings!" He is the King of the Kings that He birthed into the Kingdom of God as an emperor!

The Seventh Divine Emperor: Peter

> *"And Jesus answered and said unto him, Blessed art thou, Simon Barjona: for flesh and blood hath not revealed it unto thee, but my Father which is in heaven. And I say also unto thee, That thou art Peter, and upon this rock I will build my church; and the gates of hell shall not prevail against it. **And I will give unto thee the keys of the kingdom of heaven: and whatsoever thou shalt bind on earth shall be bound in heaven: and whatsoever thou shalt loose on earth shall be loosed in heaven"** (Matthew 16:17-19).*

Before Jesus left the Earth, He handed over the Keys of the Kingdom of Heaven to Peter, thus designating Peter as the next divine emperor. One very important mystery you must understand about the office of the emperor is that God raises divine emperors on the Earth one at a time, space, and generation. You cannot have two emperors ruling the Earth at the same time. Emperors rule worlds, so how can two rule one world at the same time? Adam was the first one, then Noah, Abraham, Moses, David, Jesus and now Peter! You see, God gives all of us access to imperial power because we are joint heirs with Jesus who is a divine emperor.

All of us are kings, but He raises one major divine emperor at a time in a generation to keep birthing kings. A king cannot birth an emperor. A king can only birth a prince. A prince cannot birth a king, a king must birth a prince. When God said to Abraham, *"Kings shall come out of thee..."* (Genesis 17:6) He was basically telling Abraham, *"You are the emperor on Earth now!"* That is also how we know that Jesus is a divine emperor because the Bible says concerning Jesus,

> *"...Unto him that loved us, and washed us from our sins in his own blood, And **hath made us kings and priests** unto God and his Father; to him be glory and dominion for ever and ever. Amen"* (Revelation 1:5-6).

When the Bible says Jesus *"made us kings"* that right there is God calling Jesus an emperor. How can He make us kings if He is not an emperor? That defines Jesus' imperial status and office when He was on Earth. Before He ascended into Heaven, He established Peter as the next emperor. You see, when Jesus gave Peter the keys to the whole kingdom of God under Heaven, He was making Peter an emperor. Look more carefully at what Jesus told Peter,

> *"And I will **give unto thee** the **keys of the kingdom of heaven:** and **whatsoever thou shalt bind on earth** shall be bound in heaven: **and whatsoever thou shalt loose** on earth shall be loosed in heaven"* (Matthew 16:19).

What Jesus gave Peter here was not just authority, but dominion. Jesus gave Peter the Keys of the Kingdom of Heaven to execute Heaven's agenda on the Earth. As the divine emperor over the Earth, Peter had great authority and power to bind or stop things on Earth, or loose, permit and allow certain things to happen on the Earth with the total backing of Heaven!

Why Jesus Choose Peter to be the Next Emperor

> *"And when there had been much disputing, Peter rose up, and said unto them, Men and brethren, ye know how that a good while ago **God made choice among***

*us, that the Gentiles **by my mouth should hear the word of the gospel,** and believe"* (Acts 15:7).

Jesus recognized and discerned that Peter was the next emperor because of all the apostles it was Peter who had the revelation of who Jesus was. Peter was given the revelation of the emperor before him, Jesus, by the Father Himself. I am a divine emperor because I also received the revelation of the emperors before me: Jesus and Peter. The Lord taught me the revelation of why Peter was chosen to be the next emperor because He was setting me up to be the divine emperor of this generation. To choose the next emperor, Jesus asked a very important question that only Peter could answer.

*"He saith unto them, But whom say ye that I am? **And Simon Peter answered and said, Thou art the Christ, the Son of the living God"*** (Matthew 16:15-16).

No one could get that question right unless they had personal dealings with the Father Himself! This is because the Bible says, *"... and no man knoweth the Son, but the Father..."* (Matthew 11:27). Only the Father knows the Son and only He can reveal the Son. So, when Peter answered Jesus, *"Thou art the Christ, the Son of the Living God,"* Jesus knew immediately that the Father had been talking to Peter. That is why Jesus said to Peter,

*"... Blessed art thou, Simon Barjona: for flesh and blood hath not revealed it unto thee, **but my Father which is in heaven"*** (Matthew 16:17).

Peter was the only one of all the twelve apostles who had the revelation of Son of God. The only one who could be the divine emperor after Jesus had to have the revelation of Jesus' identity from the Father Himself. This is because emperors are really princes with God. They had direct dealings with the Father. None of the other apostles had this revelation and that is why Jesus entrusted the Keys of God's Kingdom to Peter,

*"**And I will give unto thee the keys of the kingdom of heaven:** and whatsoever thou shalt bind on earth shall be bound in heaven: and whatsoever thou shalt loose on earth shall be loosed in heaven"* (Matthew 16:19).

The Keys of the Kingdom of Heaven were given only to Peter because He was to be the leading emperor. Later in Matthew 18, Jesus gave the other apostles power to bind and loose. That is why Jesus said to all the apostles, *"Verily I say unto you, Whatsoever ye shall bind on earth shall be bound in heaven: and whatsoever ye shall loose on earth shall be loosed in heaven"* (Matthew 18:18). He gave them all the power to bind and loose, but you must understand that is not the same as the keys Jesus gave to Peter directly because Peter alone had the revelation that Jesus was the Messiah and the Son of God.

Lovest Thou Me More than These?

Jesus taught me that another reason Peter became the next emperor is that he loved Jesus more than the other apostles. Many believe that John was the one who loved Jesus most, but that is not what the Bible says. People think that because the Bible says John was the disciple Jesus loved. *"Now there was leaning on Jesus' bosom one of his **disciples, whom Jesus loved**"* (John 13:23). This disciple was John, who is believed to have been the youngest of the apostles. Five times in the gospel of John, the apostle John is referred to as the disciple *"whom Jesus loved"* (John 13:23; John 19:26; John 20:2; John 21:7,20).

But the Bible did not say, *"The disciple who loved Jesus."* The scriptures only say that Jesus loved the disciple. In John 21, when Jesus asked the question, *"Lovest thou me more than these?"* John was not the one Jesus was talking to. Jesus asked Peter that question in the presence of all the other apostles. He did that to designate Peter as the leading emperor. Why do you think Jesus asked Peter this question in front of all the other apostles? He was designating rank! Why didn't He ask John that question? He did not ask John because He was not the one who loved Jesus the most. Peter was the one who loved Him the most!

*"So when they had dined, **Jesus saith to Simon Peter,** Simon, son of Jonas,*
***lovest thou me more than these?** He saith unto him, Yea, Lord; thou knowest*
that I love thee. He saith unto him, Feed my lambs" (John 21:15).

Peter loved Jesus more than all the other Apostles, and that is why Jesus asked him that question. It was not John. Jesus revealed to me in a face to face appearance that Peter loved Him more than the other apostles because he always loved and acted first! God established that pattern as in the epistle of John, *"We love him, because he first loved us"* (1 John 4:19). God's love for us is the greatest love we can ever experience because He loved us first. This became a divine pattern. He who loves first loves best! The mystery of this revelation is that none of the apostles loved Jesus the way Peter did. Peter always loved first. He always acted first.

Love operates first, love acts first, love does not wait. Even though Jesus loved John, it does not mean John loved Jesus back that way. John did love Jesus but not as much as Peter did. Peter loved Jesus the most because he acted first every time! When they were caught in the storm on the sea and saw Jesus walking on the water, who spoke first to Jesus? Peter!

*"And Peter answered him and said, Lord, if it be thou, **bid me come unto thee** on*
*the water. And he said, Come. **And when Peter was come down out of the ship,***
***he walked on the water, to go to Jesus"** (Matthew 14:28-29).

Peter was the only one to get out of the boat to go to Jesus. The others stayed in the boat. Peter acted first! Love always acts first! And this was not the only occasion when Peter acted first. When Jesus spoke about how the rich would find it difficult to enter the Kingdom of God, Peter spoke first, *"**Then Peter began to say unto him, Lo, we have left all,** and have followed thee"* (Mark 10:28). It was Peter that noticed that the fig tree had withered, *"**And Peter calling to remembrance** saith unto him, Master, behold, the fig tree which thou cursedst is withered away"* (Mark 11:21).

When Jesus spoke of how all the disciples would forsake Him during His trial, Peter spoke up first again. *"**But Peter said unto him,** Although all shall be offended, yet will not I"* (Mark 14:29). When most of the disciples stopped following Jesus, Peter spoke up first when Jesus asked the twelve whether they also wanted to leave, *"Then **Simon Peter answered him,** Lord, to whom shall we go? thou hast the words of eternal life"* (John 6:68). And when Jesus appeared to seven of the disciples as they were fishing it was Peter that leaped out of the boat and pulled the boat to shore to meet Jesus.

"Therefore that disciple whom Jesus loved saith unto Peter, It is the Lord. Now when Simon Peter heard that it was the Lord, he girt his fisher's coat unto him, (for he was naked,) and did cast himself into the sea. And the other disciples came in a little ship ... " (John 21:7-8).

Several times Peter acted and spoke up first. Peter loved Jesus more than the other disciples and the Father saw that. That is the primary reason why the Father chose Peter. *"... and he that loveth me shall be loved of my Father ... "* (John 14:21.) God knew that of all the twelve apostles, Peter loved His Son the most. That is why the Father chose to reveal His Son's identity to Peter. This is because God still picks friends for Jesus. The Father is the one who chooses the friends of Jesus and that is why only the Father chooses who gets to sit on the right or left hand of Jesus.

There is a man of God who had a trip to Heaven and had the chance to see the twelve foundations of New Jerusalem. He saw the names of the apostles on the foundations as revealed in Revelation, *"And the wall of the city had **twelve foundations,** and in them the **names of the twelve apostles of the Lamb"*** (Revelation 21:14). He saw that Peter's name came first on the foundations and then Paul's name came next. This man of God thought John's name would at least come after Peter's name, but it was Paul's name that came next after Peter because Paul also loved Jesus greatly. Paul taught a lot on the love covenant relationship we can have with the Lord because he walked in that realm!

*"**And to know the love of Christ,** which passeth knowledge, that ye might be filled with all the fulness of God"* (Ephesians 3:19).

Even though Paul's apostleship was established much later after Jesus ascended, He is still ranked highly in Heaven because of his love walk. He gave up everything as the Bible says, *"Yea doubtless, and I count all things but loss for the excellency of the knowledge of Christ Jesus my Lord: for whom I have suffered the loss of all things, and do count them but dung, **that I may win Christ"*** (Philippians 3:8). That is why it pleased God to reveal His Son to Paul as well.

*"But I certify you, brethren, that the gospel which was preached of me is not after man. For I neither received it of man, neither was I taught it, **but by the revelation of Jesus Christ"*** (Galatians 1:11-12).

*"But **when it pleased God,** who separated me from my mother's womb, and called me by his grace, **To reveal his Son in me,** that I might preach him among the heathen; immediately I conferred not with flesh and blood"* (Galatians 1:15-16).

Paul's special relationship with Jesus also attracted God's attention. Because of Paul's intense love and pursuit of Jesus, it pleased God to reveal His Son Jesus to Paul. He allowed Paul to receive great revelations about the mystery of Christ, the riches of the glory of Christ, and many other deep revelations about the fellowship of the mystery. Even Peter mentions how Paul was graced to receive those mysteries. Peter recognized how highly Paul ranked in the hierarchy of God's Empire and gave him the right hand of fellowship. Paul received all this because of love. He also loved Christ. But still, Peter loved Jesus the most and that is why his name comes first, and that is why in all the records of the Apostles his name always comes first. This is because he loved Jesus the most.

This is what you need to understand, God and His Son Jesus love everybody. In fact, He loved us when we were yet sinners! He loves the whole world! So, it is not about whether God loves you, it is about how you love Him. Your love for Jesus is what gives you placement, rank, and position in God's Empire. It is about your love and loyalty. Love is the greatest factor that determines your placement with Jesus in His Kingdom. Many do not get this revelation of why Jesus picked Peter, because Peter made a lot of mistakes. Many ministers talk about the many mistakes Peter made but few ever talk about what Jesus said about him. *"Simon, son of Jonas, lovest thou me more than these? ... Feed my lambs"* (John 21:15). Jesus also said concerning a woman who had committed a lot of sins,

*"Wherefore I say unto thee, **Her sins, which are many, are forgiven; for she loved much:** but to whom little is forgiven, the same loveth little"* (Luke 7:47).

Peter made a lot of mistakes, but he loved God. Some teach in the church that if you sin or make mistakes in your relationship with the Lord then you do not love God. That is false. God does not operate in that way, His mercy is unfathomable! *"Her sins, which are many, are forgiven; for she loved much ..."* Actually, the person who is forgiven the most has the greatest capacity to love Jesus! Peter loved Jesus more than all the other Apostles of the lamb and that is why the Father revealed His son's true identity to Peter and that is why Jesus gave Peter the Keys to the whole Kingdom of Heaven thus making him the next divine emperor. Peter did not get the Keys to the Kingdom because he understood God's government, but because he understood by revelation, Jesus, the person who was running God's government. Peter loved Jesus and was loyal to Him and that is what a king must have. Loyalty is the highest level of integrity in a kingdom. To be loyal is to be royal!

Peter Uses the Keys Over Jerusalem and Judaea

*"But ye shall receive power, after that the Holy Ghost is come upon you: and ye shall be witnesses unto me both **in Jerusalem,** and in **all Judaea,** and in **Samaria,** and unto **the uttermost part of the earth"** (Acts 1:8).

When you study the life of Peter you will realize that before the kingdom could extend to Judaea, Samaria, and the rest of the Earth, Peter had to be involved. Jesus instructed the disciples to progressively preach the gospel to Jerusalem and Judaea, Samaria, and the rest of the world. Before each major people group could be reached, Peter had to be involved. Peter had to use the keys each time. When Peter preached the first sermon to the Jews at Jerusalem after the ascension of Jesus, three thousand souls were saved that day. And then from Acts 2 to Acts 6, Peter spearheaded a mighty move of God that shook all Jerusalem and Judea.

*"And believers were the more added to the Lord, multitudes both of men and women. Insomuch that they brought forth the sick into the streets, and laid them on beds and couches, **that at the least the shadow of Peter** passing by might overshadow some of them. There came **also a multitude out of the cities round about unto Jerusalem,** bringing sick folks, and them which were vexed with unclean spirits: and they were healed every one"* (Acts 5:14-16).

Peter Uses the Keys Over Samaria

And in Samaria, when Philip preached Jesus and the Kingdom of God, the whole city was shaken. But the seal of the Holy Spirit was not released until Peter came to Samaria. Philip certainly could have released the gift of the Holy Spirit on the Samaritans, but he did not have authority at that point in time to do so to that people group. Peter had to come with the Keys of the Kingdom to open up Samaria to the gift of the Holy Spirit.

*"Now when the apostles which were at Jerusalem heard that Samaria had received the word of God, **they sent unto them Peter and John:** Who, when they were come down, prayed for them, that they might receive the Holy Ghost: (For as yet he was fallen upon none of them: only they were baptized in the name of the Lord Jesus.) **Then laid they their hands on them, and they received the Holy Ghost"** (Acts 8:14-17).*

Peter Opens the Door to the Gentiles with the Keys

And then it was time for the Gentiles to receive the gospel. Many believers were already reaching the Gentiles, but there was no major breakthrough until the divine emperor of that day, Peter the apostle got involved. To prepare him for this great venture, the Lord came to Peter in a trance. Peter had a lot of prejudice and racism in him against Gentiles and would never have ministered to them if the Lord had not intervened.

"And saw heaven opened, and a certain vessel descending unto him, as it had been a great sheet knit at the four corners, and let down to the earth: **Wherein were all manner of fourfooted beasts of the earth, and wild beasts, and creeping things, and fowls of the air.** *And there came a voice to him, Rise, Peter; kill, and eat.But Peter said, Not so, Lord; for I have never eaten any thing that is common or unclean. And the voice spake unto him again the second time,* **What God hath cleansed, that call not thou common.** *This was done thrice: and the vessel was received up again into heaven"* (Acts 10:11-15).

In this trance, you see Peter's divine emperorship manifesting. In verse 12 Peter sees, *"all manner of fourfooted beasts of the earth, and wild beasts, and creeping things, and fowls of the air."* Adam was given dominion over the beasts of the Earth, wild beasts, creeping things and fowls of the earth in Genesis 1! Now you see Peter, another divine emperor, being given this divine power. A voice in the trance instructed him to kill them and eat. Later on, Peter understood that the Lord was instructing him not be prejudiced against the Gentiles, but to preach the gospel to them without delay. So, when he got to the house of Cornelius the Gentile, Peter did what he never would have done, he entered the house of a Gentile! That is why Peter said to Cornelius,

"And he said unto them, Ye know how that it is an unlawful thing **for a man that is a Jew to keep company, or come unto one of another nation;** *but God hath shewed me that I should not call any man common or unclean... Then Peter opened his mouth, and said,* **Of a truth I perceive that God is no respecter of persons:** *But in every nation he that feareth him, and worketh righteousness, is accepted with him"* (Acts 10:28, 34-35).

If you are to walk in this imperial grace, you must overcome any racism and prejudice in your life. You have to be weaned from your culture to pay the price to become multicultural. That is why God commanded another divine emperor, Abraham, to leave his country, his father's house and his relatives. You have to lose all allegiance to your race to walk effectively in the office of the emperor. I had to overcome that in my life to be able to do what God is doing with me now.

Peter's License to Kill

*"But a certain man named Ananias, with Sapphira his wife, sold a possession,
And kept back part of the price, his wife also being privy to it, and brought a
certain part, and laid it at the apostles' feet. But Peter said, Ananias, why hath
Satan filled thine heart to lie to the Holy Ghost, and to keep back part of the price
of the land? Whiles it remained, was it not thine own? and after it was sold, was
it not in thine own power? why hast thou conceived this thing in thine heart? thou
hast not lied unto men, but unto God.* **And Ananias hearing these words fell
down, and gave up the ghost: and great fear came on all them that heard these
things.** *And the young men arose, wound him up, and carried him out, and
buried him.*

*'And it was about the space of three hours after, when his wife, not knowing what
was done, came in. And Peter answered unto her, Tell me whether ye sold the
land for so much? And she said, Yea, for so much.* **Then Peter said unto her,
How is it that ye have agreed together to tempt the Spirit of the Lord?** *behold,
the feet of them which have buried thy husband are at the door, and shall carry
thee out.* **Then fell she down straightway at his feet, and yielded up the ghost:**
*and the young men came in, and found her dead, and, carrying her forth, buried
her by her husband.* **And great fear came upon all the church,** *and upon as
many as heard these things"* (Acts 5:1-11).

One major characteristic of a divine emperor is that God is
prepared to kill everyone and everything just to preserve His man. All
divine emperors have this power. This happened most notably with Peter
in Acts 5 when he had to deal with Ananias and Sapphira. This couple,
Ananias and Sapphira, thought they could get away with a lie, but found
out to their shock that they could not do that to a divine emperor. Both of
them died instantly the same day! Can you imagine that happening today?
Many would call Peter a murderer. But in that day, they recognized that
God was judging those two and the fear of God swept through Jerusalem
after that incident.

Paul talks about how many in the church were sick and dying because they did not properly discern the body of Christ (1 Corinthians 11:29-30). In these last days, it is going to become increasingly imperative that all believers master a major revelation the Lord gave me on weights, balances, and ranks. I have a teaching out on this subject. You have to recognize the weight and rank of men and women that God sends into the world because each star differs in glory. Recognizing these weights will help you balance them right to avoid being crushed by them!

The sun, for example, is set in place in Heaven to perform a function. God calls the sun the greater light. The sun does great good, but if you get too close to it you can die from its intense heat. If you look directly at the sun, you can lose your sight. You have to make adjustments to benefit from it. I pray this teaching on divine emperors will create the right level of reverence in your life for this awesome office. This office has a dreadful height and weight in the hierarchy of God's Empire!

God Judges Herod for Peter's Sake

Herod did not understand this mystery. He had James, a powerful apostle, killed and he thought he could do the same to Peter. He did not know that unlike James, Peter was a divine emperor with great dominion. He did not know that Jesus had given the Keys of the whole Heaven to Peter. He did not know that Peter was not supposed to die as a young man. He was to die in his old age. Jesus told Peter this, *"Verily, verily, I say unto thee, When thou wast young, thou girdedst thyself, and walkedst whither thou wouldest:* **but when thou shalt be old, thou shalt stretch forth thy hands,** *and another shall gird thee, and carry thee whither thou wouldest not"* (John 21:18). And that is exactly how Peter died. He was crucified according to church history. Herod did not know all that and made the biggest mistake of his life when he had Peter arrested.

*"Now about that time **Herod the king stretched forth his hands to vex certain of the church.** And he killed James the brother of John with the sword. And because he saw it pleased the Jews, he proceeded further to take Peter also. (Then were the days of unleavened bread.) And when he had apprehended him, he put him in*

prison, and delivered him to four quaternions of soldiers to keep him; intending after Easter to bring him forth to the people" (Acts 12:1-4).

Herod had both James and Peter imprisoned, and he wanted to execute both of them. He cut the head off of James and planned to do the same to Peter at a later date. But God, the emperor of the whole universe, overruled Herod. That is why you need to know God as your Emperor. He can overrule every satanic assassination attempt on your life! God sent an angel to rescue Peter. Now, as I have already shared with you, God is prepared to kill everyone to preserve the life of a divine emperor. So after this angel rescued Peter, he then destroyed Herod.

"And when Herod had sought for him (Peter), and found him not, he examined the keepers, and commanded that they should be put to death. And he went down from Judaea to Caesarea, and there abode. And Herod was highly displeased with them of Tyre and Sidon: but they came with one accord to him, and, having made Blastus the king's chamberlain their friend, desired peace; because their country was nourished by the king's country.

And upon a set day Herod, arrayed in royal apparel, sat upon his throne, and made an oration unto them. And the people gave a shout, saying, It is the voice of a god, and not of a man. **And immediately the angel of the Lord smote him,** because he gave not God the glory: and he was eaten of worms, and gave up the ghost. **But the word of God grew and multiplied"** (Acts 12:21-24).

Herod could kill James, but he could not kill Peter, a divine emperor. That is why the Bible says, *"He suffered no man to do them wrong: yea, he reproved kings for their sakes"* (Psalm 105:14). Right after that incident in the very next chapter, Acts 13, the Gospel started reaching the whole world! Paul received the right hand of fellowship and endorsement from Peter and started evangelizing the whole known world. Peter exercised the Keys of the Kingdom over Paul life, and opened up the whole world to his ministry! Herod could not stop that! He died trying to stop a divine emperor from fulfilling his imperial mandate, but the move of God continued! *"But the word of God grew and multiplied"* (Acts 12:24). Peter had to be alive to supervise that whole global move because he had the keys of the Kingdom of Heaven!

CHAPTER 7
Transitioning into the Emperor's Office

CHAPTER 7
Transitioning into the Emperor's Office

Trained to Reign as a King

Now I want to share with you how you can transition from being a king to being an emperor using my life as an example. Over the last twenty-eight years, the Lord elevated my walk and contact in the Kingdom by making me a high king or a divine emperor. But He started by training me to be a king. By scripture, I already understood that the moment I got saved, Jesus made me a king. But you must understand that even though you are a king, you must be trained to reign and manifest your kingship. In several experiences, Jesus proved to me and established in my heart that I was truly a king. The first thing Jesus did to develop my kingship was He made me leave home.

Leave Your Father's House

When I got saved, I began seeking the Kingdom immediately because I found out that was the first thing I had to pursue. I found this out from Matthew 6:33, *"But seek ye first the kingdom of God, and his righteousness; and all these things shall be added unto you."* I intensely sought the Kingdom of God with fasting and prayer. I fasted all the time in those days. I went through a season when I would fast for three days every week and at times I would go to a local church and do seven-day shut-ins. I was so hungry for the Kingdom. I would pray, *"Lord please teach me the Kingdom. Teach me what the Kingdom of God is. I want to learn this! What is Your*

Kingdom?" Then Jesus started disciplining and teaching me the Kingdom in several face to face appearances and through certain experiences I had in my first seven years.

In the second year of my salvation, the Lord came to me in a dream as I was about to graduate from college. His white robe was shining brilliantly as He stood in front of me. He said, *"David, are you willing to give up everything for what I have for you to do?"*

I said, *"Yes, Lord!"*

Then He said, *"You've got to get out of your father and mother's house and go to a city that I will tell you on nothing. You must give everything you own, leave, and just walk by faith."*

Now, most people are not willing to do that, but you must if you want to develop in your kingship. If you search the Bible, you will discover that everyone that God used greatly had to leave everything and go to a far place to develop in what God had called them to do! This is a major prerequisite to you walking in your kingship.

"He said therefore, A certain nobleman went into a far country to receive for himself a kingdom, and to return" (Luke 19:12).

This is why Jesus gave this parable. You must leave and go to a *"far country"* to receive a kingdom. You are a king the moment you received Jesus, but have you received a kingdom? Jesus appointed to each of his twelve disciples a kingdom after they left all to follow Him! *"Ye are they which have continued with me in my temptations. **And I appoint unto you a kingdom**, as my Father hath appointed unto me"* (Luke 22:28-29). I had to do that. Everyone who came into their kingship had to leave a place that was comfortable for them. This the first test you have to pass as a king. Abraham had to leave Ur of the Chaldees to go to Canaan. Jacob had to flee from Esau to Padan Aram. Joseph was forcibly taken to Egypt. Moses had to flee from Egypt to Midian. David had to flee to the land of the Philistines. Even Jesus had to leave home, Heaven, and go to a far place,

Earth, to receive a kingdom. When He ascended after He completed his assignment, God gave Him the Kingdom (Daniel 7:14; Matthew 28:18). In order to become a king, you must get out of the house! This is how Jesus began training me to be a king.

Breaking the Prince of Fornication

"And you hath he quickened, who were dead in trespasses and sins; Wherein in time past ye walked according to the course of this world, according to the prince of the power of the air, the spirit that now worketh in the children of disobedience" (Ephesians 2:1-2).

I had a powerful dream in the early nineties that would change my life forever. Through this dream, God intensified my kingship training. It was the time of the year when fall was slowly transitioning to winter. I was around nineteen years old and I was serving an apostle in Charleston, South Carolina at that time, a man I truly love who taught me so much. I used to live with him for a while. During those days, I would be out raking my apostle's yard. I got this dream when I was taking care of him. If you want to be great in God's Empire, you must have the heart to serve. *"And whosoever will be chief among you, let him be your servant"* (Matthew 20:27).

I had this dream in 1992 or 1993 and in this dream, I saw this huge evil spirit about nine feet tall. This spirit was completely naked and he had two sex organs. He had grey skin, and looked very evil. I also saw several young people in this dream. As I stood in front of this evil spirit, I heard a voice saying to me, *"Cast the demon of fornication out of the young people, for he has become a prince among the youth."* That was the voice of the Lord speaking to me! As I woke up from that dream those words echoed in my ears, *"He has become a Prince among the youth... He has become a prince... He has become a prince..."* I pondered these words in my mind. I thought to myself, *"What kind of words are these?"* I did not know much about the Kingdom and kingdom terms at that time.

I did not know back then that that was my first kingly assignment. My first royal assignment was to challenge a prince. I was still learning about the Kingdom at the time. I did not know anything about prince demons. You see, one of the indications of your kingship is your royal assignment. Your royal assignment is to challenge a prince. As part of your training, God will pick and choose the type of principality you must fight. Why would you be a king and not fight princes? As you prove yourself and complete your assignments, God will increase the level and rank of prince you must fight. He starts putting up other princes in front of you and will say to you, *"Fight this one!"*

*"For we **wrestle not against flesh and blood, but against principalities**, against powers, against the rulers of the darkness of this world, against spiritual wickedness in high places"* (Ephesians 6:12).

The spiritual warfare in Ephesians 6 is really about your kingship because it is only kings that put on armor, not priests. Later on, as I developed further in my kingship, I had a dream where God put me in front of a huge principality and simply said, *"Survive!"*

This particular prince was so massive that as he stood on the Earth his head disappeared into the clouds. As I looked at this being, he threw what seemed like a grenade bomb at me. I quickly snatched it up and threw it back at it! That is how the Lord has been training me for battle! *"Blessed be the LORD my strength, which teacheth my hands to war, and my fingers to fight"* (Psalm 144:1).

The Lord told me in this dream to cast the spirit of fornication out of the youth. Fornication means sex before marriage. I began to learn that fornication involves your body. Of all sins, this sin in particular affects the body profoundly. The Bible says,

*"Flee fornication. **Every sin that a man doeth is without the body;** but he that committeth fornication sinneth against his own body"*   (1 Corinthians 6:18).

As I studied more about this spirit, I discovered that when you engage in sex before marriage an evil spirit comes into your body. That is why the youth can't just stop when they start fornicating because that spirit takes control over them. Paul revealed that, *"... the body is not for fornication, but for the Lord; and the Lord for the body"* (1 Corinthians 6:13). Every other sin does not affect the body in that way because *"every sin that a man doeth is without the body."* Fornication is the only sin that involves a spirit getting in your body, *"but he that committed fornication sinneth against his own body."* Most people do not realize what is happening because these spirits are so subtle that you cannot even tell that they are inside you.

That was the voice of Jesus in the dream. *"He's become a prince... He's become a prince."* How did this happen? How did the demon of fornication become a prince? The Lord started teaching me how regular spirits become princes. From that moment, I started to understand that regular spirits are demons are not princes. They have to work to become princes. They have to work overtime to get people up under their control.

The Bible says, we *"... walked according to the course of this world, **according to the prince of the power of the air, the spirit that now worketh in the children** of disobedience"* (Ephesians 2:2). He works in the children of disobedience to make them follow him. In other words, princes are regular spirits at first until they gather enough people to fill up a principality. Jesus also used a verse in Proverbs to teach me how princes build their forts. The Bible says,

"In the multitude of people is the king's honour: but in the want of people is the destruction of the prince" (Proverbs 14:28).

From this scripture, you can see that the authority of a prince is destroyed when he lacks people. A regular spirit cannot become a prince if he lacks people. He has to get enough people under his control before he can be crowned as a prince. His spoils are the people he controls. The fornication devil was not so powerful twenty years before the 1990s. He was a spirit then, not a prince. The way spirits become princes is that they work hard to find a generation, a location, and a mass of people that are willing to accept their influence. For example, the spirit of homosexuality could not become a prince in Mississippi. It found a place more conducive to its character in Southern California and established his fort over there.

When a spirit finds millions of souls to fill up its principality, Satan says to that spirit, *"You are not a regular spirit anymore. I am going to make you a prince in my kingdom."* That is when that spirit becomes a prince. Satan gives that spirit a seat, a scepter, and sets him up in the air, in the heavenlies, so that the prince can have a greater drawing power to mind blind masses of people and seal them with his character. That is why the Bible talks about principalities in the heavenly places. *"... unto the principalities and powers in heavenly places might be known by the church the manifold wisdom of God"* (Ephesians 3:10).

If God would roll back the veil of the natural, you will see demonic princes sitting on thrones high up in the air over America. These princes have other demons ranked under them reporting to them. Over time, they set up a whole principality. A principality is the fort of a prince, a kingdom is the fort of a king, and an empire is the fort of an emperor. These princes establish these principalities, or what Jesus calls, a *"palace"* so that they can better control the souls they hold in their grip. Jesus calls princes strongmen: *"When a strong man armed keepeth his palace, his goods are in peace"* (Luke 11:21).

I began to learn all that I just shared with you when the Lord told me to cast the spirit of fornication out of the youth. That is how I began to make progress in my kingship. God makes you a king so that you can deal with principalities and powers. To develop your kingship, He gives you a demonic prince to break. As I started ministering to the youth, the spirit of fornication was broken. That is when teenage pregnancy rates began to dwindle. Before then, teenage pregnancy was endemic because the young ones were so promiscuous in those days. That prince was having a revival in those days. As a king, I executed my first royal assignment to cast the prince of fornication out of the youth! That was the first prince I broke. Over time, the Lord gave me more and greater princes to break until I matured to become an emperor where now I could break not just demon princes but king demons!

The Crown of Gold

"For thou preventest him with the blessings of goodness: thou settest a crown of pure gold on his head" (Psalm 21:3).

When I was around 20 or 21 years old, I had another experience that made me more convinced that I was a spiritual king. I was in a powerful service and the praise and worship team was so awesome. As we were worshipping, I felt a heavy weight on my head. I thought it was an anointing or something else. It was so heavy I bent over. I wondered what it was because I had never felt anything like that before. I was saying all this time, *"Lord what is this that I am feeling that is making me bend over like this? What is on my head?"* I could not see anything and when I reached my hand to my head I could not feel it with my hand but it was there!

I asked the Lord again, *"Lord what is this?"* Right then the Lord brought this scripture to me, *"Thou settest a crown of pure gold on his head."* At that time I was still studying and learning about the office of the king and the powers inherent in that office. When the Lord said that to me about the crown of pure gold, I whispered to myself, *"So this is a crown! This is a pure gold crown spiritually on my head?"* And then all of a sudden as I was talking and dialoguing with the Lord about the crown on my head the worship leader said, *"Let us all take our crowns off our head and cast them before his feet!"* I knew she had no idea what she was saying. The Holy Spirit had prompted her to say that!

From that moment, I knew that we were real kings! I knew then that Jesus had truly made me a king and a priest unto God as Revelation 1:6 said. I was fully persuaded from that point on that as kings we carry crowns on our head that cannot be seen in the natural. I knew more concretely that we were real kings with crowns sitting on thrones with scepters in our hands. Every scripture about the identity and power of kings in the Bible came alive from that point on! I knew then that our eyes are full of fire with power to scatter wickedness with just one look. As kings, our words have power! I began to come to grips with my identity as a king in God's Kingdom.

That is also when the kingly anointing became more pronounced in my life and ministry. You see, when you come into the kingly anointing, the slaying power of the Holy Ghost manifests. *"Thine arrows are sharp in the heart of the king's enemies; whereby the people fall under thee"* (Psalm 45:5). The kingly anointing is so heavy it causes people to bow and fall. There are so many other manifestations in the kingly anointing and that is why when you are around a ministry that is connected to God and his throne there is a lot of bowing and falling and getting slain in the spirit. That is why the devils would fall down and cry out when they came near Jesus. Those who came to capture Him in the garden of Gethsemane also fell back under the power because of the kingly anointing on Jesus. This is because He was a real king with a real crown on His head!

Power to Break Princes After Forty-Day Fast

After walking in my kingship for some time, I entered in to a forty-day fast. After the fast, the Lord visited me in a dream and He said, *"I am going to show you what you received off this fast. From now on, whenever you into regions, the principalities over those cities will break immediately."* That is what He said to me about twenty years ago.

Then He said, *"I will now show you what happens in the realm of the spirit when the prince is broken."* Then He allowed a screen to appear and then said to me, *"This is what happens when a prince is broken!"* As I looked at the screen, I saw myself go into a region and the principality of that region who had been there for many years was broken!

When this prince realized that he had lost his principality, he summoned another prince with a demonic tongue. With that tongue, I saw him summon another prince from another place around the world. That prince was not from America. I believe he was from a third world country and he was a more powerful prince (Matthew 12:45). I saw this prince come at light speed to his aid. When he got in the region he immediately got in the atmosphere and caused it to storm and rain. The Lord looked at me as I saw all this happen on the screen.

He said, *"When the prince is broken in any region I send you to, he will call on a stronger prince from around the world to assist him. The sign that will make you know that this prince is fighting you is that it will rain and storm."*

He looked at me with a steady gaze and repeated, *"It will rain and storm. When it rains it is not a sign that they control the region, it is a sign that they have lost the region and they are trying to get it back."*

And true to this vision, everywhere I go it rains! This happens in America, Europe, Asia, and anywhere else I go. When the prince of that region I go to is broken, it begins to rain. This has happened so often that many leaders and pastors simply know it will rain when I come to their region. In 2013, I went to Orlando to minister and it stormed and rained very heavily. The pastor of that church said to me, *"What you said has come to pass!"* And immediately Orlando began to shake as the prince as broken. I said to the pastor and to the church, *"The next sign that will prove to you that the Kingdom of God has come here is that in two days you will see on the news the biggest drug bust in this region."* I told them that the Lord had come down from Heaven and He is working in the spirit realm and in the natural to break the biggest drug ring in Orlando, Florida. In forty-eight hours it happened exactly as I decreed!

Not only that, I have seen several human sex-slave trafficking rings dismantled in many American cities after I finished that forty-day fast. While I was in Orlando in that same church, I began to proclaim and decree that God was also about to free the three-hundred million girls and some boys sold into human sex trade trafficking. I looked into the camera and confronted those in the underworld controlling those helpless girls and boys. I proclaimed under a strong kingly anointing, *"God is coming after you and He's after all those girls and boys you have bound in human slave trafficking."* I then told the church, *"In a few days you will see the biggest nationwide bust of human slave trafficking. You will see hundreds of girls freed."* Two days later, it happened in over seventy cities in America! Hundreds of girls were released. That was the power of the king in manifestation!

Transitioning into the Imperial Realm

All this time that Jesus was training me in my kingship, I did not realize that He was training me not just to be a king with Him, but to be a prince with God. He was training me to be a divine emperor! In my earlier years, I did not catch on to what He was doing until I became more mature in the Kingdom of God. It took a series of events in my life to help me catch on to what He was doing. You see, the Godhead deals a lot with mysteries. A lot of what they do in our lives is shrouded in deep mystery, and as a king you must go on a quest to understand those mysteries God is unveiling in your life, *"... because it is given unto you to know the mysteries of the kingdom of heaven..."* (Matthew 13:11). As a king unto God, the mysteries of the Kingdom belong to you! God desires that you understand them.

"It is the glory of God to conceal a thing: but the honour of kings is to search out a matter" (Proverbs 25:2).

The first thing Jesus did to activate me into the imperial realm is that He gave me the Keys of the Kingdom that He gave Peter. Then He gave me the revelation of the highest anointing in the Empire of God: the imperial anointing. He then commissioned me as God's End-Time General and the Face to Face Prophet for our generation. Through these events and experiences, the Lord set me up in the office of the divine emperor. I want to share more details of these experiences with you. This will help you better understand how the Lord broke me into the imperial realm!

Jesus Gives Me the Keys of the Kingdom

This was the penultimate event that really broke me into the imperial realm. I had walked with the Lord for seven amazing years. During these years, the Lord tutored me in mysteries of the Kingdom of Heaven and gave me several royal assignments to break principalities in

America and other nations of the world. But nothing prepared me for what He was about to do in my life in my seventh year.

It all started when the Lord appeared to me in a dream in 1997. I was deep in sleep when all of a sudden I saw myself and the Lord Jesus in a vision of the night. As usual, He had on that gorgeous white robe that He loves so much.

At first, He was just standing with me, then He started walking silently. When I saw Him walking, I remembered a decision I had made some time ago, when I purposed in my heart not to ever do what Peter did on the Mount of Transfiguration, when he spoke out of turn and got rebuked by the Father (Matthew 17:1-6). I said to myself, *"I'm just going to be quiet until He talks to me."* So, whenever Jesus appears to me, I behave wisely. I just wait quietly and follow His lead. So, when the Lord started walking I started walking with Him. Then He took six steps ahead of me and stopped. He stopped, I also stopped. He stood in front of me and looked into my eyes I saw a trust for me in His eyes that I had never seen before.

Then He said, *"David, I am giving you the Keys of the Kingdom of Heaven. These are the keys I gave Peter when he was alive. But he is dead and I need a man in your generation to carry them today. Whatever you bind, I, Jesus, will personally back you up. Whatever you loose, I, Jesus, will personally back you up. These are not the keys or the authority I have given to every believer to bind and to loose. These are the special Keys to the Kingdom of all of Heaven! Wherever you go and loose a move, I, Jesus, will personally work with you and back you up!"*

Then I woke up! My whole body was pulsating from the divine glory and power that came off the Lord's body as He talked to me. I knew something most glorious had just happened. The words Jesus spoke echoed in my heart, *"... I, Jesus, will personally back you up!"* That is how He said it. That is how He talks! *"I, Jesus, will personally back you up!"*

Months later I was reading through the book of Revelation and came across this scripture, *"I Jesus have sent mine angel to testify unto you these things in the churches...*" (Revelation 22:16). I said, *"Wow! He still talks like that! I, Jesus!"*

I did not know then what all this entailed. I did not know then that, like Peter, I was being set up as the next divine emperor in this generation when Jesus gave me the Keys to the Kingdom of Heaven! It was during the winter when this happened. I called one of my pastors to come and take me to the church to pray. I like to pray about every visitation I receive from the Lord. As we were driving to the church, I narrated everything Jesus told me in the dream to him. He was so excited. That night there was a very strong heavy blizzard in the city. It was snowing very heavily in St. Louis as we drove to the church. I said, *"I'm going to try this right now."* I prayed and said, *"Lord, I just saw you in the dream. You just gave me the same keys you gave Peter. Lord, if it's true what just happened, I should be able to stop this snow."*

I know I did not have a lot of faith in what I was saying that night, but I continued praying. I said, *"Jesus, with the Keys of the Kingdom you just appeared to me. I got to know that this works."* Then I looked at the snow and said, *"With the Keys of the Kingdom, I command this snow to stop!"* It was not five minutes later, it was not three minutes later, it was not one minute later, in seconds it stopped! The snow stopped so suddenly we could hardly stop exclaiming in shock and awe.

Later that day on the radio the announcers were gushing over how the snow storm stopped suddenly and how the sun was now shining brightly. They were very happy because they had forecasted a very heavy snow storm. I am not exaggerating. God is my witness in Heaven, that blizzard stopped suddenly! And it did snow, it was a blizzard, but it stopped immediately as I used the Keys of the Kingdom! That is imperial power! Emperors, you know, also have power over creation! This is what gave me boldness and confidence to walk in the power of those keys!

Entire Regions Set Free with the Keys of the Kingdom of Heaven

Ever since Jesus gave me those keys in 1997, we have seen whole regions taken over by the Power of God. We have seen an entire mental institution emptied, nursing homes, and prisons emptied. This is all documented. We have seen massive deliverances take place over entire cities with hundreds of thousands of people getting saved, healed and delivered! We could not build churches fast enough and big enough to hold the people that came out that glorious move. This is because wherever you preach the Kingdom of God and break the prince ruling the millions of people in a city, you get the spoils of his principality. The spoils of the prince are the souls! All the souls come to you. Every city I go to and I use the keys, amazing things begin to happen! Entire cities and regions are turned to the Lord as the princes are broken!

With these keys, I began to loose finances on people all over the world. Before this happened, I was only using these Keys to loose healings and mass deliverances over entire regions then the Lord came to me and said, *"Why don't you use the keys to loose finances over my people?"*

Up to that point in time, I did not even realize I could do that, but once the Lord pointed that out to me and I started doing what He said, we saw great finances being loosed on the people of God. When I use those keys over people who really sow sacrificially, they become millionaires and billionaires overnight.

With these keys, I have seen princes broken even more easily over entire regions. Many years later, the Lord came to me and gave me more wisdom about the power of these keys.

In this visitation, He said to me, *"David, this is why when I send you to a place, the leaders there have to listen to you - even major leaders who have been in ministry longer than you. If they do not listen to you, they will go down. It does not matter if they are bigger than you at the time. It does not matter. They have to listen to you because I have granted you the power of a kingdom, a billion-year-old system. You have been given the keys to that here on Earth."*

Jesus Defends My Imperial Office

I did not realize that even then Jesus was setting me up to walk in the emperor's office. All that He said to me was shrouded in mystery. It took many years for me to fully understand that the Lord promoted me from being a king to being an emperor the moment He gave me the Keys to the Kingdom. He was granting me the power of a billion-year-old system! He was giving me the power of an entire Earth. This is why I have been explaining to you in the earlier chapters the dreadful nature of the office of the divine emperor. You have seen in the life of the seven divine emperors how God came against all those that dared to attack them. It is truly a fearful thing to fall into the hands of the Lord!

God is determined to destroy anything and everything that threatens his divine emperors. He did this for Noah, Abraham, Moses, David, Jesus, and Peter, and I have seen Him do this several times in my life after I received those keys. I have seen major leaders and ministries go down to nothing after they attacked my ministry. There are leaders who were attacking me that Jesus visited and rebuked. He told one of them that He would throw him into Hell when he dies if he does not stop slandering my life and ministry. I have seen this happen over and over and over again! Many people do not understand that when God gives someone the keys to His Empire that person is granted the powers of that kingdom *and* the power to establish that kingdom on the Earth.

Just like Peter, Jesus gave me the Keys to the Kingdom of Heaven because I had a revelation of who He was. I have been given the keys of the Kingdom of God on Earth. Jesus came to me in a dream and gave me those keys. How can you lie about something like that? That is why every leader, no matter how big they are when they come against me, loses. Every minister who attacked me and did great harm to me lost their people and eventually their ministries. I remember one particular leader in St. Louis who did me great harm. He was a very major leader in the Body of

Christ with one of the biggest churches in the state. He slandered my name in a way that greatly maligned my ministry. He spoke against me from his pulpit when I was out of the country.

I heard of what this leader did and was really grieved over that because he was like a father to me. Then Jesus Christ came to me in a dream and said, *"Because he has dishonored you, I am going to take his building. I am going to take everything he has including his finances."* And that is exactly what happened. This leader lost a forty-million-dollar building and thousands of members. In the book of Jeremiah, God said He would do this to His shepherds when they start going out of His will,

*"For the pastors are become brutish, and have not sought the LORD: therefore they shall not prosper, **and all their flocks shall be scattered"***
(Jeremiah 10:21).

God can and does scatter flocks from His ministers who have strayed from His divine will and who attack His high kings. Some ministers think because they are big they can do anything they want to God's dignitaries. Well, I don't need to have twenty thousand people follow me every week to walk in this imperial power and office. Jesus came to me and gave me these keys and great authority. There is no one greater or higher than Him. He is the head of the church! I did not ask for this position, He gave it to me. I did not seek power and authority. I never asked for it. I just wanted a love relationship with Him and as a result, He trusted me with the keys even when I did not fully know who I was for many years.

All I knew is that when people did something wrong to me, the Lord will come to me in a dream and say, *"They have crossed a line. I cannot allow them to do this to you."* Then He would disappear. When I wake up out of those dreams, everything He said came to pass without fail. Jesus has had to do this several times because many of these leaders who are big can destroy you. They can get doors closed to your ministry to the point where you cannot do anything. But they have never been able to stop me because my rank is greater than them and because I know who I am. I know Christ gave me these keys not to gloat in them but to change nations.

With these keys, I have launched an offensive against several demon principalities who are destroying our nation with same-sex marriage, homosexuality, cancer, drug cartels and sex trade traffic.

Mysteries of the Kingdom Entrusted to Me

These revelations I am sharing with you I did not receive from another person's book. I was preaching these mysteries of the Kingdom many years before the late Myles Munroe, for example, came out with his Kingdom book. The difference between what I teach and what the other preachers teach about the Kingdom is that I receive my message directly from Jesus face to face and through several trips to Heaven. In these trips to Heaven, the Lord allowed me to actually see the Kingdom of Heaven, The Father's throne room, the Throne of God, the Right-Hand Seat Jesus sits on, and the Kingdom God has granted Jesus which is situated in a whole different world outside of Heaven! I had to see the Kingdom of Heaven to be able to bring it down to Earth!

I am not just ministering to you these mysteries out of my study of the Word but also out from the realm of Heaven itself. In these Kingdom volumes, I am teaching you what the Lord himself told me face to face and I am also testifying what I have actually seen about the Kingdom of Heaven! I have been entrusted with this teaching ministry to dispense and unveil the mysteries of the Kingdom of Heaven. A lot of those preaching on the Kingdom teach on facets and principles of the Kingdom, but they hardly deal with the meat of the Kingdom message.

Why was I given the mystery of the Kingdom? Why did Jesus come to me in person to teach me mysteries of the Kingdom that have been lost for several centuries? He did that because He was making me a divine emperor. The Kingdom of God is really an empire, so God had to raise me as a divine emperor to dispense this revelation about His Empire. The Lord once said to me, *"David, the problem with people in the church and in your generation is they have lost my ministry and my message. Many of them preach the gospel of salvation, that's not what I preached. I didn't even preach the cross."* The Lord took me to Matthew 4:23; 9:35 and then to Matthew 24:14

and used these scriptures to teach me the Message of the Kingdom as I have revealed in the first volume of the Kingdom series.

Mystery means hidden truth. That is why the Bible says, *"But we speak the wisdom of God in a mystery, even the hidden wisdom, which God ordained before the world unto our glory"* (1 Corinthians 2:7). God hides the plain understanding of what He is doing in a mystery to blind people and the kingdom of darkness to what He is really doing. *"Which none of the princes of this world knew: for had they known it, they would not have crucified the Lord of glory"* (1 Corinthians 2:8). That is why the disciples could not understand why Jesus always spoke in mysteries. They asked Jesus why He always spoke to the multitudes in parables, *"Why speakest thou unto them in parables?"* (Matthew 13:10). Jesus replied, *"... Because it is given unto you to know the mysteries of the kingdom of heaven, but to them it is not given"* (Matthew 13:11). The mysteries of the Kingdom belong to us because God has given us the Kingdom!

Mystery Versus Revelation of the Kingdom

Jesus did not say revelation, He said the mysteries of the Kingdom! Revelation is high truth, but mystery is truth hidden deep in God! A lot of Christians are walking in revelation, high truth, but they are not walking in mystery. Many are preaching the revelation of the Kingdom, but they are not revealing the mystery of it. They can break down a parable Jesus gave by giving revelation, but that is not what Jesus gave us. He did not just give us the revelation of the Kingdom, He gave us the mystery of the Kingdom which is much deeper than just revelation. The Church always seems to stop short of something that God is doing. They are preaching revelation while God is trying to give them mystery. When you get the mystery, you get the total understanding of it, the whole counsel of God as Paul would say.

Jesus gives parables of sowers, leaven, pearls, merchantmen, and fishermen. He does not want the wrong people to understand what He is saying because He does not cast his pearls before swine. He always spoke the mysteries in parables, *"All these things spake Jesus unto the multitude in parables; and without a parable spake he not unto them"* (Matthew 13:14). He only unveils the mystery of the Kingdom to His true kings. If you are a real king, you will seek out the mystery (Proverbs 25:2). When the disciples came to Him later asking for the understanding, He gave it to them. They had to seek Him out and draw the understanding of the mystery out of Him. They would say to Jesus, *"Declare unto us the parable!"* And He did!

These mysteries Jesus entrusted to me cannot be understood just by reading the Bible. They are in the Bible, but nobody can teach what I am teaching if they have not been around Jesus. The only way they can teach on the Kingdom is after they hear me teach it. You cannot bring your brain to form these revelations, they are a mystery. They have to be taught by Christ. The whole mystery of the Kingdom unveiled is that you are a king! You were born a king from God's womb to bring His Kingdom down to the Earth. Let me share briefly some of these mysteries of the Kingdom with you.

The Mystery of the Fivefold Ministry Priesthood Offices

One major revelation that God gave me that the Church does not preach on is that the fivefold ministry offices come under priesthood and not under the Kingdom. Fivefold ministry offices are priesthood offices. The Bible says, *"And God hath set some in the church, first apostles, secondarily prophets, thirdly teachers, after that miracles, then gifts of healings, helps, governments, diversities of tongues"* (1 Corinthians 12:28). Apostles, prophets, and the other fivefold ministry offices are all set *"in the church."* The church also dealt with things pertaining to the House of God or the church which is the priesthood. This is a major classification that you have to understand before you can even begin to understand the difference between the church and the Kingdom

The Mystery of the Kings and Priests

Another major revelation that God gave me is that the church today has prioritized the church, or priesthood, above the Kingdom. We have studied our church assignments and not our Kingdom assignments. Why have we neglected our royal duties for our priestly duties? Why have you studied all your life to be a pastor and you never study to be a king? Why have you settled for a prophet's staff when God was giving you a scepter! Why have you settled for a bishop's cap when God wanted to give you a crown?

Jesus revealed to me that all believers were made kings and priests the moment they got saved. *"... Unto him that loved us, and washed us from our sins in his own blood, And hath made us kings and priests unto God and his Father ...."* (Revelation 1:5-6). You are a king and a priest, but you are a king first and a priest second. That is why Jesus commands us to *"...**seek ye first the kingdom of God,** and his righteousness; and all these things shall be added unto you"* (Matthew 6:33). When you seek the Kingdom first, everything else in your life will get in order! What is lacking in your life will be gravitationally drawn to you! But we have put the church before the Kingdom and that is the wrong order. We are a royal priesthood, not a priesthood royal! *"But ye are a chosen generation, **a royal priesthood**..."* (1 Peter 2:9).

The church calls everything the Kingdom. They do not know the difference between the Kingdom and the church. For many years, the Lord has been using me to sanctify the realm of the Kingdom. He has been using me to show the difference between God's Kingdom and God's Church, God's kings and God's priests, God's dominion and God's authority. The Kingdom and the church are two different realms, but the church has put them together. As a result, those two realms have been enmeshed causing chaos and that is why God's involvement is so limited in the church today. Jesus showed me what we are doing wrong and he gave me the solution. We are to seek his Kingdom first before the church!

The Mystery of the Two Births

Another major revelation the Lord gave me to explain the difference between the Kingdom and the church is that we came out of our mother's womb with our priesthood gifts and ministries. God ordained

Jeremiah to be a prophet to the nations from his mother's womb. Our priesthood gifts are given in our mother's womb! That is why John the Baptist was called the prophet of the highest and was anointed even in his mother's womb. If you were ordained a priest, a prophet, an apostle and so on from your mother's womb, then who are you when you are born again from God's womb? *"For whatsoever is born of God overcometh the world..."* (1 John 5:4). You are born a king from God's womb! That is why Jesus told Nicodemus, *"... Except a man be born again, he cannot see the kingdom of God"* (John 3:3). In your first birth, you received your primitive priesthood offices and in your second birth from God's womb, you received your primary assignment and office as a king to overcome this world!

The Mystery of Your Identity as a King

This is a major mystery of the Kingdom. You are king! Jesus dispensed the mystery of our kingship in a way that most of the people could not know. Only the apostles understood what Jesus was teaching. They figured it out when the Lord started telling them, *"...ye also shall sit upon twelve thrones, judging the twelve tribes of Israel"* (Matthew 19:28) and *"And I appoint unto you a kingdom, as my Father hath appointed unto me"* (Luke 22:29). They then understood that, *"Oh if I'm sitting on a throne, and if Jesus has appointed me a kingdom, then I am a king!"* The apostles had great confidence in their identity and manifested the power of the Kingdom Jesus gave them before they ever got the infilling of the Holy Ghost years later!

When I tell people that they are kings, it is the unraveling of all the parables Jesus was giving. He told them all this in a mystery, but by Revelation 1:5-6 they understood the revelation of the mysteries he was teaching them, that they were kings unto God! This the mystery of what Jesus was teaching when He said, *"... A certain nobleman went into a far country **to receive for himself a kingdom,** and to return"* (Luke 19:12). Jesus was basically saying that the Kingdom of God is like a prince who goes off to receive a kingdom for himself and comes back with the power to be a king.

The Mystery of the Controversy over the Birth and Death of Jesus

The whole controversy surrounding the whole life and death of Jesus was because He was a king. That is the mystery He kept hidden. At His birth, Herod wanted Him killed because he heard a king had been born in his domain. And at the time of His death, Pilate asked Jesus, *"Art thou a king then?"* Jesus told him without telling him, *"Thou sayest that I am a king"* (John 18:37). Jesus masterfully kept the truth of His real identity from the wrong people. He allowed His disciples to know but warned them not to tell anyone else. Jesus simply would not let the wrong people know.

Jesus confused Pilate so much with His answers that Pilate asked in exasperation, *"What is truth?"* (John 18:38). Jesus shrouded His identity with the cloak of mystery. He revealed His identity to people so subtly they would not believe Him anyway even if He told them. That is why He said to Pilate, *"My kingdom is not of this world: if my kingdom were of this world, then would my servants fight, that I should not be delivered to the Jews: but now is my kingdom not from hence"* (John 18:36). He was really telling Pilate that He was a king with a kingdom but He did not allow him to understand what He was saying.

This is like you going up to CNN and saying to them, *"I sit on a heavenly throne with Christ in Heaven."* They will just laugh at that because they do not understand that from Heaven we govern CNN and everything else. They are blind and ignorant of spiritual things, because as the Word says,

*"**But the natural man receiveth not the things of the Spirit of God:** for they are foolishness unto him: neither can he know them, because they are spiritually discerned"* (1 Corinthians 2:14).

So, when Pilate asked Jesus whether or not He was a king, Jesus replied, *"... **Thou sayest that I am a king.** To this end was I born, and for this cause came I into the world, that I should bear witness unto the truth. Every one that is of the truth heareth my voice"* (John 18:37). When Jesus said, *"To this end I was born."* He was telling Pilate in a mystery, *"Yes, I am a king and that is why I am here!"* Pilate could not get that because he was a *"natural man."* What Jesus said was foolishness to Him. Jesus' birth and death were about His identity as king. The great controversy over your life is that you are king.

The Mystery of the Office of the Emperor

When the Lord took me to Heaven in 1996 and taught me the imperial anointing, I did not even know then that He was making me an emperor. You see, from the beginning, God always sends a king to confront the kingdom of darkness and to deliver His people. That is why he made Adam a high king, a divine emperor, and gave him dominion, which is a kingdom. *"Let them have dominion..."* (Genesis 1:26). Dominion is the domain of a king. God knew that Satan was a prince with a kingdom trying to bring his kingdom to the Earth realm. God could not make Adam a priest, because it takes a king to confront another king. He would not make Adam anything less than a king because he had to fight the kingdom of Satan. That is why God told him not to eat of the tree of knowledge. God already knew that the temptation was coming from another king (Satan), to cause Adam to submit his world to Satan's kingdom.

God has a pattern of always sending a king. When He had to destroy the whole world with water, He chose Noah, another high king with imperial status to fill up the whole Earth again with his three sons. Any time God is replenishing the Earth, He chooses an emperor because He has to start an empire. Emperors cannot just birth princes because that is too low, they have to birth kings. So, when He started the process to redeem man, God choose another man, Abraham, and made him an emperor by telling him, *"Kings shall come out of thee."* God only chooses emperors when He wants to start a world.

You see, princes fill up a kingdom with their principalities and kings fill up an empire with their kingdoms. So, when He chose Abraham, He basically said, *"I am starting afresh with you. You will be a father of nations."* Then He sent Moses a king and deliverer to set Israel free from Egypt. It is the kingly anointing that delivers slaves from Satan's kingdom.

Then God sent Jesus as a high king, an emperor, to restart everything again two thousand years ago. God puts the Power of One in His emperors to walk in imperial power. God does not create a million people to start a world. He simply creates a man, a high king, an emperor, and starts a new world with Him. That is why God started a new creation or world with Jesus!

*"Therefore if any man be in Christ, **he is a new creature** (creation): old things are passed away; behold, all things are become new"* (2 Corinthians 5:17).

Jesus came as the new emperor to take over this world with powers from another world. As a divine emperor, Jesus raises new kings under him and appoints them kingdoms. God uses emperors to birth new kings to fill up or take over the Earth again! That is why God was prepared to kill all the Israelites and start over with Moses because as an emperor, Moses had the Power of One. Every emperor births kings and appoints them kingdoms to make up a whole world. That is why Jesus told the Apostles, *"And I appoint unto you a kingdom ..."* (Luke 22:29). This is why Jesus is the King of Kings and the Lord of Lords! Now, Jesus is giving out kingdoms, whole lands and territories to His kings to rule and reign over.

Now here we are, two thousand years later in our generation. A lot has been lost through the dark ages and God has to start again with another divine emperor. Over the last two thousand years, the church lost dominion and did not occupy the Kingdom Jesus took from Satan. So, in the dark ages, Satan again repopulated this world with his kingdom and now God has to raise another emperor to reclaim what Jesus was given! That is why Jesus came to me and started giving me the mysteries of His Kingdom. He was setting me up to be the divine emperor of our generation! This is why He talked to me about the imperial anointing in

Heaven because He was starting a new world and He has to start with an emperor.

I would be boasting if I did not have the authority to say all of these things through the experiences I have had. I saw Jesus, the Son of God. He came to me and gave me the Keys of the Kingdom of Heaven just like He gave Peter. I have made it a practice in my life never to think and talk of myself more highly than I ought to. (Romans 12:3). That would be presumption and self-promotion, but that is not true in my life because Jesus has come to me.

The only thing that gives me the authority and power to talk like this is the fact that I have had multiple face to face appearances from the Lord and was told these things by Him. The Son of God came to me and said what I was directly and indirectly. That is why the Bible says, *"And no man taketh this honour unto himself, but he that is called of God, as was Aaron"* (Hebrews 5:4). I cannot go out there and say I am a divine emperor unless God specifically calls me out and says, *"This is what I am giving you, this is who you are!"*

The time He revealed the imperial anointing to me, He showed me my right-hand seat and later gave me the Keys of the Kingdom of Heaven. In 1996, He took me to Heaven and gave me the imperial anointing and office of the emperor revelation. That same year, He gave me another trip to Heaven and He told me that I had a right-hand seat with Him. He actually showed me the right-hand seat that He had reserved for me! The right-hand seats are for God's high kings or emperors. In 1997, Jesus came to me in a dream and gave me the Keys of the Kingdom of Heaven. These three landmark events in my life happened around the same time in two consecutive years. Through these events in 1996 and 1997, God was setting me up to be the next divine emperor after Peter!

The Mystery of the Imperial Anointing

The Kingdom message and ministry has been lost over the last two thousand years and the Lord has given me the global mandate to restore

His Kingdom in this generation. Jesus gave me the lost message of His Kingdom and trained me first to be a king. He then took me to Heaven to teach me what an emperor is and how important it is for me to understand how that works because I am one. I did not realize all this back then in 1996 when I received the imperial anointing revelation. He was telling me basically, *"This is who you are, you are an emperor."* I did not get it back then because God speaks in hidden messages. He will tell you something without saying it. He expects you, as a king to search out the matter! *"It is the glory of God to conceal a thing: but the honour of kings is to search out a matter"* (Proverbs 25:2).

When the Lord took me to Heaven and told me what an emperor is and the imperial anointing that flows from the office and presence of the emperor He was really telling me, *"I have made you an emperor!"* But I didn't know it then. I woke up from that dream saying, *"Oh, I've got to walk in the imperial anointing."* So, that is all that I did then. I taught on the imperial anointing and walked in imperial power. I did not realize all that time that I was not just a king walking in the imperial anointing, the Lord had made me an emperor! He gave me this imperial anointing revelation in Heaven as He stood in front of me in His white robe, but all my mind could grasp was the revelation of the imperial anointing.

Mystery, as I shared with you, is a hidden truth, it is something that the Lord hides from you. He does not tell you straight up what He is doing, He tells you everything around it. For example, instead of Him saying, *"You are a duck,"* He says, *"You are green, you have feathers, you can swim."* You have to figure out what He is saying. You have to search for the glory of what He is saying because it is the glory of kings to search out a matter. He tells you these things, but He expects you to be involved. *"For we know in part, and we prophesy in part"* (1 Corinthians 13:9). God reveals part of your identity and you have to find out the other part to get the complete picture by searching for and gaining knowledge through study! He expects us to co-labor with Him to get the total truth of what He is saying.

Nobody else has the message of the imperial anointing. Nobody taught that before the Lord gave me that revelation. People are trying to teach it now because they heard me teaching on it. When I first came out with this revelation, I spoke to Sid Roth about this mystery and he confirmed a lot of what I am saying about imperial power from the Hebrew scriptures. He did some researching and told me that in the Hebrew Bible, the Kingdom of God is called the Empire of God. Just as Jesus told me the God's Kingdom is really an empire. Therefore the revelation of the imperial anointing is true.

This is the reason why when I go into regions demonic princes break immediately. I do not have to do a forty-day fast to break them because my rank as an emperor is so high I hardly have to do anything much to break them. From the time I was a teenager the mystery of the Kingdom was birthed in me. I am a true emperor, a high king raised by God. God started developing all this in me right from my teenage years when He put a crown on my head. And over the last twenty-eight years, the Lord has developed and matured the message of the Kingdom, but oftentimes God has me operate in the lower level as a king to train the new crop of kings who are coming into their kingship and to help them understand their identity as kings. Jesus, as a divine emperor during His earthly ministry, had to walk in the lower realm of a king at certain times so that the apostles could walk in that realm as well.

When Jesus took me to Heaven for no more than five minutes, He stood before me and said, *"You have taught that the kingly anointing is the highest, but I brought you here to tell you that that is not true. The imperial anointing is the highest anointing in my Kingdom."* He taught me how it operates as I revealed in the earlier chapters. Jesus told me the imperial anointing flows from the office of the emperor. God will never tell you something like that unless He is making you one! He was making me a divine emperor.

One Emperor at One Time in a Generation

The reason God did not give anybody else the revelation of the imperial anointing is because He always has only one emperor on the Earth at one time. You cannot have two emperors in the same world at the same time. Now, in the regeneration that is in the next age, there will be several high kings who will walk in the office of the emperor for all eternity. Many of you learning this mystery will walk in that! In the next chapter, I will show you how you can break into the divine emperor infinity realm by pursuing the right-hand seat position with the Lord Jesus Christ. The Lord Himself in these two scriptures offers you this eternal position:

*"And Jesus said unto them, Verily I say unto you, That ye which have followed me, **in the regeneration** when the Son of man shall sit in the throne of his glory, ye also **shall sit upon twelve thrones**, judging the twelve tribes of Israel"*
(Matthew 19:28).

"To him that overcometh will I grant to sit with me in my throne, *even as I also overcame, and am set down with my Father in his throne"*
(Revelation 3:21).

Right now you are a king with imperial anointing because you sit together with Jesus at God's right hand. But you are also called to be a king and an emperor for all eternity! When you mature to the right-hand seat relationship with the Lord, you will be an eternal high king! These high kings will be nothing but emperors! They will be high kings who are loyal friends to the king of all kings, Jesus Christ. These eternal emperors will rule and reign over entire worlds in the next age. But on the Earth, in this world, God raises a divine emperor in certain generations. Adam, Noah, Abraham, Moses, David, and Peter were all set up by God to be divine emperors in their generations. They served their generations as divine emperors.

God gives imperialship to different high kings in different generations to keep birthing kings. Before Jesus left the Earth, He gave the emperorship to Peter by giving him the Keys of the Kingdom of Heaven (Matthew 16:19). Jesus raises new kings and an emperor. They all establish the Empire of Heaven on Earth. When Jesus gave Peter the Keys to the Kingdom of Heaven, He was basically saying to him and to the rest of the apostles, *"Peter, I am giving you these keys because I am making you the emperor of all these kings. You are the emperor over the Kingdom of God on Earth. You will lead it, you will open up regions with the keys, and you have the strategic keys to open up everything. Now, the rest of you apostles also have power to bind and to loose because you are all kings, but I have given the keys to Peter because he is the emperor."*

That is the mystery of what Jesus was telling Peter and the apostles in Matthew 16:19 and Matthew 18:18! Then Jesus goes back to Heaven and he lets Peter stay on Earth as an emperor with the keys. Peter reminded the church of his position when he said, *"... Men and brethren, ye know how that a good while ago **God made choice among us, that the Gentiles by my mouth** should hear the word of the gospel, and believe"* (Acts 15:7). You see how Peter made it clear that he was chosen by God to imperially open up the nations of the world, the Gentiles, to the Gospel of the Kingdom? *"... **God made choice among us,** that the Gentiles by **MY mouth** ..."* Peter was God's choice!

Now, after two thousand years the Lord has come back and given me the Keys of the Kingdom of Heaven. When He gave me the keys, He was saying to me without telling me, *"David you are an emperor."* It took many years for me to figure that out. He gave me the same keys he gave Peter, thus laying on me the authority and imperial power to fill up the Earth again with kings so that we can take over the world again. He established me as the next emperor on the Earth by revealing to me the emperors before me. That is why I have the revelation of Jesus through the face to face relationship I have with Him and that's why Jesus gave me the revelation of why God chose Peter to be a divine emperor. He chose Peter to be the next divine emperor because he loved Jesus more than the other apostles.

That is the mystery of the Kingdom. It is a real kingdom and it really is an empire. The mystery to all the parables Jesus gave was basically that, *"Hey guys, you are kings and I am giving you a kingdom. You have powers from another world to rule this world as kings."* The whole mystery and message of the Kingdom that Jesus was trying to teach is that Heaven has now come to the Earth. God has sent his government to the Earth to rescue the world from a renegade tyrant king that took it by subtlety from the

Transitioning into the Emperor's Office

original kings, Adam and Eve. Jesus came back to restore to you the crown you lost and to make you kings over the Earth. And you are to impose His will here on Earth as it is in Heaven. You are to take back the Earth!

I Will Give You Your Kings Back

*"And I will make thee exceeding fruitful, and I will make nations of thee, **and kings shall come out of thee"** (Genesis 17:6).*

A divine emperor is a birther of kings. God told Abraham, *"And kings shall come out of thee."* That is the grace of a divine emperor because whereas kings birth princes, emperors birth kings. This is important to understand because in a dark seven-year season in my life, I lost all my staff and disciples and had to rebuild my ministry from the ground up after that period. The Lord visited me later in a dream and said to me, *"I will give you new kings."* That was a very profound statement because it takes an emperor to birth kings. Jesus was automatically telling me in a mystery, *"You are an emperor!"* He was revealing my identity and office as a divine emperor through that statement – *"I will give you new kings."* Only emperors have kings reporting to them. And I have since seen these *"new kings"* come into the Face to Face Movement.

Many young men and women have left their homes, jobs, and academic pursuits and relocated to my North America Headquarters in Taylor, Michigan. The amazing thing is they all talked about how Jesus appeared to them face to face in dreams and visions and instructed them to relocate to Taylor. God has been faithful to His Word! Even to this very day more and more "new kings" are coming over. When you enter the imperial realm as a divine emperor, you become a birther of kings! These are kings who will have their own kingdoms to rule and reign over for all of eternity. That is why the Bible says, *"And **I appoint unto you a kingdom, as my Father hath appointed unto me"** (Luke 22:29).*

Moreover, through this series of Kingdom books God instructed me to write, many kings are being birthed all over the world. Many believers have now been birthed the right way into the Kingdom of God as they came into their identity as kings. One of these *"new kings"* on my staff always goes around telling people about me and saying I'm an empire. I never told her anything. God the Father, Jehovah, came to her in a dream and told her who I was.

God's Greatest Last Day General

*"Incline your ear, and come unto me: hear, and your soul shall live; and I will make an everlasting covenant with you, even the sure mercies of David. Behold, I have given him for a witness to the people, **a leader and commander to the people"** (Isaiah 55:3-4).*

Just like David, one of the divine emperors before me, I have been called to be a general. Divine emperors are often called upon to wage certain battles to topple king demons and prince demons all over the world. Moses was called as a general to go and deliver Israel out of Egypt. God called me a general in a dream in 2001. This dream lasted only a few seconds. In this dream, I saw four stars on the ground and I picked them up. I somehow felt that there was a fifth star that I needed. At that point, God spoke audibly in the dream telling me that he would give me the fifth star when the End-Time Glory Revival begins! Later on, I found out that a five-star general is extremely rare in the United States Army. A five-star general is only released in the time of a great war.

Now, Jesus as God's general in Revelation 19 is called the King of Kings. That is not to just to designate a lot of kings under Jesus, but the diversity of the type of kings Jesus raises up. Jesus has made each of us a unique type of king. Solomon, for example, was a different type of king from David. God raised David as a divine emperor to forge His Kingdom on Earth through war. David was therefore a warrior king. Solomon, on the other hand, was called by God to establish the Kingdom dynasty and to build God a house through peace. The name Solomon itself means peaceful.

*"Behold, a son shall be born to thee, **who shall be a man of rest;** and I will give him rest from all his enemies round about: for his name shall be Solomon, and **I will give peace and quietness unto Israel in his days"*** (1 Chronicles 22:9).

Solomon was a man of rest while his father David was a man of war. They were both kings, but different types of kings. Once you understand that you are a king, then God develops and fashions the kind of king you are over the years. That is how you get to know your own niche. Now that you know that you are a king, God will begin to construct the identity, weight, and glory of your kingship. Well, I am a warrior king. God made me so. In a trip to Heaven, Jesus showed me my book. And in this book, I found written concerning my destiny, *"God's End-Time General."* That is how I discovered that I am a warrior king.

I am a general king. A general is a warrior, a commander. I like fighting. I am not like Solomon, a man of peace, I am more like David, I love battle! I love taking out demonic influences and tearing down demonic principalities and kingdoms. As His end-time general, God spoke to me and said, *"Raise me up an army!"* So, I started off by mobilizing a ten-thousand-man army. Now, more recently, God commanded me to raise Him a million man army! God has mandated me to mobilize, deploy, and dispatch the End-Time Joel Army to take over cities and nations!

Handed Over to Satan For Seven Years

Divine emperors are often handed over to Satan to be tried before they can operate more fully in their calling. David was provoked by Satan to count Israel, Jesus was led by the Spirit into the wilderness to be tried by Satan, and Satan asked to sift Peter him like wheat! God does this to develop and toughen His divine emperors and generals. When the Lord was training me to walk into my office as a divine emperor, He gave me over to Satan, the Prince of the World.

This was during one of my yearly checkups with the Lord at the judgment seat. Early in my walk with the Lord, I spent a long season in prayer asking the Lord to grant me a yearly spiritual checkup so that I can know whether I am on track with Him or whether I have fallen short of what He desires of me. In one of these yearly checkups, the Lord had me appear before His judgment seat in Heaven and said to me, *"I have to deliver you over to Satan because I have chosen you to be a general in my army and you have to learn a certain realm."* There are many other things he shared with me at that time that I have chronicled in my book, *My Trip to Heaven, Face to Face with Jesus.*

For seven years I had to deal with this dark prince. I lost everything – literally everything in those seven years. But in that dark season of my life, I also learned more things about the devil that I could ever have known otherwise. The Lord had me go through that experience to prepare me for what He's having me do today, confronting king demons and bringing God the Father down to the Earth, face to face, with all mankind. For seven years, Satan would appear to me and I saw this terrible darkness in his eyes. Every time he would come by I noticed that his eyes had become darker and more wicked. During that time, Jesus would also appear to me to comfort and strengthen me because you need strength to go through that kind of trial.

When Jesus would visit me I would ask Him questions. This was my training to fight Satan, Lucifer, the arch enemy of God, not just the principalities and king demons under him. I once asked Jesus during that time, *"Lord, why are his eyes so dark and getting darker every time I see him?"*

Jesus looked at me and said, *"David, many people think Satan fell and that was it. But what they do not understand and what you saw in his eyes is that he is continually falling. He has not stopped falling from that being of light he was. He is still falling; he's still getting darker!"*

Then Jesus gave me this scripture, *"For, behold, the darkness shall cover the earth, **and gross darkness the people:** but the LORD shall arise upon thee, and his glory shall be seen upon thee"* (Isaiah 60:2).

Then He said, *"Do you now see the reason the world keeps getting darker? It's getting darker because Satan is getting darker."*

That is why the Bible also says, *"But evil men and **seducers shall wax worse and worse**, deceiving, and being deceived"* (2 Timothy 3:13). The darker Satan gets, the darker the world becomes because he is the prince of this world. He is still falling! The full manifestation of who he is has not even happened yet. That is why the only punishment suitable for his nature is the bottomless pit because he is continually falling. This is the kind of training I had to go through to become God's end-time general.

We Are More Than Conquerors

Now that God has transitioned me from being just a king to becoming a divine emperor, I confront and take out more king demons and their kingdoms. When I was in South Korea in 2013, the Lord had me confront the king demon holding North Korea in his grips. God called the prince ruling North Korea a king demon. He asked me to break him. Why would He ask me to deal with a king demon if I was not a divine emperor? As I have taught you, God makes you a king to break princes and He makes you an emperor to break king demons. This is the key to changing the world. It takes a government to fight another government. It takes a kingdom to fight another kingdom. You must understand why it takes an emperor to overcome a king. A king can fight another king, but victory is not certain until the battle is over. It can be a victory, a pyrrhic victory. A pyrrhic victory is when you win at a great loss to your life. To be completely certain of victory, you have to outrank the other person.

That is why Jesus said, *"When a strong man armed keepeth his palace, his goods are in peace: **But when a stronger than he shall come upon him, and overcome him,** he taketh from him all his armour wherein he trusted, and divideth his spoils"* (Luke 11:21-22).

You have to be stronger than whatever you are dealing with to have flawless victory. When you have higher rank, you are stronger! You have to be stronger by walking in a higher rank to be able to overcome! You and I are more than conquerors in all things and in all battles! *"Nay, **in all these things we are more than conquerors** through him that loved us"* (Romans 8:37). That means God has programmed us to be sure of victory every time! Jesus always leads us in victory! *"Now thanks be unto God, which always causeth us to triumph in Christ..."* (2 Corinthians 2:14). There will be a clear, flawless victory when an emperor fights a king and when a king fights a prince!

When God sends me into a region with the government of His Kingdom, these princes and king demons ruling those regions leave immediately! I always have victory because of my spiritual rank as emperor. As a divine emperor, I confronted and broke that king demon over North Korea and decreed by the Spirit that the war between South and North Korea would stop in five years. I gave that decree in 2013 when I was in South Korea. And now, exactly five years later, we have seen the North Korean leader walk across the demilitarized zone and embrace the South Korean Leader. In the ensuing summit between the two leaders, they decided to end the war! All this happened because I broke that king demon with imperial power as a divine emperor!

Called to Restore the Ancient Face to Face Realm

Divine emperors have direct dealing with God the Father. God has direct face to face contact with them. These pontiffs have the unique grace to bring God down on the Earth! Moses and Jesus particularly walked in this grace. Like Moses and Jesus before me, I have been mandated to bring God down on the Earth, openly, face to face with mankind. To be able to fulfill this global mandate, God made me go through a rigorous twenty-year process to mature into full sonship so that I can work with Him. To bring God down face to face on the Earth, God has had me bridge our generation to the lost ancient face to face realm.

When God has a divine emperor on Earth, He is able to execute His global plans through that person for that generation. One specific global mandate of my office as a divine emperor is the restoration of the face to face relationship we once had with the Father and His Son. For many years since Jesus came to me in a dream when I was seventeen years old and delivered me from my dangerous lifestyle as a gangster, the Lord Jesus Christ has appeared to me more than a thousand times. In 2008, the

Lord commanded me to write a book describing some of those face to face appearances and the doctrine. He made a covenant with me that he would appear to anyone who reads that book! I obeyed God and wrote that book, *Face to Face Appearances from Jesus* and its sequel, *My Trip to Heaven – Face to Face with Jesus* under a strong anointing.

Today, the face to face book has been translated into several languages of the world and Jesus has faithfully appeared to masses of people and entire nations through this book. In South Korea, for example, the Face to Face Movement broke out over there when the pastor of a seventy-thousand-member church bought the book and translated it into the Korean language. When he released the book, Jesus began to appear to hundreds of thousands of people in South Korea. They asked me to come over just because of that and for the time that I was there tens of thousands of people had to be turned away because of the huge turnout. They were waiting out in the cold in the early morning hours just to get inside the building! The pastor told me that they had all come to the face to face meetings with me because Jesus had appeared to all of them! I did not realize then as I do now that God could do that because I am a divine emperor. Global mandates can only be effectively executed by divine emperors.

At the beginning of my ministry, the Lord appeared to people individually through my ministry and through the book he commanded me to write, *Face to Face Appearances from Jesus*. The mandate has now broadened in scope. The Lord told me, *"You are not only to introduce people to me individually, I am now telling you to bring a nation out to meet with me."* My ultimate destiny is to arrange a meeting between America and God. I am to bring America to meet God.

The Face to Face Prophet

*"And there arose not a **prophet since in Israel like unto Moses,** whom the LORD knew face to face"* (Deuteronomy 34:10).

The Lord told me in a dream, *"I have now given you what Moses had to arrange a meeting between the nation and I."* That was when the Holy Spirit led me to the scripture in Exodus 19 where Moses brought Israel to meet with God. *"And Moses brought forth the people out of the **camp to meet with God"*** (Exodus 19:17). During that season of my life, the Father came to prepare me to spearhead this movement. In a dream, He came down on Earth in a blazing flame of fire and talked to me out of the fire. He told me three times, *"I am with you."* He then changed my middle name, which was Edward, to Emmanuel. That name Emmanuel means "God with us," (Matthew 1:23). My name was changed to align with my mandate. Father told me that He was now on Earth working with me.

In Deuteronomy 34:10 we read that, *"...there arose not a prophet since in Israel like unto Moses, whom the LORD knew face to face."* There were many powerful men and women God raised up before and after Moses, but none of them had the realm of power Moses walked in. Joshua, who followed Moses, did not have that kind of power with God even though he was powerful. That is why the Bible says, *"... there arose not a prophet SINCE..."* That word "since" means that the Mosaic type of ministry is a very unique, rare, and powerful one.

During a visitation, the Father explained to me that the face to face prophet is raised up every two thousand years. This is an ancient realm of ministry, it is not normal. Face to face is a very high realm. Moses was not a normal prophet - he was a face to face prophet and that is why that scripture says there *"arose not a prophet since"* in Israel. That means the type of prophet he is was never raised up again until two thousand years later when Jesus came. A face to face prophet operates in unprecedented and unparalleled realms of power. Moses, as the first fruit of the Face to Face Movement, walked in this type of power. God established a covenant with the Mosaic ministry and lineage to do marvels that had not been done on the Earth before!

*"And he said, Behold, I make a covenant: **before all thy people I will do marvels, such as have not been done in all the earth, nor in any nation: and all***

the people among which thou art shall see the work of the LORD: for it is a terrible thing that I will do with thee" (Exodus 34:10).

Face to face prophets have this covenant with the Lord. How many prophets do you know eclipsed what Moses did until Jesus came? Who else did God use to discipline a Pharaoh and a whole nation with miracles of judgment such as frogs covering the whole land of Egypt, and locusts destroying the land? Moses split the Red Sea and closed it back up over the Egyptian army. He caused the Earth to open up to swallow the rebellious leaders in the Israelite camp. How many prophets do you know who do this? Yes, most prophets of our generation walk in powerful spiritual gifts such as the word of knowledge and some miracles, but there are none on the scene who come anywhere close to what Moses did. This is because a face to face prophet walks in amazing signs and wonders.

God Chooses Me as the Next Face to Face Prophet

This is now the third time that God is coming back face to face to the Earth. In the first Face to Face Movement with Moses, God came down to deliver Israel from their enemies. In the second Face to Face movement, two thousand years later, God sent Jesus to remove the sin problem that hindered us from seeing God's face. God was in Christ, in the flesh, reconciling the world to Himself! That is why at the death of Jesus the veil in the temple was ripped open. God could now come out and manifest openly to man.

God is coming down again in our day in much the same way He came in the days of Moses, but in a greater manner. This time God is coming down to the Earth as a husbandman and as the Lord of the Harvest to reap the end-time harvest of souls. With Him on the Earth, face to face with man, the greatest harvest ever is about come in! (Hosea 6:3; John 15:1; Matthew 9:37-38; James 5:7). Jesus took a little boy to Heaven just to give me the revelation of the last end-time move. In this trip to Heaven, Jesus revealed to this little boy that the last end-time move is not just an outpouring of the Holy Ghost, it is an outpouring of Jehovah. The Latter Rain Movement is an outpouring of God the Father Himself!

Jehovah God Himself is about to come down to Earth, face to face with mankind. Jesus said to this little boy, *"Come with me, I want to show you the end-time greatest Move of God that is going to hit the Earth. It is David's destiny to lead this on Earth."* I was so humbled to hear this. I really do not fully understand why Jesus chose me. All I know is that I fell in love with Him. I am called to bring our nation back to God. That is what the Face to Face Movement is all about. It is a movement that brings people to meet with God and to turn their hearts back to God. The Face to Face Movement will prove to the whole world that the Lord God of our Fathers, the God of Abraham, Isaac, and Jacob and the God of Moses and Elijah is still alive.

It is Happening Again!

And now, after another two thousand years, our generation has been selected for the greatest Face to Face Movement ever! We know that two thousand years have passed by since our Lord Jesus came to the Earth. In the year 2006, I spent a long season shut in a church praying, fasting, and fellowshipping with the Lord. One day, Jesus physically walked through the walls of the church. The power and glory coming off His body threw me back and knocked me down. At times it takes several days just to recover when He does that.

In this visitation, Jesus said to me, *"David, the time has now come where not only I Jesus will manifest myself as I have been doing through your ministry, but now me and my Father are going to begin coming down on Earth working with you notably and openly in the eyesight of America and the world like He did with Moses and with me during my earthly ministry. This will take place before whole cities, regions, and nations, starting mainly in America."*

Then Jesus said these amazing words to me, *"You are the prophet that God has chosen to lead this Face to Face Movement. You are a face to face prophet."*

This came as a revelation to me. I had no idea that I was a face to face prophet and I did not even know what that meant. Jesus had to teach me about who a face to face prophet is because the fivefold ministry today does not teach on this. Someone came to me after this visitation and told me a prophecy given by a major prophet in America. This person prophesied that God had revealed to him that in the last days he will raise up a ministry like that of Moses and that a black man will be leading that movement.

During this visitation, the Lord also said to me, *"As the Father came down on the Earth in a thick pillar of cloud in Moses' day, and also when I walked the Earth, He will do the same with you for the End-Time Revival and Latter Rain Movement."* This is so amazing because in an earlier visitation, the Lord told me He had given me what Moses had. Just like Moses, I was born around the time the abortion edict became law in America in 1972. You see, abortion is the new Pharaoh and Herod that is trying to kill children in the womb just like the period preceding the first two Face to Face Movements when the devil was trying to stop deliverers from being born. It is the devil doing what he did in the days of Moses and in the days of Jesus when at their birth an edict was released to kill all the male seed born at that time.

I am so glad that my mother did not abort me. She had nine children and I was the seventh. She could have aborted me legally. Ever since the *Roe v. Wade* Supreme Court decision legalized abortion, more than sixty million babies have been aborted. It is the same pattern. Moses was born in Egypt and two thousand years later Jesus was brought to Egypt to protect him from Herod. Two thousand years later I was born in a city in Tennessee called Memphis around the time the abortion edict was coming out.

Interestingly, in the time of Moses, Memphis was a principal city in Egypt and the seat of the Egyptian kings. The famous Egyptian pyramids are located near this city. I was not born in Egypt in Africa, but I was born in a city called Memphis in the State of Tennessee, USA. In my hometown, Memphis, TN, there is a sixty-five-million-dollar pyramid building located downtown called the Memphis Pyramid or the Great American Pyramid. You simply cannot make this up! It is divine. It is supernatural! Our heavenly Father never deviates from His divine patterns. He has meticulously planned the ages and predetermined that every two thousand years a face to face prophet should be raised up to spearhead a Face to Face Movement. Every two thousand years you see this same pattern playing out, first with Moses, then with Jesus, and now with me.

The Lord then spoke to me about the four-hundred-year period that preceded the third Face to Face Movement that is on the Earth today. He said to me, *"A four-hundred-year period just passed by. This is the four hundredth year of America's existence. David, four hundred years passed by before the first appearance from the Lord in Spokane, Washington. There is a four-hundred-year interval before the Father comes down just like in Moses' time and in my time."*

I really thought America had existed for two hundred years up until that point in 2006. I began to research our history right after the visitation and I discovered that on April 10, 2006, King James I granted a charter to a group of investors which gave them the right to settle anywhere from present-day North Carolina to New York State. They called the first settlement Jamestown. The first time the Father appeared in the clouds working with me in America was in June of 2006, four hundred years after the first colonists received a grant to occupy this land. How amazing is that? *"Jesus Christ the same yesterday, and to day, and for ever"* (Hebrews 13:8).

God works in patterns! There is a two thousand year pattern and a four-hundred-year period before each Face to Face Movement. The Lord in this visitation also said to me, *"Tell America, Father is coming down to deliver this country."* Our Father is on Earth to bring deliverance to masses of people who are bound by sex trade trafficking, homosexuality, and drug empires. We are seeing great deliverances take place in several cities ever since Father came on Earth working with me. This is just the beginning of what God is about to do.

The Face to Face Movement is bigger than a ministry. A ministry or administration is given to an individual, but a movement of God encompasses and outranks every ministry. Every ministry must submit to a movement or operation if it is from God. In the Face to Face Movement, God promises to come to the Earth to meet face to face with mankind. God told me He would progressively reveal His face over the cities and nations of the Earth. The full manifestation of this movement is when God Himself comes down physically on Earth and talks out of the clouds.

God is Appearing Openly Face to Face Working with Me

The Lord Jesus told me in a visitation, *"My Father and I, we are going to start coming down to work with you. We will start appearing openly in the clouds before all America, before all three hundred and seventy million Americans."*

Then the Father said to me, *"I will come down like I did in Moses' time. But I will do this gradually so I do not scare Americans."* That is what he told me. And I have noticed how since 2006 when the Father first appeared in Seattle the visitations have been more and more notable.

The next stage of the Face to Face Movement is that the Father will speak out of the cloud in front of everybody. You will not just see a face form in the cloud and then dissipate. Our God will prove that He is God in our generation. In every region that He visits in this manner, massive deliverances will take place. This has already been happening in every region that He has appeared in the clouds working with me, but it is going to intensify. For example, you will see millions of sex trade victims rescued and major drug ring syndicates dismantled on a national and worldwide scale.

God the Father told Moses, *"And the LORD said, I have surely seen the affliction of my people which are in Egypt, and have heard their cry by reason of their taskmasters; for I know their sorrows. **And I am come down to deliver them out of the hand of the Egyptians...**"* (Exodus 3:7-8).

The Father is here on the Earth to break these demonic princes and powers holding entire regions and nations captive. He has come down to deliver! You will also see the prince of homosexuality broken and I am telling you that you will see hundreds of thousands of homosexuals and lesbians set free. They will be delivered because Father is on Earth.

*"And the glory of the LORD shall be revealed, **and all flesh shall see it together:** for the mouth of the LORD hath spoken it."* (Isaiah 40:5).

*"For I know their works and their thoughts: it shall come, **that I will gather all nations and tongues; and they shall come, and see my glory"*** (Isaiah 66:18).

Last year, the Lord told me that we have only experienced two percent of what He is about to do! The Father is appearing face to face openly to our generation to bring in the End-Time Great Harvest! These are exciting times!

CHAPTER 8
The Imperial Seat

CHAPTER 8
The Imperial Seat

The Greatness of the Kingdom

Now I want to teach you about the greatest and most important aspect of the Kingdom of God. I have taught you a lot of what Jesus has revealed to me over the past twenty-eight years of my life, but, I believe that this particular revelation of the right-hand seat of God is the apex of what you need to aspire to in the Empire of God! This chapter relates to the highest calling of God's Empire for you! Now, let us look at a very important text in Daniel:

*"But the judgment shall sit, and they shall take away his dominion, to consume and to destroy it unto the end. And the kingdom and dominion, **and the greatness of the kingdom** under the whole heaven, shall be given to the people of the saints of the most High, whose kingdom is an everlasting kingdom, and all dominions shall serve and obey him"* (Daniel 7:26-27).

In this passage, we learn about three dimensions within the Kingdom of God. These three dimensions are the Kingdom, the Dominion, and the Greatness of the Kingdom. As the Bible says, *"... and the Greatness of the kingdom under the whole heaven, shall be given to the people of the saints of the most High.*" You must understand that God's Kingdom has been given to you! If you are one of the *"saints of the Most High,"* then the Kingdom has been given to you. The Lord Jesus told the elders of Israel, *"Therefore say I unto you, The kingdom of God shall be taken from you, and given to a nation bringing forth the fruits thereof"* (Matthew 21:43). The government and Kingdom of God is on the shoulders of Jesus Christ! God and the Lord Jesus Christ give the Kingdom to people. That is also why Jesus said, *"Fear not, little flock; for it is your Father's good pleasure to give you the kingdom"* (Luke 12:32). The Kingdom can be given!

When a young prince comes of age, there comes a time when his father, the king, delivers that kingdom over to him. He is given the kingdom, just like the Father gave Jesus the Kingdom, *"And there was given him dominion, and glory, and a kingdom..."* (Daniel 7:14). So, you must understand that when the Bible says that the kingdom has been given to us, it is not just talking about some weak sorry stuff. This is major. We have been given God's Kingdom! He has handed His Kingdom over to us! This is far beyond any son or daughter of a King here on Earth receiving a kingdom from their father. Jesus would not call you a king if that was not true. You are truly a king, and as a king, you have a kingdom. The point is that in the American and the western church, we have so diminished and minimized the words of Jesus and we have so much ignorance about the depths and importance of what He said. The reason we are not conscious of the depth and potency of the words of Jesus is because we have not seen it manifested in power in our day as we should. But when you begin to see the Kingdom of God come in power and demonstration of miracles, signs, and wonders, you will begin to see how amazing it is when God says He has given you the Kingdom.

Kingdom and Greatness in the Kingdom

There is a difference between the Kingdom and Greatness in the Kingdom. I have been teaching you up till now about the Kingdom and Empire of God, but in this particular chapter, I am going to reveal to you what Jesus taught me about the Greatness in the Kingdom. To better understand this message, you must first understand the importance of ranks in the God's Empire. There is rank in Heaven, and there is rank in the Kingdom of God. There is also rank in the Godhead. Jesus said, *"My Father is greater than I"* (John 14:28). During His earthly ministry, Jesus taught extensively on who would be the greatest in the Kingdom of God.

When you start talking about the greatness of the Kingdom, you are talking about the realm that God deems as the highest pinnacle or apex of the Kingdom of God. God has not only given you His kingdom, He also desires to give you the Greatness of the Kingdom! However, we must also understand that although this realm is open for everybody, only a select few ever make it into the Greatness of the Kingdom. Everybody can get into the Kingdom, but not all saints get the Greatness of the Kingdom even though it is available to all.

I have been to Heaven and I have seen these things I am sharing here, and I want to give you a record of what I have seen so that you can understand that these realms in the Kingdom of God are for you. Our Father has prepared these things for us to walk in. Do you know that having the Greatness of the Kingdom, versus just having the Kingdom of God, enables you to get more done here on Earth? When you come into the Greatness of the Kingdom, you get more done! You torment more devils! You can take more cities and take out more principalities! In my book, *My Trip to Heaven,* I explain in the first chapter, the eight different relationships we can mature into in our walk with God and the Lord Jesus Christ. As you grow in your walk with God, you mature from just being a disciple, to becoming a servant of the Lord, then a friend, son, bride, and lover of the Lord Jesus Christ. The next realm you can attain in your walk with God is the right-hand seat!

Now, this is the point, the further along you mature in your walk with God, the more you can get done here on the Earth. A friend with God has greater negotiating power with Him than just a servant of God. The right-hand seat relationship is the highest of all the relationships you can attain with the Lord Jesus Christ before you move into a personal covenant relationship with God the Father Himself! The greater you are in the Kingdom of God, the more authority, weight, and rank you have to displace principalities and powers and bring the Kingdom of Heaven down to the Earth. This is why this chapter is so important. When Jesus first gave me this revelation about the Greatness of the Kingdom, it completely transformed my life, and it will transform yours, too!

Everything I have been sharing in this book is a combination of what I have learned over the past twenty-eight years, ever since Jesus Christ appeared to me when I was seventeen years old and started training me face to face, and also through the different experiences I have had in Heaven and the things He told me when I was there. All that I have learned changed my life, but nothing changed my life more than what I am sharing with you here! I will never be the same, ever, because of this message. What you are going to learn here in this chapter is the apex of everything. I really want you to understand the weight of this revelation of the Greatness of the Kingdom.

The disciples were taught by Jesus that there are ranks and levels in God's Kingdom. As I told you, there is rank in the Godhead, among God the Father, Jesus, and the Holy Ghost. There are boundaries. There are certain things Jesus will not do, and He will not cross certain boundaries where He does not have the jurisdiction or the authority to do so. In America, this is difficult to understand because saints exalt the Lord Jesus, but they do not know much about the realm of God the Father. In talking about the Godhead, many like to quote the scripture in John where the Bible says, *"Jesus saith unto him, Have I been so long time with you, and yet hast thou not known me, Philip? he that hath seen me hath seen the Father; and how sayest thou then, Shew us the Father?"* (John 14:9). You've got to understand what Jesus meant by that.

Rank in the Godhead

Most people think that when Jesus said, *"I and the Father are one,"* that means they are both equal in rank, but they are not! A husband and wife are one, but they are not equal in rank. The Bible says the husband is the head of the wife. *"But I would have you know, that the **head of every man*** *is Christ; and the **head of the woman is the man; and the head of Christ is God***" (1 Corinthians 11:3). This verse clearly describes the rank between man and Christ, the husband and his wife, and Christ and God, His Father. The husband is ranked above the wife even though they are one. And even though there is oneness in the Godhead, there is still rank and God is the head of Christ. Jesus Christ is ranked above the Holy Spirit, because the Holy Spirit only says what Jesus tells Him to say. Jesus revealed this to His disciples in John 16:

*"Howbeit when he, the Spirit of truth, is come, he will guide you into all truth: **for he shall not speak of himself;** but whatsoever he shall hear, that shall he speak: and he will shew you things to come. He shall glorify me: **for he shall receive of mine, and shall shew it unto you**"* (John 16:13-14).

The spirit of equalization is so endemic in America that it's very difficult to teach on these subjects. For example, some men in church tell the pastor, *"You know I put my pants on just like you. We are both the same."* Well yes, they are both men and they are all brethren, but they operate in different authority realms. When you start getting into Greatness in the Kingdom, you get into honor, authority, and recognizing ranks. Jesus understood this, and that is why He is so great. Jesus denoted the rank that existed between Him and the Father when He said, *"The Father is greater than I."* He always gave honor and reverence to God!

The Bible also says, *"Then cometh the end, when he shall have delivered up the kingdom to God, even the Father; when he shall have put down all rule and all authority and power. For he hath put all things under his feet. **But when he saith all things are put under him, it is manifest that he is excepted, which did put all things under him.** And when all things shall be subdued unto him, then shall the **Son also himself be subject unto him that put all things under him,** that God may be all in all"* (1 Corinthians 15:24,27-28).

So, in this passage, you see how God put all things under Jesus' feet until all rebellion in the Kingdom of God is overcome. Once Jesus puts down all opposition to the Kingdom of God, He also, the Son, will Himself be made subject to the Father! All throughout scripture, rank is clearly established in the Godhead, in marriage, in work relationships, in families and in kingdoms and nations on Earth.

You know, when I was in Heaven, I saw how much Jesus loves the Father. He absolutely adores and loves the Father, without question. And He submits to God. Yes, they are one, but there is rank in their relationship. He is equal with God in divinity, but not equal in rank. Do you see that? He thought it not robbery to be equal with God like Lucifer did through pride. Jesus made himself of no reputation. That is why Jesus told the disciples, *"Be as the younger."* That is what makes you great in the Kingdom, and that is the Greatness of the Kingdom! The Bible says, *"Wherefore God also hath highly exalted him, and given him a name which is above every name"* (Philippians 2:9). When Jesus made Himself of no reputation and took on the form of a servant, God the Father Himself exalted Jesus, and gave Him the highest place and position in Heaven for all of time! Jesus did not break rank, He kept rank during His ministry here on the Earth and He still does so in Heaven.

Jesus the Potentate of Heaven

During a trip to Heaven, Jesus said to me concerning God the Father, *"David, He's an emperor. He is not just a king. He is more than a king. He is an emperor and He has many kings up under Him."*

Jesus is one of the kings under God the Father, but next to Him in position and rank. Jesus is the enacting potentate and the King of Kings over God's whole Empire. *"Which in his times he shall shew, who is the blessed and only Potentate, **the King of kings**, and Lord of lords"* (1 Timothy 6:15). It was Father Himself who seated Jesus as His own right hand as the potentate of heaven. That is why the Bible says, *"...he raised him from the dead, and **set him at his own right hand** in the heavenly places"* (Ephesians 1:20).

When I was in Heaven I saw this. In God's Empire, there is a huge throne that God sits on in the throne room, and next to God is a right-hand seat. It is not a throne, it is a seat. The Bible never said that Jesus was enthroned on the right hand of God, it says that He was "seated." If God ever allows you to go to Heaven, you will see that there is a small seat that is positioned on the right side of God's throne. Jesus was not enthroned, He was seated. Jesus received His own kingdom from the Father and this is located outside of the Holy City, New Jerusalem. Jesus has a throne, but not in God's Empire because one of the ways of royalty is that there is not more than one throne in a kingdom!

In God's Kingdom, Jesus is the "acting potentate" and He sits beside God in a seat, a guest of honor seat, in the same manner that Joseph sat next to Pharaoh. *"And Pharaoh said unto Joseph, Forasmuch as God hath shewed thee all this, there is none so discreet and wise as thou art: Thou shalt be over my house, and according unto thy word shall all my people be ruled: **only in the throne will I be greater than thou**"* (Genesis 41:39-40). As you can see from this scripture, Pharaoh made Joseph next in command to him. Joseph was the second in command to Pharaoh, as the enacting potentate. I am giving you all these scriptures to let you know that there is a boundary that Jesus does not cross in the Godhead!

The Danger of Strife in the Kingdom

*"And Jesus knew their thoughts, and said unto them, **Every kingdom divided against itself is brought to desolation;** and every city or house divided against itself shall not stand: And if Satan cast out Satan, he is divided against himself; how shall then his kingdom stand?"* (Matthew 12:25-26).

That is why Jesus told the Pharisees that a kingdom divided against itself cannot stand. That is why, especially in the church, very little is being accomplished because everybody is divided against each other. In the Kingdom of God, there has to be unity and the only thing that brings about unity is love and honor birthed out of love. You must understand that honor and rank keep the Kingdom together. It keeps unity in the Kingdom.

Honor is the recognition of somebody. No matter how old I get, my father and mother will always be my father and mother. I never disrespect them; I always honor them. No matter where I go, and no matter how successful I get, I cannot dishonor my parents. That is honor. True honor is to acknowledge the authority that is above you, and the authority that is under you. It is to recognize rank in a balanced way. If you do not understand rank, honor, and authority, you cannot get into the realm of the Greatness of the Kingdom. You can have the Kingdom, but not the Greatness of the Kingdom!

*"And **there was also a strife among them**, which of them should be accounted the greatest"* (Luke 22:24).

Divisions in the Kingdom of God are caused by strife, jealousy, and competition because people are always striving for positions. But you must understand that this kind of spirit is demonic! The Bible says,

*"But if ye have bitter envying and strife in your hearts, glory not, and lie not against the truth. This wisdom descendeth not from above, **but is earthly, sensual, devilish.** For where envying and strife is, there is confusion and every evil work"* (James 3:14-16).

Envy, strife, and jealousy are all devilish and counterproductive to the Kingdom. Greatness in the Kingdom does not come through striving ambitiously to climb to the top. Greatness in the Kingdom is attained by striving ambitiously to get to the bottom! How would you like to be in a church where everybody is tripping over each other to serve each other, instead of striving against each other to get to the biggest position in the church? That is how God desires us to be in His Kingdom.

People who are great understand humility. They understand that striving for the highest position, the wrong way, is not the Kingdom way. The Bible says, *"Endeavoring to keep the unity of the Spirit in the bond of peace"* (Ephesians 4:3). Endeavoring in this context means also striving but doing so in the right way. So, instead of striving to get the biggest position, and to be the greatest in the wrong and ambitious way, we must strive to walk in love and serve each other. Can you imagine churches like that where everybody is saying, *"What can I do to serve you today? What can I do to make this better? How can I serve you today?"* This will make the church greater, ministries will grow faster, and pastors will have fewer problems because the Kingdom is now incorporated into the House of God. This is Greatness in the Kingdom of God.

Standing at the Judgment Seat of Christ

"For we must all appear before the judgment seat of Christ; that every one may receive the things done in his body, according to that he hath done, whether it be good or bad" (2 Corinthians 5:10).

I can assure you, that at the end of your life when you go to Heaven and stand before the judgment seat of Jesus Christ, you will find out how much we have missed God because of ambition, strife, and contentions! I have stood in front of the judgment seat of Christ. That seat is not big. It is a very small seat and the Lord judges you and tells you things about yourself. Most of us do not want that, but in order to be great you got to have that. Most people who are great are accountable. People who are not accountable cannot be great! People who are not willing to be told they are wrong, or for God to get in their face and expose the secrets of their hearts, cannot be great.

Greatness in God's Empire is not what most believers perceive greatness to be. You've got to define greatness from the perspective of Jesus, and that is why Isaiah by the Spirit said, *"For as the Heavens are higher than the Earth, so are my ways higher than your ways, and my thoughts than your thoughts."* God's definition of things is vastly and infinitely different from the way we define things. Our ways of thinking are totally wrong and opposite to God's.

I have learned through many years of walking with the Lord, that the things we call great, he calls nothing. When I was in Heaven, I saw some of those we would consider great men, who had some of the biggest ministries down here on Earth, occupying the lowest and least places in Heaven! Yes, they were in the Kingdom, but they were in the least part of the Kingdom. In His teachings, Jesus referred to great and least positions in the Kingdom of Heaven. Jesus said to His disciples,

> *"Whosoever therefore shall break one of these least commandments, and shall teach men so, he shall be called the least in the kingdom of heaven: but whosoever shall do and teach them, the same shall be called great in the kingdom of heaven"*
> (Matthew 5:19).

In Heaven, there are saints who are called the "least" and those who are called "great." You see, in the Kingdom of Heaven, there are ranks of the least, and ranks of the greatest. God has given us the Greatness of the Kingdom, but you choose which part of the Kingdom you will occupy! These men of God I saw in Heaven were very big down here and everybody sang their praises, but in Heaven they are nothing. In Heaven, they are called the least. It is like somebody telling you that you are the janitor, or you have the lowest position in the company or organization.

There will be those who will be called the least in Heaven, because of how they lived here on Earth. Now, you will not be offended at being called the least the way you would here on Earth because your emotions are perfected in Heaven! You would be content with that, because of how you lived on Earth. So, you will not be angry or flare up when are you are addressed as the least. God has a way of taking the pain of it away, but you will feel the pain initially when you stand before the judgment seat.

Desiring the Judgments of the Lord

Now, this is the thing you must realize, if you stand before Christ's judgment seat now, you can change that! If you die in that state of *"the least,"* then no matter how big you were on Earth, in Heaven you will be small. We can ask for and receive the judgments of the Lord right now. As the Bible says, *"For if **we would judge ourselves, we should not be judged. But when we are judged, we are chastened of the Lord,** that we should not be condemned with the world"* (1 Corinthians 11:31-32). Did you see that? We have an opportunity to pre-empt the judgments of the Lord right here on Earth! You can ask the Lord to judge you now! This helps to expose what is wrong with you so that you can change while you are still alive. Going through this process of judgment enhances your relationship with the Lord and also makes your election and calling sure!

*"Wherefore the rather, brethren, give diligence to make **your calling and election sure**: for if ye do these things, ye shall never fall"* (2 Peter 1:10).

That is why I asked the Lord to ruthlessly judge me while I am alive here on Earth. There was a time in my life when I took time off to pray for a season asking the Lord to give me a yearly spiritual check-up. He has been so faithful to do this in my life! At the end of every year, I go through the judgments of the Lord and that is why I have made so much progress in my walk with Him. I have been through the Lord's judgments and believe me, it did not feel good at all. It felt bad. I mean really bad, like David said, *"Make me to hear joy and gladness; that **the bones which thou hast broken** may rejoice"* (Psalm 51:8). He broke my bones. It felt bad, but it changed my life! That is what changed me, His judgments!

You have to let the Lord Jesus Christ examine your life. You cannot hide from Him anyway. He knows what is inside of you, even things you cannot believe that you will or can do. Peter is a great example of this mystery. The Bible says, *"Jesus said unto him, Verily I say unto thee, That this night, before the cock crow, thou shalt deny me thrice. Peter said unto him, Though I should die with thee, yet will I not deny thee. Likewise also said all the disciples"* (Matthew 26:34-35). Peter and the disciples did not know they had it in them to deny Jesus. They could never imagine that they would do that to the Lord whom they loved dearly. But Jesus knew the secrets of their heart. And the Lord desires truth in the inward parts! Jesus saw denial on the inside of Peter and the other disciples. That is what the judgment of the Lord does. It unearths what is buried and covered up deep within you!

At the judgment seat of the Lord Jesus Christ, He tells you what you will do in the future. He shows you the crevices and inner secret faults lying underneath the surface that can cause a major destructive earthquake in your life. You see, an earthquake does not happen immediately. Before an earthquake happens, fault lines begin to open up underneath the Earth and it just takes the right pressure to cause the earthquake to erupt. That is why the Bible says,

> *"The fear of the LORD is clean, enduring for ever: **the judgments of the LORD** **are true and righteous altogether.** More to be desired are they than gold, yea, than much fine gold: sweeter also than honey and the honeycomb. Moreover by them is thy servant warned: and in keeping of them there is great reward. **Who can understand his errors? cleanse thou me from secret faults"***
> (Psalm 19:9-12).

David said, *"Who can understand his errors? cleanse thou me from secret faults"* (Psalm 19:12). Secret faults are the fault lines underneath your heart that have not yet come out yet, but His judgment reveals those things inside you so that you can allow Him to deal with you. This births and produces humility in you. I did not become humble because I wanted to be humble, His judgments humbled me. All of us at our very best are prideful and arrogant! It takes God helping you with His judgments and giving you the grace to develop humility in your heart to expose and counterbalance pride in your life!

Ranks in the Kingdom

> *"And there was also a strife among them, which of them should be accounted the greatest"* (Luke 22:24).

In this scripture, we see the disciples contending about who was the greatest among the apostles. These kingpins, as I call them, would not even be talking like this if they did not know there was rank in Heaven! They knew about ranks in Heaven because Jesus always talked to them about the Kingdom of God. Jesus taught them often about the Kingdom and how the Kingdom had ranks of the least and ranks of the greatest in it (Matthew 5:19). Jesus also spoke about the position John the Baptist held in the Kingdom of God when He said, *"Verily I say unto you, Among them that are born of women there hath not **risen a greater than John the Baptist:***

*notwithstanding **he that is least in the kingdom of heaven** is greater than he"* (Matthew 11:11).

In our dispensation, we have the opportunity to be even greater than John the Baptist in the Kingdom of Heaven! How can you occupy this realm in Heaven if you do not know about your royal identity as a king in God's Kingdom? You see in those scriptures that Jesus talked to them about the greatest and the least many times. We just overlook these mysteries because we have not been taught the Kingdom.

Greatness in the Kingdom

So, the apostles were striving about Greatness in the Kingdom and Jesus had to correct them and let them know that, yes, there is Greatness in the Kingdom, but that they were going about it the wrong way. He pointed out to them that they were striving for greatness the worldly way like the way people do here on Earth when they are trying to climb the corporate ladder. Jesus began to teach them how to attain the greatness of the Kingdom.

*"And he said unto them, **The kings of the Gentiles** exercise lordship over them; and they that exercise authority upon them are called benefactors. **But ye shall not be so: but he that is greatest among you, let him be as the younger;** and he that is chief, as he that doth serve"* (Luke 22:25-26).

Jesus had to teach them His way. His way is humility. In the same context in Matthew, Jesus said to His ambitious disciples, *"Whosoever therefore shall **humble himself as this little child**, the same is **greatest in the kingdom** of heaven"* (Matthew 18:4). You can learn more about humility by reading my book, *Victory Over Pride, Triumph in Humility.*

Greatness in the Kingdom of God is like being the youngest person or child or servant. You must understand that this is a major revelation! Jesus said the greatest should be as the younger. You know how when you are young, your older siblings make you do the dishes and chores that nobody else wants to do? You have to be like that child if you want to great in the Kingdom of God. When you are a child you are no different than a servant. That is why the Bible says, *"Now I say, That the heir, **as long as he is a child, differeth nothing from a servant,** though he be lord of all"* (Galatians 4:1). A child is a servant in God's Kingdom!

In the Kingdom of God, when you take the position of a servant, you are like a child and you are the younger. That is how Jesus Christ Himself attained the greatest position in the Kingdom of God at the right hand of God! Isaiah and Paul spoke about the servanthood of Jesus as follows:

*"Behold, **my servant** shall deal prudently, he shall be exalted and extolled, and be very high"* (Isaiah 52:13).

*"But made himself of no reputation, **and took upon him the form of a servant,** and was made in the likeness of men"* (Philippians 2:7).

As a child, everybody in the house treats you as a servant. You are made to wash dishes, take out the trash, and do all the menial jobs. Jesus wants you to make it your choice to be like the younger person. Put yourself in that position. In other words, take the position of the one who is always bossed around and being told to do something. Now, most of the time we do not like being treated like that. Our flesh wants none of that! But Jesus said if you want to be the greatest, you have to learn to be the younger. That is why when I go around people I always make sure my place is, *"I am the younger. I am the least."* This is very important to learn. *"Be as the younger."* You can be forty years old, but still "be as the younger."

To be as the younger means to be in the position of the younger person. In a lot of places, many people have the pride of age. They say for example, *"Well I'm older than you so you should do that."* They expect things because they are older than you. But that is what Jesus is correcting here. If you really want to be the greatest, you have to be as the younger no matter how old you are! The point is not that you should act childish, but it means to be in a humble position, that a younger person or servant is always in. That is why Jesus said, *"But ye shall not be so: but he that is greatest among you, let him be as the younger; and he that is chief, as he that doth serve"* (Luke 22:26). Kingdom thinking is much different from the way the world thinks! Being a servant makes you the chief, it makes you the greatest!

Seeking the Things Above

Are you ready for your life to change? Are you sick of focusing on this life here on Earth? You've got to be sick of focusing here. God will definitely bless you here as He promised, but ultimately life is not just about prosperity and material possessions. Today the church is totally off course! They focus on the wrong things. What I am about to share with you is life, and this is what you need to strive for! Paul said by the Spirit,

> *"If ye then be risen with Christ, **seek those things which are above,** where Christ sitteth on the right hand of God"* (Colossians 3:1).

That means we are not to seek things down here on Earth. We are to seek those things which are above! You can get the powers of the world above, and the world to come, and walk in these powers right here on Earth! *"And have tasted the good word of God, and the powers of the world to come"* (Hebrews 6:5). We are to seek those things which are above. That means that you can get things that are up there in Heaven and bring them to Earth! That is how the apostles changed the world. They got the powers of another world and walked in them here! Jesus told Pilate that the Kingdom of God is not of this world,

> *"Jesus answered, **My kingdom is not of this world:** if my kingdom were of this world, then would my servants fight, that I should not be delivered to the Jews: but now is my kingdom not from hence"* (John 18:36).

Jesus gave the apostles powers of another world, to walk in this world to transform it. This is what the church needs to understand, that until we walk in the powers of the world to come, this world will not change! Regions will not change. Cities and nations will not change until we walk in the powers of the world above!

So, what exactly does this scripture tell us to seek? *"If ye then be risen with Christ, seek those things which are above, where Christ sitteth on the right hand of God"* (Colossians 3:1). It does not say just anywhere in Heaven, such as the prophet's mansions. Most of the prophets in heaven, like Jonah, Hosea, Daniel, and the others, have their beautiful mansions next to each other on the same street. They live on the same block. I saw them during my trips to Heaven. It is absolutely tremendous! There are many places in Heaven that you can seek, but in Colossians 3 we are told specifically what we are to seek. We are to seek those things above, ***"Where Christ sitteth on the right hand of God."*** In that one place, right there, is life! At the right hand of God is everything! David said,

"Thou wilt shew me the path of life: in thy presence is fulness of joy; ***at thy right hand there are pleasures for evermore"*** (Psalm 16:11).

There are pleasures at the right hand of God! The ultimate intimacy! Your pursuit in this life should be to seek the things that are above, in that location where Christ is sitting at the right hand of God! The majority of believers do not understand what it means when the Bible says to seek that place, but in this chapter I will share with you what that means, and I can assure you that your life will never be the same again if you make this the premier pursuit of your life! With this knowledge, you will send the devil out of your life with his tail between his legs! With the Greatness of the Kingdom established in our life, we will see entire regions freed from the oppression of demonic princes and powers!

That I May Win Christ

"But what things were gain to me, those I counted loss for Christ. Yea doubtless, and I count all things but loss for the ***excellency of the knowledge of Christ Jesus*** *my Lord: for whom I have suffered the loss of all things, and do count them but dung,* ***that I may win Christ.*** *I press toward the mark for the* ***prize of the high calling of God in Christ Jesus"*** (Philippians 3:7-8,14).

The mystery of the Greatness of the Kingdom is embedded in the third chapter of Philippians. Most of us do not understand this chapter, yet we quote it all the time, as I did for at least fifteen years. I studied this passage and quoted it in my messages, but it never opened up to me, until Jesus Christ revealed to me what it meant. Paul was making a very profound statement when he said by the Spirit, *"I press toward the mark for the prize of the high calling of God in Christ Jesus."*

The point is that the high calling of God is *in* Christ Jesus. I used to think that the high calling was something we attain here on Earth. I thought that the highest calling was the apostolic ministry or any one of the fivefold ministries. I really did think that the high calling was some type of pinnacle point of ministry because over here in America when we refer to calling we think of ministry. That was my focus until the Lord changed that and gave me understanding. Paul gave up everything to win Christ. He said, *"That I may win Christ."* Do you know that Jesus Christ is someone to be won? We do not look at Jesus as a prize, but He is. God gave Himself as a reward to Abraham in Genesis. The Bible says,

*"After these things the word of the LORD came unto Abram in a vision, saying, Fear not, Abram: **I am thy shield, and thy exceeding great reward"***
(Genesis 15:1).

God was basically telling Abraham, *"I am not just giving you something such as a throne or a scepter or a gift. I am giving you myself. I am a prize you have won through your faithful walk with me."* God rewards those who diligently seek Him. He Himself is the greatest of the rewards. I like how Jesus said, *"He that loveth father or mother more than me **is not worthy of me**: and he that loveth son or daughter more than me **is not worthy of me"***
(Matthew 10:37). Jesus was here revealing part of the prize one has to pay to win Him. I love how He said, *"… is not worthy of me."* *"Worthy of me personally,"* is what Jesus is saying. Christ is someone to be won! He is a prize and He is the Father's greatest prize!

Now, Paul had been in the third Heavens and he knew what this was. He gave up everything for this. When you understand what I am about to share with you, you will also give up everything. In fact, you will give up life, in this life, for this! When I saw this it was not hard for me to give up the jets, the millions of dollars and wealth that God so graciously gave me. It was nothing to me when God sent an angel to me in a dream and said, *"Give it all up."* It was not difficult to do so, because my focus was on winning Christ.

Focusing on the Hereafter

You see, people who do not have a revelation of the *hereafter* cannot give up anything in this world. But when you know what is ahead of you then you will not have any difficulty suffering the loss of all things to win Christ. Jesus Christ himself had this disposition, as the Bible says, *"Looking unto Jesus the author and finisher of our faith;* **who for the joy that was set before him** *endured the cross, despising the shame, and is set down at the right hand of the throne of God"* (Hebrews 12:2). Jesus had His sight on the *hereafter!* That is why He did not resist His enemies when they were judging and mistreating Him. The Bible says,

> *"Jesus saith unto him, Thou hast said: nevertheless I say unto you,* ***Hereafter shall ye see the Son of man sitting on the right hand of power,*** *and coming in the clouds of heaven"* (Matthew 26:64).

Most people cannot give up anything in this life because they are too focused on the here and now. After Paul's several trips to Heaven, he became totally consumed with the hereafter. In fact, from that point on, Paul was eager to leave this world to be with the Lord. The only thing that kept him on the Earth was because he knew the people he ministered to needed him on Earth. But for that, he was prepared to leave the Earth and be with the Lord!

> *"For I am in a* ***strait betwixt two,*** *having a desire to depart, and to be with Christ; which is far better: Nevertheless* ***to abide in the flesh*** *is more needful for you"* (Philippians 1:23-24).

Paul gave up everything in this world to win Christ. Everything! When you visit Heaven your focus will change. You will give up anything and everything in this life for the hereafter! You need this in your life! I want to pray, right now, that you begin to have trips to Heaven.

Lord, I ask that you take everyone reading this book to Heaven before they die, in the name of Jesus. Take them to Heaven so they can see the glories of that realm. I pray and I release this revelation and apostolic manifestation on their lives in Jesus' name!

The Excellency of the Knowledge of Christ

*"Yea doubtless, and I count all things but loss for the **excellency of the knowledge of Christ Jesus** my Lord: for whom I have suffered the loss of all things, and do count them but dung, that I may win Christ"* (Philippians 3:8).

Paul gave up everything not for just the knowledge of Christ, but for the *excellency* of the knowledge of Christ! There are levels and dimensions even in the knowledge of Christ. Paul was not just interested in knowing Christ, he wanted the excellency of that knowledge! That means the highest and greatest dimension of knowledge. God can know you by name, but there is another realm of knowledge where God can also know you by face. Having a face to face relationship gives you the highest realm of knowledge! This was his pursuit in life. Paul then said,

"Brethren, I count not myself to have apprehended: but this one thing I do, forgetting those things which are behind, and reaching forth unto those things which are before" (Philippians 3:13).

Paul reached forth *"unto those things which are before"*. This is talking about what's in front of you, future, hereafter. You have to reach for this. This must be the pursuit of your life. You must seek this! Then Paul says,

"I press toward the mark for the prize of the high calling of God in Christ Jesus." (Philippians 3:14).

The word "high" comes from the Greek word "anō" which means *upward, above*. The word "calling" is the Greek word "klēsis" which means *an invitation*. So, the high calling means the upward calling or invitation to seek that which is in the heavenly places. As I said earlier, I used to think that ministry was the high call, but if Paul says, *"I press toward the mark,"* what is he pressing towards? He stated specifically that he was pressing toward the mark for the prize. He mentions the word "prize." Prizes are meant to be won, right? And earlier Paul said, *"... that I might win Christ"* (Phil 3:8). That whole passage is talking about Paul winning Jesus on a certain level that he had not yet.

The High Calling of God in Christ Jesus

The high calling of God in Christ is not the high calling of Jesus Christ! It is the high calling of God the Father Himself! This is the realm of relationship that God is inviting you to pursue. It is a calling from God to win this. What do you win? Jesus! But we cannot have the right honor and reverence for this call if we do not know what that scripture means. So we just say, *"Well I got Jesus. I am saved."* No, that is not what this is referring to. Paul is talking about the excellency of the knowledge of Jesus Christ. This is about winning Jesus on the highest level! The excellency of the knowledge of Jesus Christ is the high calling of God on your life! This is not just having knowledge of Christ. It is having the excellency of the knowledge of Jesus Christ at the highest level you can ever attain! God's call for you is to win Jesus on the level that I am about to share with you.

You see, God owns this realm of winning Christ. You must understand that just as only Jesus can reveal the Father, only the Father can reveal the Son. *"All things are delivered unto me of my Father: **and no man knoweth the Son, but the Father;** neither **knoweth any man the Father, save the Son,** and he to whomsoever the Son will reveal him"* (Matthew 11:27). God the Father is the one who reveals the Son, our Lord Jesus Christ, and it is the Father who draws us to the Son. Jesus taught this when He told His disciples,

"No man can come to me, except the Father which hath sent me draw him: and I will raise him up at the last day. It is written in the prophets, And they shall be all taught of God. Every man therefore that hath heard, and hath learned of the Father, cometh unto me ... And he said, Therefore said I unto you, that **no man can come unto me, except it were given unto him of my Father"***
(John 6:44-45, 65).

That is why when Peter correctly identified Jesus as the Christ and the Son of the Living God, Jesus told him, *"...Blessed art thou, Simon Barjona: for flesh and blood hath not revealed it unto thee, but my Father which is in heaven"* (Matthew 16:17). It was the Father who revealed who Jesus was to Peter! And it is the Father who determines who has paid the price to win Christ and to receive the greatness of the Kingdom!

This high calling of God in Christ Jesus is not even for you to be a king in God's Kingdom. Now, I have been teaching you about being a king and your calling to be an emperor - that is great, but that is not the greatness of the Kingdom or the high calling of God in Christ. God's greatest call on your life is not just to be a king. Jesus made you a king the moment He died for you. Your kingship came with your salvation. The bible says,

"And from Jesus Christ, who is the faithful witness, and the first begotten of the dead, and the prince of the kings of the earth. Unto him that loved us, and washed us from our sins in his own blood, ***And hath made us kings and priests unto God and his Father;*** *to him be glory and dominion for ever and ever. Amen"*
(Revelation 1:5-6).

Jesus made you a king the moment He died for you and washed you from your sins in His own blood. The Greatness of the Kingdom is beyond your kingship. The greatest blessing and calling on your life from God Himself, is to win Christ! Jesus is also calling you to win Him. And the whole purpose of Jesus is to bring you to the Father. Jesus told the disciples that no one goes to the Father except through Him because God was in Christ reconciling the world to Himself. Jesus draws all men to Himself so that He can lead them to the Father. Now, to better understand what you are to win in Christ, let us examine more scriptures on this subject.

The Right-Hand Seat

*"Then came to him the mother of Zebedee's children with her sons, worshipping him, and desiring a certain thing of him. And he said unto her, What wilt thou? She saith unto him, **Grant that these my two sons may sit, the one on thy right hand, and the other on the left,** in thy kingdom. But Jesus answered and said, Ye know not what ye ask. Are ye able to drink of the cup that I shall drink of, and to be baptized with the baptism that I am baptized with? They say unto him, We are able. And he saith unto them, Ye shall drink indeed of my cup, and be baptized with the baptism that I am baptized with: **but to sit on my right hand, and on my left, is not mine to give,** but it shall be given to them for whom it is prepared of my Father"* (Matthew 20:20-23).

Now, you've got to understand that these people could talk to Jesus about seats and positioning in God's Empire because they understood these protocols and aspects of the Kingdom. They understood that it is a great honor to sit on the right or left hand of the king. Now, in the western civilization or culture, we do not understand this type of Kingdom language, because we do not study these Kingdom terms. James, John, and their mother knew that it was possible to gain the greatness of the Kingdom because they were around when Jesus was teaching on the Kingdom of God for three years. They were so consumed with the Word of the Kingdom that it became the pursuit of their life! They were now seeking the Kingdom and the Greatness in the Kingdom.

Jesus was always teaching about the greatness of the Kingdom, sitting on thrones, and what they had to do if they wanted to be great in the Kingdom. They were acclimated to the realm of the Kingdom because that was the main message Jesus taught and preached. So, the mother of Zebedee's children could ask Jesus to allow her two sons, James and John, to sit on His right and left hand. She knew that the greatest honor in a kingdom is for you to sit directly next to the king or emperor.

Jesus had to explain to her that he could not fulfill that request because that kind of positioning was not in His jurisdiction. Jesus always sanctified the Lord God in the eyes of those He talked to. Jesus was always careful not to cross boundaries and jurisdiction. That is why He taught extensively on the ranks in the Godhead.

The Bible says, *"And he saith unto them, Ye shall drink indeed of my cup, and be baptized with the baptism that I am baptized with: **but to sit on my right hand, and on my left, is not mine to give**, but it shall be given to them for whom it is prepared of my Father"* (Matthew 20:23).

Jesus was basically telling them, *"I can't give you that. Only my Father can."* The high calling of God is a realm only the Father can establish in your life. The Father is the one calling you to this realm. He is the one giving you the invitation. The Father has called you to win Jesus on a level that is extraordinary and beyond this life! Winning Christ is beyond normal Christianity and beyond boring dead religion. Do you want this?

The Revelation of the Right-Hand Seat

*"The LORD said unto my Lord, **Sit thou at my right hand**, until I make thine enemies thy footstool"* (Psalm 110:1).

*"So then after the Lord had spoken unto them, he was received up into heaven, **and sat on the right hand of God"** (Mark 16:19).

"Hereafter shall the Son of man sit on the right hand of the power of God"* (Luke 22:69).

*"Who being the brightness of his glory, and the express image of his person, and upholding all things by the word of his power, when he had by himself purged our sins, **sat down on the right hand of the Majesty on high"*** (Hebrews 1:3).

*"Looking unto Jesus the author and finisher of our faith; who for the joy that was set before him endured the cross, despising the shame, **and is set down at the right hand of the throne of God"*** (Hebrews 12:2).

I learned about the greatness of the Kingdom at the right hand of God through a trip to Heaven. Now you must understand that I did not understand any of this because I grew up in America and grew up westernized. I did not have any concept of the Kingdom of God or the greatness of the Kingdom. The Lord Jesus Christ himself had to teach me this mystery face to face after I pursued the Kingdom of God passionately in my teenage years. One year the Lord took me to Heaven to show me my heart for Him, and how much I loved Him, and what I had received after giving up everything to come after Him the way I did! He showed me my reward for sacrificing everything to follow Him.

When we got to Heaven, the Lord Jesus asked me, *"David, do you know what the right hand means?"* I began to tell Him what I knew about the right hand. The only thing I knew about the right hand, was what we call your right-hand buddy, your right-hand friend. That is all I could respond to the Lord. I told Him that the right hand is, you know, your right-hand man, someone who is close to you. I understood that it meant your friend.

The Lord said, *"Well, it is much deeper here in Heaven. Whenever you are honored by the right-hand position, you are honored to sit next to the Emperor of the whole Empire."*

I was so amazed by the teaching the Lord was giving me. In other words, the right-hand position is a position of favor and honor for all eternity! It is the greatest place that you can ever hope or desire for! It is the greatest joy and it is beyond this world!

Do you remember that every time Jesus was persecuted He said *"hereafter?"* He always had His mind on the "hereafter." ***"Hereafter*** *shall the Son of man **sit on the right hand** of the power of God"* (Luke 22:69). Why did He always talk about the right hand? The Bible says, *"Looking unto Jesus the author and finisher of our faith; **who for the joy that was set before him** endured the cross, despising the shame, and is set down at the right hand of the throne of God"* (Hebrews 12:2). It was a *"joy set before him."* He anticipated entering into that position of closeness to the Lord God with great joy! He looked forward to this so much that there was nothing He could not endure to be able to get that close to his Father! He told two of his perplexed disciples who were walking on the road to Emmaus,

*"Ought not Christ to have suffered these things, **and to enter into his glory?"***
(Luke 24:26).

He understood that suffering was part of the price He had to pay to gain the greatness of the Kingdom! The Lord kept mentioning the right-hand position because we are to seek that realm. *"If ye then be risen with Christ, seek those things which are above, where Christ sitteth on the right hand of God"* (Colossians 3:1). This is major! Your whole call is to seek this and to want this. But we get caught up in messages of prosperity. You've got to understand that if you get this, everything else will come to you!

The Right-Hand Seat at the Throne

While we stood in Heaven, the Lord said to me, *"This is what you have gained as a result."* And I looked and I saw a chair, and not only a chair, but there were many others. After this visitation, I was still in unbelief until the Lord took someone else to Heaven and gave them a message for me. When the Lord took this person to Heaven, He told him several things and showed him around Heaven, but the main thing He said to him was in regards to the right-hand seat position He told me about.

Jesus said to this person, *"I brought David here and showed him something, but he does not quite believe it. I want you to affirm this to him."*

He came back and told me the same thing Jesus told me. He told me, *"God has given you a right-hand position at his throne."* I still could not fully understand this until I read Rick Joyner's book, *The Final Quest*. You need to read that book.

In the book, *The Final Quest*, Rick Joyner talks about how Jesus took him to the highest point in Heaven and showed him those who were the greatest in the Kingdom of Heaven, and also how Jesus Himself has a right-hand seat next to the Father. Jesus also showed Rick that there were many other right-hand seats. Only a few people who had lived on the Earth attained that position. The people on the right-hand seats finished right by loving God with all their heart. This is how Rick describes his observations of those who attained the highest ranks and those who did not.

Higher Ranks

> *"In this first multitude I saw many other men and women of God both from history and from my own time. I stopped and talked to many of them, and was shocked that* **so many I expected to be in the highest positions were in the lowest rank of the kingdom.** *Many shared the same basic story – they had fallen to the deadly sin of pride after their many victories, or fallen to jealousy when other men were anointed as much as they were. Others had fallen to lust, discouragement, or bitterness near the end of their lives and had to be taken before they crossed the line into perdition. They all gave me the same warning: The higher the spiritual authority that you walk in, the further you can fall if you are without love and humility.*
>
> *… Those who stumbled did so in many different ways. But those who prevailed all did it the same way: They did not deviate from their devotion to the first and greatest commandment – loving the Lord,"* (The Final Quest by Rick Joyner, excerpts from Pages 124-125).

While in Heaven, Rick also discovered that the biggest group of people who occupied the right-hand seats were housewives and working women. Can you believe that? Rick Joyner had the opportunity to talk to some of the saints in Heaven. There was this particular saint sitting on one of those seats that Jesus pointed out to Rick. This saint was a bum on the street when he was alive on Earth. Do you want to know how he got the right-hand position? He was a bum on the street, got saved, and started witnessing to people. His name is Angelo. You really need to get the book, *The Final Quest* and read all about how this man got the right-hand position. I will quote some of what Jesus revealed to Rick Joyner about Angelo,

"Angelo began to love everyone and everything. He would rejoice more over an apple than some of my people do over a great feast. He was faithful with all that I gave him, even though it was not very much compared to what I gave others, including you. I showed him to you in a vision because you passed by him many times. Once you even pointed him out to one of your friends and spoke of him"

"I did? What did I say?"

"You said, 'There is another one of those Elijahs who must have escaped from the bus station.' You said he was 'religious nut' who was sent by the enemy to turn people off of the gospel."

This was the worst blow that I had yet suffered in this whole experience. I was more than shocked, I was appalled. I tried to remember the specific incident, but could not – simply because there were so many others like it. I had never had compassion for filthy street preachers, considering them tools of Satan.

"I'm sorry, Lord. I'm really sorry".

"You are forgiven," He quickly responded..

"… He had a lot to give to My people, but they would not come near him. Even my prophets avoided him. He grew in the faith by buying a Bible and a couple of books that he read over and over. He tried to go to churches, but he could not find one that would receive him. If they would have taken him in, they would have taken Me in. He was my knock upon their door".

I was learning a new definition of grief.

"How did he die?" I asked.

"He froze to death trying to keep alive an old wino who had passed out in the cold," (The Final Quest by Rick Joyner, excerpts from Pages 164-166).

This bum, Angelo, is now highly esteemed and positioned in Heaven, but on Earth he was not honored. In fact, even Rick spoke disparagingly of him. The Lord basically told Rick that he mistreated this great king while on Earth. The churches would not even receive this great king. You must understand something at this point, what we call great here is not great up there! Jesus told Rick that Angelo could not find a church that would receive him. Jesus told Rick that if he had discipled Angelo, he would have had much fruit in Heaven. But yet Angelo gave his life to make sure an old wino was warm! That is why Angelo has that high position of the right-hand seat in Heaven. He got that position because of love. Love is the greatest thing that will put you there. Your love for the Lord earns you greatness in the Kingdom of God. Everyone in Heaven who attained the right-hand position did not deviate from one major thing, their love for the Lord.

We get so sidetracked and caught up in things such as positions, fame, promotion, pride and material possessions. All this moves us away from the foundations and rudiments of the Lord Jesus Christ. Loving him, loving people right, treating each other right, living right with each other. That is the real call of God in Christ Jesus for you. During my trip to Heaven, Jesus showed me my seat in Heaven! When I saw my seat, I asked Jesus, *"Lord how did I get that?"* He answered, *"Because of only one thing, your love for me. Your love for me."*

The Right-Hand Seat is Not for Everyone

*"And he saith unto them, Ye shall drink indeed of my cup, and be baptized with the baptism that I am baptized with: **but to sit on my right hand, and on my left, is not mine to give, but it shall be given to them for whom it is prepared of my Father"*** (Matthew 20:23).

*"And they said unto him, We can. And Jesus said unto them, Ye shall indeed drink of the cup that I drink of; and with the baptism that I am baptized withal shall ye be baptized: **But to sit on my right hand and on my left hand is not mine to give; but it shall be given to them for whom it is prepared"*** (Mark 10:39-40).

174

Before I had this experience, I did not understand when other people went to Heaven and saw a number of these positions on the right hand. I thought there could only be one chair because we think that God sits on this one throne and Jesus His Son sits on the only right-hand seat beside the Father, but that is not true. There are many of these seats next to Jesus, and those who have attained the right hand position next to God sit there. Those who sit on God's right hand are high kings. Those who will sit at the right hand of Jesus just as He sits on God's right hand will be emperors or high kings. They are those who were loyal friends to the king while on Earth. They will reign as emperors over worlds for eternity!

The right-hand seat position is not for everyone. If you remember, Jesus told James and John that only the Father determines who sits there. The Father also determines the positioning and rank of the seats. This is not for everybody. It is only for the people who are willing to love the Lord Jesus and win Him. They are willing to give up everything! They are willing to lose everything, everything! They are willing to count it as nothing.

*"But what things were gain to me, those I counted loss for Christ. Yea doubtless, and I count all things but loss for the excellency of the knowledge of Christ Jesus my Lord: **for whom I have suffered the loss of all things,** and do count them but dung, that I may win Christ"* (Philippians 3:7-8).

You see, we value our lives too much and that is why many believers are falling short of this high calling. If you struggle over winning Christ, then you are not worthy. We struggle especially over people we are too close to. The godly relationships God gives us produce ungodly soul ties, because many chose their families over winning Christ. God gave us our father, mother, sister, brother, wife, children and all that, but, we develop these ungodly soul ties, where we cannot obey God or do what He tells us to do because we are too close to them. We love them more than we love the Lord which makes us unworthy of Him. As the Bible says,

*"He that loveth father or mother **more than me is not worthy of me**: and **he that loveth son or daughter more than me is not worthy of me"** (Matthew 10:37).

That is what Jesus is saying. If you cannot love me more than you love your family, you are not worthy of me! Most people cannot have the greatness of the Kingdom because they are too caught up even in the economy. Many worry about their finances and their jobs, but I don't. I do not care! It does not matter to me at this point in my life. This quest to win Christ must consume you. It has to be your one focus, just like Jesus, who kept saying, hereafter you will see the Son of Man sitting at the right hand of power! Every time He was persecuted and every time they dishonored Him, He had this one thing in his mind,

*"Looking unto Jesus the author and finisher of our faith; **who for the joy that was set before him** endured the cross, despising the shame, and is **set down at the right hand of the throne of God"** (Hebrews 12:2).

That is all that Jesus looked forward to. The joy set before him was to sit at the right hand of God! What he sought for and obtained, is now *your* high calling to pursue! God is calling you to seek those things that are above where Christ sits at the right hand of God. This is the greatness of the Kingdom! And the people who pursue this call are the people God can trust with the greatest part of his Kingdom, because they love God beyond, their father, mother, brother, sister, wife, and children.

You know some people cannot obey God because of their children. They are too caught up and tied up with them. And many love their spouses more than they love God. Yes, these are godly relationships, but you are not to have an ungodly soul tie with them. Anything that you love more than the Lord, your business, your job and everything else that takes the place of you spending time with God and loving Him, makes you unworthy of the greatness of the Kingdom. Too many people are too busy, too caught up in this life, and too busy making money to pay bills. If you are doing this, then you are missing the path of life. Winning Christ is the path of life! If He becomes your passion, you can win Him!

There are Many Right-Hand Seats

*"And he saith unto them, Ye shall drink indeed of my cup, and be baptized with the baptism that I am baptized with: **but to sit on my right hand, and on my left,** is not mine to give, **but it shall be given to them for whom it is prepared of my Father"** (Matthew 20:23).*

In this passage, Jesus said, *"… **it shall be given to them** for whom it is prepared of my father."* Them! That means that God has planned for many people to occupy the right-hand seats! There are many right-hand seats, but based on the fact that billions and billions of people have lived from the time of Adam up until now, there is going to be a limited number of people. In fact, during Rick's visit to Heaven, this is what the Lord said to him concerning the number of right-hand seats available.

"At one point the Lord looked toward the galleries of thrones around him. Many were occupied, but many were empty. He then said, "These thrones are for the overcomers who have served me faithfully in every generation. My Father and I prepared them before the foundation of the world. Are you worthy to sit on one of these?"

"… The Lord asked, "But do you want this seat?"

"I do with all my heart," I responded.

The Lord then looked at the galleries and said, "Those empty seats could have been filled in any generation. I gave the invitation to sit here to everyone who has called upon My name. The seats are still available. Now the last battle has come, and many who are last shall be first. These seats will be filled before the battle is over…" (The Final Quest by Rick Joyner, excerpts from page 127-128).

Many centuries and generations have passed by and there are still empty seats up there! That is why you have to make this the pursuit of your life. You must pursue and seek the greatness of the Kingdom which is the right-hand position with all your heart! To gain this position, you have to win Christ. While Rick was up in Heaven, he saw that Apostle Paul gained that position, because Paul was taken to the third Heaven and shown the right-hand seat and what it was!

When Jesus was persecuted, He didn't talk about how much power, authority, and dominion He would have after He rose from the dead. He basically said, *"I am going to be on the right hand of the Father. I am going to be sitting right next to the Father."* You must understand that the right-hand seat does not just represent a position of authority, but a position of closeness which gives you the authority. It is a position of intimacy! It is a position of closeness to God! The Kingdom of God is built on the king. The Kingdom of God is about God Almighty. We have made church all about entertainment, and we have been spoiled from the rudiments of Christ. We have been spoiled from wanting Him alone! The church needs too much tickling. The church is too fixated on material possessions.

The Seat Versus the Throne

You've got to understand the seat versus the throne. Jesus did not have the right-hand seat at the beginning, even though He was in the beginning with God. He did not have the position He now has with the Father. It was after He rose from the dead that Jesus said, *"...All power is given unto me in heaven and in earth"* (Matthew 28:18). That means that before He rose from the dead, He did not have all power. So you've got to understand, that at the beginning, there was this right-hand seat next to God and the only person who could get that position would be God's closest friend and confidant! God could trust this person to do anything He asked of Him in the Kingdom. So right now, Jesus is not just God's son, He is God's closest confidant! That is why He ever lives to make intercession for you, at the right hand of God. If Jesus intercedes for you, believe me, He will get God's attention for you, because He is God's closest friend! God takes His advice.

Lucifer saw that right-hand seat, but he bypassed it because the right-hand seat is not just a seat of rule, it is a seat of intimacy next to the one who rules. Lucifer did not want the relationship, He wanted the power. Concerning Lucifer, the Bible says, *"For thou hast said in thine heart, I will ascend into heaven, I will exalt my throne above the stars of God: I will sit also upon the mount of the congregation, in the sides of the north"* (Isaiah 14:13). That is what Satan was all about! He was about self-exaltation. He wanted the throne and not the seat! He said, *"I will exalt my throne,"* he wanted the throne! That is why you have to watch people who want positions and power and do not want a relationship with you. They are wicked. Their whole life is motivated by pride and upward motion and self-promotion.

I have several churches under my apostleship around the world and I have ordained bishops. I had one young man who came to me years ago asking me to ordain him as a bishop in my organization.

I asked him, *"Why do you want this? Why should I even ordain you to be a bishop?"* I told him that his spirit was not right, because I do not just ordain people to be bishops. *"Why do you want this?"* I asked him again.

"Because this popular name is out," he responded.

You know how the title bishop has become popular in the church today.

I said to him, *"Don't you know that a bishop is really just an overseer?"* You see the bishop is really not a God-given office. It is only an office to be desired by men, which makes it less than the fivefold ministry, but the Roman Catholic Church has exalted this title and made it so ostentatious with all the big caps, gold shields, and gold chains.

Many of these ministers are all about the gold chain, the cap, bishop ring, and all that, but they do not walk in power. *"Having a form of **godliness, but denying the power** thereof: ..."* (2 Timothy 3:5). Jesus had to deal with this same spirit during His earthly ministry. Commenting on the ostentatious display of clerical positions by the Pharisees and Scribes, Jesus said,

"But all their works they do for to be seen of men: they make broad their phylacteries, and enlarge the borders of their garments, And love the uppermost rooms at feasts, and the chief seats in the synagogues, And greetings in the markets, and to be called of men, Rabbi, Rabbi"* (Matthew 23:5-7).

Amazingly, it is the same today! It's all about the garments and chains and caps and titles but no power! You did not see the apostles in the book of Acts behaving like this. Jesus warned them not to. These apostles did not come walking down the aisle with huge hats, bishop crosses, and big staffs. No, that was not how they operated. These apostles had power! They would walk down the streets and their shadow would heal the sick! That is the kind of power they had. Those were the aisles they walked down. Paul spoke of this when he said,

*"But I will come to you shortly, if the Lord will, and will know, not the speech of them which are puffed up, but the power. For the **kingdom of God is not in word, but in power**"* (1 Corinthians 4:19-20).

Paul called these men who craved positions, *"puffed up."* Paul was only interested in the power these men of God demonstrated, not just in their positions and titles. The church today is in a big mess. We glory in position and titles. That is a Luciferian spirit because all Satan wanted was position, power, and authority; he did not want the right-hand seat. But all Jesus wanted was to be close to the Father for all eternity. He said, *"Hereafter shall the Son of man sit on the right hand of the power of God"* (Luke 22:69). That is all Jesus was focused on. He did not talk about how God would give him a kingdom, a throne and all that, even though God did give Him all of that and more. Jesus only talked about his position at the right hand of God, because it is a seat of intimacy.

While He was in Heaven, Jesus was in the bosom of the Father. To get the seat, Jesus knew that He had to leave Heaven, go down to the Earth, humble Himself as a man and as a servant, and become obedient even to death. He obeyed God and went through the most shameful death one could ever imagine because of the *"joy that was set before him."* He endured the cross because of his focus, the right-hand seat, the seat of the closest intimacy with the Father. And that is why the Father exalted Him and gave Him the highest position and place in His Empire, the right-hand seat. Jesus got the Greatness of the Kingdom. Lucifer did not want the right-hand seat, he just wanted authority, power, and the throne. Now he is condemned to suffer eternal damnation because of his misplaced priorities.

Your High Calling

To win Christ, He has to be your focus. This is your call. This is your destiny! This is the high calling of God for your life, to win Christ Jesus in a way you have never known before. And you can have this! I have personally experienced this and I can tell you that winning Christ is beyond life, it is greater than life. At this point in my life, nothing means more to me than this! I do not have to come on the scene in a major way down here on the Earth. I am ready to go now. There is nothing in my heart that blocks this focus of my life. This is all I look forward to. I have the same testimony Jesus had, hereafter I shall sit on the right hand of Jesus. That is my calling from God!

My high calling is not just to be great in ministry. There are people down here on Earth that God is bringing into glory, and that brings them greatness in ministry, and they think that is it. That is definitely not it! It is a fleeting moment, just one generation, whereas the Greatness of the Kingdom is a position attained for all eternity. To attain the Greatness of the Kingdom, Christ must become your focus. Jesus alone, not ministry, not anointing, not money, not a business, nothing else must come before Christ! This is life! Life is pointless without this!

I will never forget the first time Jesus appeared to me when I was smoking dope, drinking, partying, and pushing kilos of cocaine. When Jesus appeared to me face to face, He changed my life. And from that point, it has not stopped and I still want more. I cannot get enough of this face to face relationship with Jesus! We need too much in this earthly realm. Just like Paul told the Colossians, we must mortify our members on the Earth. You must, *"Set your affection on things above, not on things on*

181

the earth" (Colossians 3:2). We need too many other things and that is causing us to deviate from the main thing, winning Christ. Jesus told Martha,

"But one thing is needful: and Mary hath chosen that good part, which shall not be taken away from her" (Luke 10:42).

Only one thing is needful and that is to be here in this place that we are talking about, the right hand of God, at the feet of Jesus, next to Him! Only one thing is needful. You do not need a car. You do not need a house. You really do not need any of that. What you need is to win Christ. You need to pursue and seek passionately the high calling of God in Christ Jesus! You must seek the things above where Christ sits - the right-hand seat position of God. You must seek this. his is the Kingdom and the Greatness of the Kingdom. When you seek that above all else, then everything else will come. Everything else you have ever dreamed of will happen. But this is the greatest of all things!

He has to be the prize you seek to win. He has to be your prize, and if He is a prize then He is something to be won, right? That means you got to do something to win. And one of the things you must do to win Him is to have nothing else competing for Christ in your heart. Singleness of heart in pursuing him is a major component of winning Christ. That is why Paul jettisoned everything else he had, his pedigree, his race, his social status, and his relationships and pressed aggressively after Christ. God told Abraham, *"I am your shield and exceedingly great reward"* because he was willing to sacrifice everything for God, even his own son, Isaac. You must be worthy of the Lord to win Him. This is what I live for. This is all I want! I want nothing else and for the last twenty-eight years of my life, this has been my pursuit. I honestly did not think I could get this, but I did. This place is available and you can have it, too!

Pursuing Christ with Passion

In his book, *The Final Quest*, Rick Joyner explains how he found out, to his great surprise, that praying women and mothers occupied more of the seats than any other single group (Joyner, 127). Do you know why? I believe that women are more passionate in pursuing this, and they are more sensitive to the presence of the Lord. Men, unfortunately, walk in so much pride and that is why men have to let God deal with them on pride! If you do not deal with pride in your life, then you will mess this up. You have to lose pride and arrogance and all that hardness of heart. You got to have a passion and a heart like David did for God! David often sang of his passion for the Lord. *"O God, thou art my God; early will I seek thee: my soul thirsteth for thee, my flesh longeth for thee in a dry and thirsty land, where no water is"* (Psalm 63:1). That is how badly you must want this. David was a man after God's heart and he pursued the Lord relentlessly! *"When thou saidst, Seek ye my face; my heart said unto thee, Thy face, LORD, will I seek"* (Psalm 27:8).

Passion makes you go after God! How hard do you pursue? This is everything and I want you to have it, too. I can go home now. I am prepared to be offered up. Honestly, at this point in my life, I do not want anything but to finish what He has called me to do. After I am done with my assignment on Earth, I want to go. I do not want to stay here a second longer because life here means nothing to me. I have crossed over into a place years ago where there is no return for me. My mind does not think here anymore! Once you have been to Heaven one time or two times or as many times as I have, you will not want to come back here. You will not.

Once you are exposed to the glories of Heaven, you do not want anything else. I do not want anything here. There is nothing here for me, nothing! Everything is over on the other side for me. And I have made it this way because of my sacrifice. Like Paul, I have counted everything as loss, everything, not just one time but many times over. Unless you are prepared to lose any and everything for the Lord, including money success and any type of vision or project you have, you cannot have this. Everything you are and everything you have has to die! What I am talking about has to be the call on your life!

Your call has to be Jesus. It has to be Jesus. And it has to be the Lord in a way that you have not experienced yet. I am talking about a dimension in Jesus, just as Madame Guyon said, *"Experiencing the depths of Jesus Christ."* I am talking about experiencing Christ in a way that you did not even think possible. This love relationship is really amazing and it has changed my life and the way I look at life. I do not want anything else. I have denied myself to follow Jesus. I can honestly say from the bottom of my heart that I do not want anything else in life but this. This is my pursuit, this is my vision, this is my call and this is yours too!

CHAPTER 9
The Emperor's End-Time Plan to Win the World

CHAPTER 9
The Emperor's End-Time Plan to Win the World

*"And when they found them not, they drew Jason and certain brethren unto the rulers of the city, crying, **These that have turned the world upside down are come hither also"** (Acts 17:6).*

*"And he said unto them, **Go ye into all the world,** and preach the gospel to every creature" (Mark 16:15).*

*"And **this gospel of the kingdom shall be preached in all the world for a witness unto all nations;** and then shall the end come"* (Matthew 24:14).

The Latter Rain World Wide Harvest

God has an end-time plan to win the whole world! God wants the whole world! Five years ago, He gave me His action plan to take over the world. You must understand that all seven billion people on the Earth shall be shaken and they shall all experience the power of God as the Kingdom of God invades their lives. The world is about to be turned upside down in our generation because the Prince of this World, the devil, is about to be broken! Jesus did all this two thousand years ago and authored a divine pattern that still works today. We must never forget that Jesus is the author and finisher of our faith. *"Looking unto Jesus the author and finisher of our faith"* (Heberws 12:2). Once we follow His pattern, we shall see the whole world shaken and saved in our lifetime and this generation!

We are embarking on the greatest move of God that has ever hit the Earth! I am so excited about this because we are in the greatest time in history. We are witnessing the dawning of a new glory, a new power from God that has been given to us to impact the world and turn it upside down. Beloved, we are about to turn the world upside down.

The Lord visited me recently and said, *"David, I am going to give you the strategy to turn the world upside down and it will happen again in your generation."* The world was first turned upside down in the time of the Acts of apostles, as the Word says, *"And when they found them not, they drew Jason and certain brethren unto the rulers of the city, crying, these that have turned the world upside down are come hither also"* (Acts 17:6). In this passage, we see that it was the heathen, unbelievers, that recognized that the whole world had been turned upside down by the twelve apostles. This is exactly what is about to happen in a greater measure because God is not simply into repeating what He did in the past, He is into increase. *"Of the increase of his government and peace there shall be no end"* (Isaiah 9:7).

When the Lord visited me about this end-time harvest, He gave me the promise of it and also the plan and strategy. And through this strategy, we are about to see the glory of God invade our generation like we have never seen before. I want you to understand that we are in the final Move of God, which is the Latter Rain! The Latter Rain is the last Move of God! God told Moses in Exodus about the two major signs He will perform when He sends him to Pharaoh.

*"And it shall come to pass, if they will not believe thee, neither hearken to **the voice of the first sign**, that **they will believe the voice of the latter sign**"*
(Exodus 4:8).

He promised Moses two signs, the first and latter sign. I refer to the life of Moses because the Mosaic Army is the first of five armies that the Joel 2 Army is comprised of. The Mosaic army is the army that God Himself leads. God himself came down physically in the days of Moses to fight for Israel as Jehovah the Man of War.

Jehovah told Moses that if Pharaoh does not respond to the first sign, he will definitely yield to the voice of the latter sign! So you see Moses walking in major miracles in Egypt, but the magicians of Egypt duplicated most of the earlier miracles Moses performed. However, they could not duplicate the latter miracles and signs God performed through Moses. And that is how it is going to be in this last hour as the Move of God thickens and increases with glory.

We are about to go into a deeper power realm of kratos, or dominion power of creation! This will be the outpouring of the Latter Rain and the kind of glory that satanic powers will not be able to follow and duplicate! Witchcraft cannot duplicate and follow this next move that is about to hit the world. They may be able to follow the voice of the first signs, but definitely not the voice of the latter signs! We are the generation that is propelling the voice of the latter sign which is the Latter Rain Glory from God! I am excited and literally jumping in my seat as the spirit releases this word because we are about to see this thing hit the Earth and I cannot wait. And you should not be able to wait, either! What God is about to do is phenomenal! It is unprecedented!

God the Father Visits Me in a Dream

Five years ago, the Lord spoke to me and said, *"David, I have not come down on the Earth with you for nothing."* And as you may very well know, the Lord Jesus and his Father have been coming down face to face in the clouds in a phenomenal way, in the cities He sends me to. Jehovah also visited me personally in 2010 in a massive tornado cloud and I heard His audible voice coming out of this great cloud and saying to me, *"I am with you on the Earth now."* Now, you must understand that the Lord Jesus Christ and the Holy Spirit have been with me continually and working

189

with me before this happened. The Father came to me on the Earth and said, *"I am on earth with you now and I approve of your public, national and international ministry."* This was after twenty years of working with the Lord and the Holy Spirit. And just five years ago, the Lord began to explain why He's come down to the Earth in this open manner.

The point I want you to understand is that God and His Son always have a purpose for their visitations and appearances. They do not just appear for fun. They have a purpose to fulfill. When the Father first came down, He explained why to Moses. The Bible says, *"And the LORD said, **I have surely seen the affliction of my people which are in Egypt**, and have heard their cry by reason of their taskmasters; for I know their sorrows; **And I am come down to deliver them out of the hand of the Egyptians, and to bring them up out of that land unto a good land and a large**, unto a land flowing with milk and honey; unto the place of the Canaanites, and the Hittites, and the Amorites, and the Perizzites, and the Hivites, and the Jebusites"* (Exodus 3:7-8). He didn't come down just to make Moses happy, no, He came down with a specific purpose to deliver Israel out of Egypt and relocate them to the land of their destiny Canaan.

When the Lord Jesus Christ appeared to Paul, He had a definite goal in mind. Jesus said to Paul in that appearance, *"But rise, and stand upon thy feet: **for I have appeared unto thee for this purpose, to make thee a minister and a witness** both of these things which thou hast seen, and of those things in the which I will appear unto thee; Delivering thee from the people, and from the Gentiles, unto whom now I send thee, To open their eyes, and to turn them from darkness to light, and from the power of Satan unto God, that they may receive forgiveness of sins, and inheritance among them which are sanctified by faith that is in me"* (Acts 26:16-18). Do you see this? He did not just appear to Paul to give him an "encounter" as we love to say. No! He had a purpose. He appeared to Paul to empower him to deliver the nations from the power of Satan and turn them to the Lord!

The Husbandman is on Earth to Reap the Harvest

Five years ago, the Lord began to disclose to me His plan to take over the world. He told me He had come down to the Earth to reap the harvest! The Father explained to me in this visitation that He is not just a king, but an emperor, and as a result, everything He does has a world emphasis. God has come down for the whole world! He has a global worldwide vision to reap the harvest. A man of God recently had a vision where he saw the Father climbing down a ladder from Heaven to Earth wearing the clothes of a gardener! The Lord revealed to this man of God that the Father, as the husbandman, had come down to reap the harvest of the Earth. You see, Father is not just sitting on a throne in Heaven. He has come off the throne in His identity as the Lord of the Harvest and the husbandman to reap the harvest. The Father is a husbandman as the Bible says,

> *"Be patient therefore, brethren, unto the coming of the Lord. Behold, the husbandman waiteth for the precious fruit of the earth, and hath long patience for it, until he receive the early and latter rain"* (James 5:7).

Jesus called Father a husbandman, *"I am the true vine, and my Father is the husbandman"* (John 15:1). Jesus also called Jehovah the Lord of the Harvest, *"Pray ye therefore the Lord of the harvest, that he will send forth labourers into his harvest"* (Matthew 9:38). As the husbandman, the Father is presently on Earth to reap the end-time harvest of souls!

When the Lord laid down His plan to win the world, I wanted to go ahead and share the plan but He told me, *"Do not share it now. I want you to wait for five years and then I will give you the strategy of what I am about to do."* That is why the Lord has been appearing all over North America these last few years, but you must understand that is just the beginning. That is not even two percent of how He is going to manifest Himself openly to our generation. None of this was happening until 2006 when the Lord told me that He had come down to the Earth to work with me by appearing openly face to face to our generation. The Father told me, *"I am back on the Earth like I was in the ancient days in the Bible. Whenever I come to the Earth, I come to win the Earth back to myself."* That is why the Bible says, *"To wit, that God was in Christ, **reconciling the world unto himself"*** (2 Corinthians 5:19). God has come to reconcile the world to Himself. God never does anything on just a city-wide level only. If Jehovah comes off His throne and comes to the Earth, it is always about winning the world.

God has a global perspective. He has a world vision. Jesus told Nicodemus, *"For God so loved the world, that he gave his only begotten Son"* (John 3:16). It was a world strategy. God's strategy in releasing Jesus to the Earth was to win the world, not just a city. Whole cities, nations, and continents are about to fall like dominoes to the Lord! Even when Jehovah came down to the Earth to redeem Israel from Egypt, He had a global purpose. He told Pharaoh,

*"And in very deed for this cause have I raised thee up, for to shew in thee my power; **and that my name may be declared throughout all the earth"*** (Exodus 9:16).

To this day, the whole world knows what God did to Pharaoh when he brought Israel out of Egypt. And to this day Hollywood is still releasing movies about the miracles of judgment God brought on Earth that established His renown and glory on a worldwide scale. What God is about to do is a worldwide move.

The Latter Rain is a Global Movement

This is an imperial global movement, not just a local movement. The Father is on the Earth to win the whole world and He revealed His plan and strategy to me. He has now given me the go-ahead to release this plan to the world. He gave me a keyword when He was revealing the strategy to me. He said, *"Remember my pattern."* I now want to share God's divine pattern for taking the world. A lot of the Charismatic and Pentecostal leaders think that the Holy Ghost Outpouring is the only element that will change the world, but you must understand that the outpouring of the Holy Ghost in a believer life is only part of the last stages or steps to turning the world upside down. When the Lord visited me, He said, *"Tell them that they do not have the whole thing right."* I really used to think, just like the Charismatic Movement thinks, that the last day Move of God is just going to be a revival or another outpouring of the Holy Spirit. But I must tell you that it is much greater than that.

You see God has already poured out His Spirit and His ancient pattern for winning the world is the same and has not changed. The Lord said to me as He introduced the strategy to me, *"Many of my people in the church have tried to change the world and turn it upside down, David. But they cannot do it because they do not understand what they are fighting. They think that having a revival in the church is what is going to change the world. That is not going to change the world."*

Then He began to give me the steps to how He turned the whole world upside down. He said, *"Some of the movements have one or more elements, but they do not have all the elements that it took to turn the world upside down."*

It is imperative that you understand that before the apostles got filled with the Holy Ghost and turned the world upside down, the Godhead took other preceding steps. We simply do not realize that, but the Lord appeared to me and gave me the strategy and the various steps to it took to win back the world.

Saints, the move of God has begun to reap the last harvest and to bring an *upside-down revival*. We call this move an "Upside-Down Revolution to the world." The people of the world are going to say about us, *"Those people who have turned the world upside down have come here, too."* This is about to happen and I am excited about it. Now, these are the strategic steps God took to take back the world from the kingdom of darkness.

God's Pattern and Strategy to Win the World

First Step: All Persons of the Godhead Need to be Involved

"For God so loved the world, that he gave his only begotten Son, that whosoever believeth in him should not perish, but have everlasting life" (John 3:16).

"Now when all the people were baptized, it came to pass, that Jesus also being baptized, and praying, the heaven was opened, And the Holy Ghost descended in a bodily shape like a dove upon him, and a voice came from heaven, which said, **Thou art my beloved Son;** *in thee I am well pleased"* (Luke 3:21-22).

The Lord explained to me the first step. He said, *"David, what the leaders of your generation who want to turn the world upside down lack is Face to Face."*

I said, "Lord, what do you mean?"

He said, *"The first step in turning the world upside down is that I came down face to face."*

That is why the Bible says, the emperor, Father, had to get involved to save the world. The first step to turning the world upside down is that you need to have face to face involvement from God. The Bible says, *"For* **God so loved the world,** *that he gave his only begotten Son, that whosoever believeth in him should not perish, but have everlasting life" (John 3:16).* That is how world domination was commenced by the Kingdom of God. God sent His Son on the Earth in His body, in the flesh, face to face.

*"**And the Word was made flesh, and dwelt among us,** (and we beheld his glory, the glory as of the only begotten of the Father,) full of grace and truth"*
(John 1:14).

Jesus came down on Earth face to face with man and walked among us. It took Face to Face with the Godhead to start the movement to win the world back. Face to Face is the key and this is what our generation needs to understand! The whole ministry of Jesus was God Himself coming on Earth face to face, not just Jesus. You must understand that all three persons of the Godhead were on Earth with Jesus.

Jesus Himself said, *"My Father worketh hitherto, and I work"* (John 5:17). The Father and Son were working together on Earth. In fact, Jesus would not do anything on Earth without the Father's involvement. Jesus explained this vital key of his ministry to the Jews when He said,

*"Verily, verily, I say unto you, **The Son can do nothing of himself, but what he seeth the Father do**: for what things soever he doeth, these also doeth the Son likewise"* (John 5:19).

Jesus was working directly with the Father on Earth to win the world back. Jesus also told Philip, *"Believest thou not that I am in the Father, and the Father in me? the words that I speak unto you I speak not of myself: **but the Father that dwelleth in me, he doeth the works"*** (John 14:10). Jesus co-labored with the Father to win the world!

The Holy Ghost was also involved on Earth face to face with Jesus. The Holy Spirit overshadowed Mary in the process of conceiving Jesus in her womb as prophesied by Angel Gabriel, *"And the angel answered and said unto her, **The Holy Ghost shall come upon thee**, and the power of the Highest shall overshadow thee: therefore also that holy thing which shall be born of thee shall be called the Son of God"* (Luke 1:35). At the commencement of Jesus' ministry, John the Baptist saw the Spirit descend in bodily form upon Jesus and said, *"And I knew him not: but he that sent me to baptize with water, the same said unto me, **Upon whom thou shalt see the Spirit descending, and remaining on him**, the same is he which baptizeth with the Holy Ghost"* (John 1:33). The Spirit of God rested permanently on the Lord during His earthly ministry. Jesus had the Spirit without measure on His life!

Jesus also said, *"**But if I cast out devils by the Spirit of God**, then the kingdom of God is come unto you"* (Matthew 12:28). Jesus worked with the Holy Spirit to cast out devils! He performed miracles in the power of the

195

Spirit, *"And **Jesus returned in the power of the Spirit** into Galilee: and there went out a fame of him through all the region round about"* (Luke 4:14). That is when Jesus said, *"The Spirit of the Lord is upon me, because he hath anointed me to preach the gospel to the poor; he hath sent me to heal the brokenhearted, to preach deliverance to the captives, and recovering of sight to the blind, to set at liberty them that are bruised, To preach the acceptable year of the Lord"* (Luke 4:19). The Spirit of God anointed Jesus to preach and to heal and to cast out devils.

All three persons of the Godhead were on Earth, but Jesus, the Son of God, was the one who was more visible. Jesus manifested the Godhead in a body His Father prepared for Him. *"Wherefore when he cometh into the world, he saith, Sacrifice and offering thou wouldest not, **but a body hast thou prepared me**"* (Hebrews 10:5). When God sent Jesus to the Earth, He prepared a body for Him and the fullness of the Godhead indwelt Jesus bodily! Paul made this powerful declaration,

> *"And without controversy great is the mystery of godliness: **God was manifest in the flesh**"* (1 Timothy 3:16).

God Comes Down Face to Face with Moses

Every time there was a strong move of God in the Old Testament, the Father came down physically face to face. The Lord said to Moses, *"And be ready against the third day: **for the third day the LORD will come down in the sight of all the people** upon mount Sinai"* (Exodus 19:11). Face to Face was first mentioned in the Old Testament when God worked with Moses to bring Israel out of Egypt. *"The LORD **talked with you face to face** in the mount out of the midst of the fire"* (Deuteronomy 5:4). God came down on Earth in a Spirit form. The children of Israel saw Him come down physically in fire and they heard His voice! That really scared them.

> *"And it came to pass on the third day in the morning, that there were thunders and lightnings, and a thick cloud upon the mount, and the voice of the trumpet exceeding loud; so that all the people that was in the camp trembled. And mount Sinai was altogether on a smoke, **because the LORD descended upon it in fire:***

and the smoke thereof ascended as the smoke of a furnace, and the whole mount quaked greatly" (Exodus 19:16,18).

"And all the people saw the thunderings, and the lightnings, and the noise of the trumpet, and the mountain smoking: and when the people saw it, they removed, and stood afar off. And they said unto Moses, Speak thou with us, and we will hear: but let not God speak with us, lest we die" (Exodus 20:18-19).

The people could not deal with the physical presence of God and chose – tragically – to deal with God through Moses. That is what I call the *Ancient Violation.* Israel essentially rejected the direct face to face relationship with God. They chose the prophetic over the face to face relationship in much the same way our generation today is doing. But God would not let that stop Him. In the New Testament, God basically said, *"Okay, I will change this up. I will send my Son to the Earth. We the Godhead will come down to man, but in a body."* God sent His Son Jesus to the Earth in the flesh, face to face. ***"And the Word was made flesh, and dwelt among us,** (and **we beheld his glory,** the glory as of the only begotten of the Father,) full of grace and truth"* (John 1:14). So, God was on Earth with Jesus and Jesus, with the Godhead dwelling in Him, walked among us. *"For in him dwelleth all the **fulness of the Godhead bodily**"* (Colossians 2:9). Paul also said in his letter to Timothy, *"And without controversy great is the mystery of godliness: **God was manifest in the flesh**"* (1 Timothy 3:16).

Face to Face is the Key to the End-Time World Harvest

For years we have quoted this scripture without understanding, *"If my people, which are called by my name, shall humble themselves, and pray, and **seek my face,** and turn from their wicked ways; then will I hear from heaven, and will forgive their sin, and will heal their land"* (2 Chronicles 7:14). God himself said, *"Seek my face."* SEEK MY FACE... SEEK MY FACE... We are to seek God's face. *"Seek the LORD and his strength, seek his face continually"* (1 Chronicles 16:11). And that is why the Church leaders today are failing to turn the world upside down with prayer and fasting. They are missing the face to face component and they go into prayer without humility. God said that before praying, His people should humble themselves! God wants humility first before prayer. If you are not walking in humility, then when you pray God cannot use you to win the world. So, God told Solomon, *"If my people, which are called by my name, shall humble themselves, and pray, and seek my face ..."* The first step is that we are to humble ourselves and the second step is to pray and then we are to seek His face.

Prayer and seeking God's face are two different things. *Seeking God's face is not just going to Him in prayer. It means to look for the face of God. It means to look for God's personal involvement physically, face to face in a situation.* Moses sought this! *"And he said unto him, If thy presence go not with me, carry us not up hence"* (Exodus 33:15). You know the Hebrew word for "presence" (H6440 pânîym) also means "face!" Moses would not move without God's personal face to face involvement. Moses got his heart's desire. God's face was continually seen upon Israel as they moved to the Promised Land.

"And they will tell it to the inhabitants of this land: for they have heard that thou LORD art among this people, that thou LORD art seen face to face, and that thy cloud standeth over them, and that thou goest before them, by day time in a pillar of a cloud, and in a pillar of fire by night" (Numbers 14:14).

God came down physically on Earth and all the nations of the world knew this. They knew that God was on Earth with Moses and with the children of Israel. *"And there arose not a prophet since in Israel like unto Moses, whom the LORD knew face to face"* (Deuteronomy 34:10). When you seek His face, you want Him to come down like Isaiah said,

"Oh that thou wouldest rend the heavens, that thou wouldest come down, that the mountains might flow down at thy presence" (Isaiah 64:1).

How would you like for that to be said about the church of the twenty-first century? How would you like for it to be said on CNN, "God is on Earth with these people!" Today they do not believe God is on Earth with us. That is why they do not fear God because it is face to face that gives the validation they are looking for. And now we are beginning to see God's face to face involvement with us on Earth. You must understand that to turn the world upside down, you must have face to face involvement from God. Jesus explained that this is what the movements of today are missing and that is why they are not able to turn the world upside down.

I must explain why none of the movements are taking over the world. By movements, I mean the apostolic, Pentecostal, prophetic, evangelical, charismatic, and all the other movements operating in the church today. And there are awesome movements of the Lord such as what is happening in Redding with Bill Johnson, and also the Call with Lou Engle, however, none of these movements are taking the world. Everything they are doing is not working. Now, these movements are blessing the Body of Christ, but they do not have the power to penetrate and take over the world! We just need to honest about it. You see, I am just not going to keep doing all this twenty-first century kind of ministry, holding services and revivals and doing all this work that has no world impact. We just need to stop deceiving ourselves. How is it that twelve men turned the world upside down in their lifetime and all we can do is fill up an arena with a hundred thousand people, but we cannot even win a city? Something is wrong with that picture.

All Three Persons of the Godhead Are on Earth Now

Before God does a world move, He shows up Himself. That is something the leaders of most of these movements do not teach and that is what I am teaching. All the three persons of the Godhead are on Earth for a reason. We know that the Holy Spirit is here and has been here ever since Pentecost, but the Holy Spirit is not the one who causes the world to be turned upside down. He has a part to play, but He is not the only person of the Godhead who has to be involved to win the world as the leaders of today think. The leaders of the church today believe the outpouring of the Holy Ghost is what is going to change the world. Well, you see them rolling and dancing and laughing in the Spirit and jumping up and down in the Holy Ghost outpourings, but the world is not getting saved. This is because it is not just the dunamis power of the Holy Spirit that can save the world. You have to go back to God's strategy when He first sent Jesus to the Earth to save the world.

This is the first and most important step of God strategy to win the world. All three of the Godheads need to be on Earth at the same time! That is what the movements of today do not have. They skip to the Holy Spirit because they do not follow God's strategy and order in the New Testament. To win the world, God the Father and His Son, Jesus, together with the Holy Ghost got personally involved. All three of them were on the Earth. God was working with Jesus and the Holy Spirit was on Jesus.

In the four gospels, we see that when Jesus started His ministry, Heaven opened up to Him, and as the Father spoke to Him out of Heave, the Holy Spirit descended like a dove and rested on Him. All three of the Godheads were involved in a global movement to win the world back. Until we have all three of them involved, the world will not be taken. It is not just the outpouring of the Holy Spirit that will win the world. We also need to have the Father and Jesus down on earth too! That is what the Face to Face Movement has been all about. All the three persons of the Godhead must be on Earth to be able to bring in the worldwide harvest.

Second Step: Aggressive Recruitment of Disciples to be Kings

*"And Jesus, walking by the sea of Galilee, saw two brethren, Simon called Peter, and Andrew his brother, casting a net into the sea: for they were fishers. And he saith unto them, **Follow me, and I will make you fishers of men.** And they straightway left their nets, and followed him. And going on from thence, he saw other two brethren, James the son of Zebedee, and John his brother, in a ship with Zebedee their father, mending their nets; **and he called them**. And they immediately left the ship and their father, and followed him"*
(Matthew 4:18-22).

The second step to turning the world upside down is that Jesus started recruiting a staff of disciples by numbers. He chose twelve apostles and discipled them to be kings with the message of the Kingdom. He had to do this because these would be the men who would rule what he conquered after He left. So, God sent His Son Jesus Christ to the Earth and when He was of full age He went to certain men, face to face, and said, *"Follow me."* Jesus immediately started aggressively recruiting disciples or a staff, as we call them today, to do the work. Jesus did not take over the world until the team of disciples was in place.

Today we need to move people from the believer to the discipleship realm. He recruited these disciples with the simple command, *"Follow me,"* and transformed them into fishers of men. The kind of disciples Jesus produced was not the kind of flimsy and weak disciples we produce. Today we invite disciples to our weekly Bible studies and try to teach them the spiritual gifts. We teach our disciples only basic minor subjects that do not matter. Jesus, on the other hand, made these recruits students of the Kingdom. He discipled them to become spiritual kings! He trained them to be kings who walk in exousia power.

And Jesus did not go into the synagogues to recruit these men. He recruited fishermen, tax collectors, and people who were not raised up in the traditional and religious set up of that generation. He did not even recruit any of the elders of the church of that day. The elders and religious leaders of that day were relentlessly and manically opposed to His ministry, anyway. He purposely recruited raw, unpolished, common people who would follow Him and be willing to be trained by Him. He even recruited tax collectors known by all to be sinners. *"And as Jesus passed forth from thence, he saw a man, named Matthew, sitting at the receipt of custom: and he saith unto him, **Follow me.** And he arose, and followed him"* (Matthew 9:9). In fact, He recruited people who considered themselves unworthy and unclean. For example, when He recruited Peter the Bible says,

*"When Simon Peter saw it, he fell down at Jesus' knees, saying, **Depart from me; for I am a sinful man, O Lord**... And Jesus said unto Simon, Fear not; from henceforth thou shalt catch men"* (Luke 5:8,10).

You must understand that these recruits were unlearned and considered ignorant by the religious leaders of that day as the Bible says, *"Now when they saw the boldness of Peter and John, and perceived that **they were** *unlearned and ignorant men, they marvelled; and they took knowledge of them, that they had been with Jesus"* (Acts 4:13). Throughout His ministry, Jesus kept on recruiting more and more disciples apart from the twelve apostles. He recruited seventy other disciples as the Bible says,

*"After these things the Lord **appointed other seventy also**, and sent them two and two before his face into every city and place, whither he himself would come"*
(Luke 10:1).

By the end of His earthly ministry, He had raised up five hundred disciples apart from the first twelve. This is the second phase of God's strategy. And we have started this. We have already mobilized teams of new recruits and discipled them in the Kingdom. Some of those I trained have emptied out whole hospitals and performed amazing miracles signs and wonders.

Jesus immediately began to train the disciples in the ways of royalty. He gave them the mysteries of the Kingdom as the Bible says, *"He answered and said unto them, Because **it is given unto you to know the mysteries of the kingdom of heaven,** but to them it is not given"* (Matthew 13:11). After three years of this intense training, the Bible says, *"Then answered Peter and said unto him, Behold, we have forsaken all, and followed thee; what shall we have therefore? And Jesus said unto them, Verily I say unto you, That ye which have followed me, in the regeneration when the Son of man shall sit in the throne of his glory, **ye also shall sit upon twelve thrones**, judging the twelve tribes of Israel"* (Matthew 19:27-28). Jesus was acclimating these disciples to the fact that they were eternal kings. He told them they would sit on thrones. He taught them that they had spiritual power as kings.

Jesus gave them the exousia power of the Kingdom to exercise authority over devils and heal diseases. He then sent them out in teams of two to operate in this spiritual power. The Bible says, *"And he called unto him the twelve, and **began to send them forth by two and two;** and gave them power (Exousia) over unclean spirits"* (Mark 6:7). He gave them very extensive powers of exousia over all devils and to cure all diseases! When He commissioned the twelve disciples, Jesus said to them,

*"And as ye go, **preach, saying, The kingdom of heaven is at hand.** Heal the sick, cleanse the lepers, raise the dead, cast out devils: freely ye have received, freely give"* (Matthew 10:7-8).

He told them what to preach and what to do and then sent them out into the cities. That is the three-pronged process of mobilize, deploy, and dispatch. That is the same pattern we are employing today. Jesus mobilized and deployed the disciples, and then and dispatched them to cities and villages to invade those regions with the Kingdom of Heaven.

These disciples were healing the sick, casting out devils, and raising the dead even when they did not have the Holy Spirit. I really do not understand why the church does not do this today. Why is it that our leaders do not teach on the power of exousia to cast out devils and heal the sick? Jesus trained the disciples to cast out devils and heal the sick in His name. He gave them what is known as the "power of attorney"' to exercise authority or exousia in His name. The disciples were amazed at how effective and powerful the exousia power was. *"And the seventy returned again with joy, saying, Lord, even the devils are subject unto us through thy name"* (Luke 10:17). They cast out devils with the power Jesus gives.

There is power that Jesus gives and there is power that the Holy Spirit gives. The Bible is clear that the power Jesus gives is called exousia. ***"Behold, I give unto you power (EXOUSIA) to tread on serpents and scorpions,*** *and over all the power of the enemy: and nothing shall by any means hurt you"* (Luke 10:19. This is the governmental power of the Kingdom to confront and cast out all the power of the enemy. There is no power of the enemy that is not subject to this exousia power Jesus gives! The word for power that Jesus gives is exousia and the word for power that the Holy Spirit gives is dunamis. These are two different realms of power. Jesus taught the disciples how to walk in exousia when He was on Earth with them and then after He resurrected He released the dunamis power of the Holy Ghost on the disciples. But He gave them exousia first. God told me when He gave me His strategy, *"Remember my pattern."* God's pattern is to walk in exousia first and then dunamis.

Jesus taught the disciples how to be kings and then sent them out with exousia power. He revealed to them that they were kings from another world when He said, "And I appoint unto you a kingdom, as my Father hath appointed unto me" (Luke 22:29). He was discipling them in kingship when He told them to say wherever they go that the Kingdom of Heaven is there. Only kings do that. That is why Jesus commanded them saying,

> *"And as ye go, **preach, saying, The kingdom of heaven is at hand**"*
> (Matthew 10:7).

And that word "preach" does not mean to get an organ, grab your ear, and start hacking. That word means to decree as a king! Jesus was basically telling the disciples to decree everywhere they go that another kingdom, the Kingdom of Heaven, had come to that region. The moment they made that decree that region was taken over by Heaven. And that is why when the disciples went out, all the regions were stirred up as they cast out devils and healed the sick. *"And they departed, and went through the towns, preaching the gospel, and healing every where"* (Luke 9:6). This is the same pattern we must follow. This is the ancient way and the ancient message. Jesus aggressively recruited the disciples and then taught them the Kingdom of God. Right after that, they started walking as kings.

Fourth Step: Casting Out the Prince of the Whole World

> *"But if I cast out devils by the Spirit of God, then the kingdom of God is come unto you. Or else how can one enter into a strong man's house, and spoil his goods, **except he first bind the strong man?** and then he will spoil his house"*
> (Matthew 12:28-29).

> *"**When a strong man armed keepeth his palace, his goods are in peace:** But when a stronger than he shall come upon him, and overcome him, he taketh from him all his armour wherein he trusted, **and divideth his spoils"***
> (Luke 11:21-22).

"Now is the judgment of this world: **now shall the prince of this world be cast out"** (John 12:31).

This next step is very crucial to winning the whole world. This is known as the strongman principle. Jesus said, *"No man can enter into a strong man's house, and spoil his goods, except he will first bind the strong man; and then he will spoil his house"* (Mark 3:27). How can you take over the world when the Prince of the World, Satan, is ruling and controlling it? Jesus revealed a major spiritual law that before anyone can take over a domain, the person ruling that realm needs to be displaced before one can have access to all the spoil that was controlled by the strongman. That is what is wrong with our cities and that is why many of the churches are having great difficulties in winning over cities. You've first got to bind the strongman. Jesus had to do this! And so right about the time that Jesus was about to be crucified, God came down and spoke out of the clouds. The Bible says, *"Father, glorify thy name. Then came there a voice from heaven, saying, I have both glorified it, and will glorify it again"* (John 12:28).

God told Jesus He had done two things. First, He had already glorified Jesus because the Bible says that Jesus Christ was crucified from the foundation of the world. *"And all that dwell upon the earth shall worship him, whose names are not written in the book of life of the* **Lamb slain from the foundation of the world"** (Revelation 13:8). Jesus was glorified before the foundation of the world, so the Father was basically telling Jesus, *"I have already done it and I am about to do it again."* The second thing the Father told Jesus is that He *"will glorify it again."* The Bible says, *"This he said, signifying what death he should die"* (John 12:33). Jesus knew that through His death, burial, and resurrection, He would be glorified again as He destroys the kingdom of darkness. God the Father spoke openly and publicly to Jesus because He was on Earth working with the Lord. You must understand that God was on Earth working with most of those men who turned the world upside down.

The Bible says, *"Father, glorify thy name. Then came there a voice from heaven, saying, I have both glorified it, and will glorify it again."* (John 12:28) Jesus asked the Father to help Him wrap up the conquest of the world by glorifying His name. We know what happened in the book of Exodus when God began to glorify His name through Pharaoh. The moment Jesus asked the Father to glorify Him, Jehovah responded, *"I have both glorified it, and will glorify it again."* I need you to understand that I am not asking Jehovah to come down on Earth and appear face to face and talk out of the clouds just because I want Him to honor me in front of the people. Of course, I do want Him to honor me before people because I desire only the honor that comes from Him. I do not want honor from men on Earth.

I must make that clear because Jesus told the Jews, *"I receive not honour from men. How can ye believe, which receive honour one of another, **and seek not the honour that cometh from God only?"*** (John 5:41,44). I seek the honor that comes from God only. A lot of ministers today get to where they are going because they have a lot of people around them honoring them. A lot of them do not have the honor that comes from God and that is why they do not have the kind of supernatural glory my ministry carries.

Now, I am not saying that there is anything wrong with having the favor of men, what I am saying is that most ministries are run by the favor of men and when they fall out of favor with those people who gave them platforms their ministries crater and implode on them. I built my life and ministry by the favor and honor that comes from God alone. My life and ministry is not built by the kingmakers of our generation and that is why they cannot make or break me. God has put me where I am and no one can take me down when God is on Earth working openly with me. The whole world is going to come and see what God is doing working with me. I do not need the validation and commendation of men. That is why Jesus told the elders of Israel, *"How can ye believe, which receive honour one of another, and seek not the honour that cometh from God only?"* (John 5:44). I pray that you will not be like that.

Crave and desire the honor that comes only from God and you will be stable and secure in life and ministry. I see a lot of young preachers today who aggressively pursue platforms and seek for men to endorse and establish their ministries. You are not going anywhere in this end-time movement with that kind of mindset. Those kind of ministries built on the platform of men are dead or dying. If you really want a ministry that is going to win the world, you've got to have something real. You can build a church and operate off the platform of men in the priesthood realm, but to win the world you need much more than that. You need God working with you!

The world is not going to come and listen to somebody who can just grab their ear, moan and yell. The world is not coming out to see someone just prophesying names and calling out street addresses. They already have their psychics and witchcraft workers doing that for them. I believe in spiritual gifts and I operate powerfully in them myself, but I must tell you, that is not what is going to win the world. The Gospel of the Kingdom is what is going to win the world. What is going to bring in the harvest is the Kingdom. Until you start thinking like a king, you cannot move in this kind of glory to turn the whole world upside down! The world was taken over by a royal power and a royal spirit and if you are not royal you cannot get it back. That is why the Bible says we are a royal priesthood (1 Peter 2:9).

And I am telling you, dear reader, God the Father is going to speak out of the clouds as He did in the days of Moses and He did with Jesus. Do you know what will happen when He speaks out of the clouds? What will happen is the same thing that happened when He spoke out of the clouds to Jesus. The Prince of the World will be cast out! After God spoke out of the clouds to Jesus, the Lord began to explain what happened to those standing by. Jesus said,

*"This voice came not because of me, but for your sakes. Now is the judgment of this world: **now shall the prince of this world be cast out**. And I, if I be lifted up from the earth, will draw all men unto me"* (John 12:30-32).

The moment Father spoke out of Heaven, the prince of the world, Satan was cast out of the whole world. That is what Jesus was explaining to the Jews. When God spoke to Jesus out of the clouds, Jesus pointed out that the Prince of the World was cast out. God as the Emperor of all Emperors does not have to rebuke a demon. He just spoke and His word shook the Earth so hard that Satan the Prince of the World himself fled. I want you to imagine Satan having a tight grip on the world and just letting it go and running away when Father spoke. That is what happened. The fourth step is for the Father to cast the Prince of the whole World out so that Jesus can then go on and get the spoil. It is a one-two punch.

Fifth Step: Jesus Spoils the Kingdom of Darkness

"And I, if I be lifted up from the earth, will draw all men unto me"
(John 12:32).

"Blotting out the handwriting of ordinances that was against us, which was contrary to us, and took it out of the way, nailing it to his cross; And having spoiled principalities and powers, he made a shew of them openly, triumphing over them in it" (Colossians 2:14-15).

*"Wherefore he saith, **When he ascended up on high, he led captivity captive,** and gave gifts unto men. (Now that he ascended, what is it but that he also descended first into the lower parts of the earth? He that descended is the same also that ascended up far above all heavens, that he might fill all things"*
(Ephesians 4:8-10).

After the Father cast out the Prince of the World, Jesus said, *"And I, if I be lifted up from the earth, will draw all men unto me"* (John 12:32). What Jesus was basically saying is, *"I am now going to be lifted up through my death burial and resurrection and by the cross, I will spoil the principalities and powers. Now that the Father has bound the strongman, I can now take spoils of the strongman which means all the men under his control will come to me."*

You see how the Father and the Son worked in tandem. It was a one-two punch. Father takes out the Prince of the whole World, Jesus takes out the principalities and powers under the prince. That is so glorious. And now when Jesus ascended He took all the souls that were captured and held in the bowels in Hell out with Him. That is why the Bible says, *"When he ascended up on high, **he led captivity captive"*** (Ephesians 4:8).

Matthew records that the graves were opened by the resurrection power of the Lord! *"And the graves were opened; **and many bodies of the saints which slept arose**, And came out of the graves after his resurrection, and went into the holy city, and appeared unto many"* (Matthew 27:52-53). After Father took out the Prince of the World, Jesus destroyed the principalities and powers in Satan's kingdom with the cross and then took the spoil of souls from them. And that is why and how Jesus took captivity captive. It only happened after Satan was cast out when God spoke! The Father took out the kingdom of darkness from the top while Jesus devastated them from below. Jesus could only descend into to Hell to spoil the kingdom of darkness after the Father cast out the Prince of the World. And in His ascension, He took captivity captive. In His ascension, He transported all the souls of men held captive down through the ages into the Kingdom of Heaven. *"And I, if I be lifted up from the earth, will draw all men unto me"* (John 12:32).

Sixth Step: Disciples Empowered with Dunamis

"And I will pray the Father, and he shall give you another Comforter, that he may abide with you for ever" (John 14:16).

*"And, behold, I send the promise of my Father upon you: but tarry ye in the city of Jerusalem, **until ye be endued with power (dunamis) from on high"***
(Luke 24:49).

*"But **ye shall receive power (dunamis), after that the Holy Ghost is come upon you:** and ye shall be witnesses unto me both in Jerusalem, and in all Judaea, and in Samaria, and unto the uttermost part of the earth"* (Acts 1:8).

In this sixth step, the Lord gives the disciples an addendum of power, the power of the Holy Ghost. After acclimating the disciples to the realm of exousia power, the Lord introduced them to the next person of the Godhead, the Holy Spirit and the power He gives. He told the disciples the kind of power they would receive when the Holy Ghost comes upon them. And that is exactly what happened on the day of Pentecost. And now with the power of the Holy Ghost, they would become witnesses for Him all over the world.

Seventh Step: Disciples Sent to Win the World

*"And he said unto them, **Go ye into all the world**, and preach the gospel to every creature. And they went forth, and preached every where, the Lord working with them, and confirming the word with signs following. Amen"* (Mark 16:15,20).

After they received the baptism of the Holy Ghost with the endowment of dunamis power, the apostles went everywhere and preached the Gospel of the Kingdom of God with signs following. In just twenty years, these apostles turned the whole world upside down. It did not take the disciples ninety years to win the world. In just one generation, they were able to penetrate and win the world with the Kingdom. The Romans officials said, *"These that have turned the world upside down are come hither also"* (Acts 17:6). The disciples also multiplied as the Bible says, *"And the word of God increased; and the number of the disciples multiplied in Jerusalem greatly; and a great company of the priests were obedient to the faith"* (Acts 6:7). Because of the Kingdom discipleship program Jesus took the disciples through, they were very effective in winning the world. In the book of Acts, we see how these disciples progressively won over all of Jerusalem and Judea and shook Samaria and then turned the whole world upside down in their lifetime. And it did not take all their life to do it.

God's Action Plan for the End-Time World Harvest

Now the time has come to do all this again. The Lord Jesus said to me, *"Now you are to release this strategy upon the Earth again. I am on Earth again to win the whole world. All seven billion souls will be impacted and revolutionized to make a decision."*

And Jehovah said to me, *"I am already with you on Earth face to face. The next dimension is that you must aggressively recruit disciples, not just to be part of a church, but to be part of the Kingdom movement."*

You must understand that these must be people who want to be discipled to be kings. That is what Jesus died for! *"And from Jesus Christ, who is the faithful witness, and the first begotten of the dead, and the prince of the kings of the earth. Unto him that loved us, and washed us from our sins in his own blood, **And hath made us kings** and priests unto God and his Father; to him be glory and dominion for ever and ever. Amen"* (Revelation 1:5-6). Jesus died to make us kings. I have a direct commission from the Father to aggressively recruit disciples, teach them the Kingdom, and then send them out to win the world.

Recruit Two Hundred On-Fire Disciples

The Lord then said to me, *"Take two-hundred of the people on your staff, the most on-fire ones and have them aggressively go out and recruit more disciples. I will work with them to bring people to them."*

We have already started doing this. I have already recruited and sent out the first two hundred on-fire disciples out of the staff I have. And the Lord worked with them to win even more disciples. Jesus has been appearing to people before we even go to them. We are telling people, "You need to join this movement to win the world." We are not asking anybody to leave their church and we are not asking pastors to drop their ministry because pastors and other ministry leaders are a part of the end-time movement to win the world. Leaders everywhere are excited about what God is saying we have to do. When they hear this plan they say, *"David, this is phenomenal. This is going to win the world."*

The Lord told me, *"First start with two-hundred of your staff, who will then aggressively recruit and win ten people."* The people they are to recruit are Christians who want to be a part of this Move of God to change the world. The vision of this movement is to change the world. You see, when the first apostles in Acts changed the world, they did not have television, radio, internet, or any kind of social media. What they did is what I call *Grassroots 101*. They traveled to cities and villages preaching everywhere. They were face to face with the people. That is what we need to go back to. The problem with our generation is that there is an overreliance on TV and radio and other media outlets to present the gospel.

You need to understand that the Face to Face Movement is not just about Jesus and the Father appearing to you face to face. The next dimension of the Face to Face Movement is you being sent face to face to every single person on the planet! That is the essence of Face to Face.

The Lord said to me, *"You go to them one by one like I went to them. Start with one on one ministry".*

Jesus told the apostles, *"When you see me, you see the Father."* So when you go to people face to face, you are presenting Jesus face to face to the people. That is why Jesus told the apostles, *"He that receiveth you receiveth me"* (Matthew 10:40). The first stage of Face to Face is the Lord and the Father coming and manifesting themselves to you. *"He that hath my commandments, and keepeth them, he it is that loveth me: and he that loveth me shall be loved of my Father, **and I will love him, and will manifest myself to him"*** (John 14:21). You must desire and pursue this relationship until you get it. Then, like John, you can boldly declare to the nations,

*"**That which we have seen and heard declare we unto you,** that ye also may have fellowship with us: and **truly our fellowship is with the Father, and with his Son** Jesus Christ"* (1 John 1:3).

The first stage of Face to Face is you beholding the glory in the face of the Lord Jesus Christ, but the second stage of Face to Face is you going to the world to present the Lord to them face to face. Paul called this the *fellowship of mystery* as the Bible says, *"To whom God would make known what is the riches of the glory of this mystery **among the Gentiles; which is Christ in you, the hope of glory"*** (Colossians 1:27).

The media is critical to regional transformation. Media is a very wonderful tool to reach masses of people at one time, but it must be enforced with actual face to face contact with people on the ground. Even in warfare, no matter how successful an air campaign is in destroying the enemy, the army people will tell you that the war is never won in the air. Every battle can only be fully consummated with "boots on the ground." That is why Jesus, after winning the battle of the air when he overcome the devil during his forty-day fast, had to physically walk about the cities and villages afterward preaching the Gospel of the Kingdom. Matthew records,

*"And **Jesus went about all Galilee**, teaching in their synagogues, and preaching the gospel of the kingdom, and healing all manner of sickness and all manner of disease among the people"* (Matthew 4:23).

Once the prince of the air is dislodged and cast out, the victory in the air must be proclaimed on the ground face to face with the people and that is why Jesus commanded the disciples after his resurrection, *"**Go ye into all the world, and preach the gospel to every creature"*** (Mark 16:15).

The Two Hundred Should Recruit Ten More People

As the Lord was outlining this powerful strategy to win the world to me He said, *"Take the two-hundred and have them aggressively recruit ten people each. Have them do that in thirty days."*

That is how I know this is working because after I recruited the two-hundred people, they got two thousand people recruited in no time. Before we can reap the end-time harvest, we also have to engage the Lord of the Harvest through prayer. We have to ask the Lord of the Harvest to release more laborers. The Bible says, *"Then saith he unto his disciples, **The harvest truly is plenteous, but the labourers are few; Pray ye therefore the Lord of the harvest, that he will send forth labourers** into his harvest"* (Matthew 9:37-38). This is why the Lord commanded me to raise up a million man army! It will take a massive army to take over the world and bring in the harvest.

In this strategy session, the Lord instructed me to have each disciple recruit ten more people. It is imperative that you understand that instructions are the way of life. *"For **the commandment is a lamp**; and the law is light; and reproofs of instruction are the way of life"* (Proverbs 6:23). The Bible also says, *"Take fast hold of instruction; let her not go: keep her; for she is thy life"* (Proverbs 4:13). This is the way we are going to win the world, by the multiple of ten! You see, Jesus started with twelve disciples and then increased that to seventy and then one-hundred and twenty, and then five hundred. Eventually, in the book of Acts, Luke records, *"... and the number of the disciples multiplied in Jerusalem greatly"* (Acts 6:7). For our generation, the Lord instructed that we increase with the number ten.

The Two Thousand Should Recruit Ten More People

For the next step the Lord commanded me, *"Now give them the Kingdom message and then release them to recruit ten people. That will equal twenty thousand in thirty days."* And I must tell you that this is already beginning to happen now!

The Twenty Thousand Should Recruit Ten More People

The Lord then told me, *"Take the twenty thousand and have them recruit ten people each which will equal two hundred thousand. Then have them come to a football stadium and tell them what I told you. I will start giving you cities to target and whole cities will come to me in one month."*

That is so glorious. The Lord explained to me in this visitation using the state of Colorado, which has more than five million people, as an example.

He said, *"What you will then do is to unleash two hundred thousand people with the Kingdom in Colorado. Release the disciples on the ground to pray for and heal the sick and raise the dead."*

I believe you can now see how exciting this is going to be. And a lot of this is already happening. You can win people through social media such as Facebook and Instagram, but you must also meet people on the ground face to face! The Lord's strategy is amazing. I had my team in Colorado recently and they experienced many miracles and saw many wheelchairs emptied. I did not have to be there. Every disciple should be walking in power to change people's lives.

The Two Hundred Thousand Should Recruit Ten More People

The Lord continued to share this glorious strategy with me. He said, *"After the two hundred thousand people, whole cities will start coming to me in one month."* That is what He told me about that stage of multiplication. But He said, *"You will not stop multiplying there."*

You see, we are to multiply in much the same way God told Adam to multiply and fill the Earth! The Earth is already filled with people, we are to multiply disciples to reach them and this is the strategy to do so. Each person is to multiply by ten. The Lord continued, *"You take the two hundred thousand and have them get ten. That will give you two million people."*

Can you imagine two million people on fire for God winning cities for Him? With two million people, you can go to a city like Chicago which has almost three million people, and each disciple will have to reach less than two people! In just a day the whole city can be turned over to the Lord!

God already told me that this will work. It is already working. I am not just sharing with you what we are about to do. We have already started. In just one month we recruited almost three thousand people. And with the three thousand we have almost recruited twenty thousand people. Now the leaders are calling me and telling me, *"David this is going to work."*

The biggest church in the whole United States is Joel Osteen's church, Lakewood, and this church averages fifty-two thousand people on site every week. Some people think that is a success and I thank God for all the great work that church is doing to touch lives all over the country and the world, but I must tell you that for where they are that is not the kind of success God wants. I want you to know that with us winning whole cities with this strategy churches are going to become not just twenty thousand but one hundred thousand and even more. Church leaders are going to have to build bigger arenas to hold over one hundred thousand people a week. This will not just happen in one place, I am talking about multiple places.

The Two Million Should Recruit Ten More People

The sixth step is that the two million disciples should get ten recruits each. That results in twenty million people to be discipled in the Kingdom. This is a crucial step. The growth is never to stop until the whole world is reached. Most ministries plateau after they reach a certain number, but that is not what will happen with this strategy. The Lord was adamant that the growth will continue and will not stop until the objective is accomplished. The objective is to reach the whole world! *"And this **gospel of the kingdom shall be preached in all the world** for a witness unto all nations; and then shall the end come"* (Matthew 24:14).

The Twenty Million Should Recruit Ten More People

In the seventh step, the twenty million will recruit ten more and that makes the total now two hundred million people! That is almost all of America because America is almost three hundred and seventy million people. Now we will be ready to invade whole nations and turn them over to the Lord. This is the stage from which we will disciple nations. You must understand that the Lord is very much into nations. Do you know that our inheritance includes nations? The Bible says, *"Ask of me, and I shall give thee the heathen (Nations) for thine inheritance, and the uttermost parts of the earth for thy possession"* (Psalm 2:8). When we get to the two hundred million people number, America will fall to the Lord in no time.

The Two Hundred Million Should Recruit Ten More People

When the two hundred million people get ten more, that will be two billion people! Now the Kingdom will be reaching the uttermost parts of the world. The whole world will be covered at this point. There are about seven billion people on the Earth now, and if the two billion recruits get ten more, that will be twenty billion people. And you know we do not have twenty billion people on this planet. We will swallow up and turn this world upside down at this stage. This is what Jesus died for and this is what He inherited when He ascended up to Heaven before the Father.

Daniel saw this and said, *"I saw in the night visions, and, behold, one like the Son of man came with the clouds of heaven, and came to the Ancient of days, and they brought him near before him. And there was given him dominion, and glory,* **and a kingdom, that all people, nations, and languages, should serve him:** *his dominion is an everlasting dominion, which shall not pass away, and his kingdom that which shall not be destroyed"* (Daniel 7:13-14). From this point on, we will see the kingdoms of this world become the Kingdom of our God and His Son Jesus Christ (Revelation 11:15).

The End-Time World Harvest

What I just shared with you is happening now. This strategy is being implemented right now. And now I am releasing the message of the Kingdom Jesus gave me to every disciple through Kingdom School of Ministry DVDs and CDs and also through books like the one you are reading. When the disciples hear that Kingdom message, they will know that as soon as they gave their lives to Jesus they received the exousia governmental power of the Kingdom to cast out all devils and heal the sick. And they will be ready to do what Jesus told the first twelve disciples, *"Heal the sick, cleanse the lepers, raise the dead, cast out devils: freely ye have received, freely give"* (Matthew 10:10). These disciples will change people with exousia. This has started and I am so excited about how this strategy is unfolding. The Lord said to me, *"You start holding Kingdom campaigns in arenas where all the miracles will happen as well. Gather the disciples and the laborers and you start giving them directions as a general to unleash them upon all cities and providing for them a way to get there."*

Now we have had so many other ministries and evangelists pack out arenas and stadiums with people, but they do nothing with the masses that come. They do not do what Jesus did. They do not mobilize them to take over cities and that is the problem. And I address all leaders right now, you should not mobilize all these people to your meetings so you can say you had a big meeting and a wonderful time in the Lord. There has to be a purpose, and I am not talking about a temporal purpose. It has to be an eternal purpose, the kind God has.

That is what we are doing. We will be doing the same thing God did to win the world. The world is about to be shaken to its foundations as God's action plan is deployed across the fifty states of America.

The Mission Starts in America

The Lord instructed that this strategy to win the world be deployed and executed first in the United States of America. We are not excluding the other nations. All the people of God in all the other nations can be included and get started now, but God said to me, *"You start in America first. Recruit two hundred thousand Americans to invade the cities of America."* And that is what we have started to do. Once we are done here, we will then begin to invade all the nations and continents of the world.

Just as Capernaum was the headquarters of the Lord Jesus during his earthly ministry, St. Louis is going to be the base and headquarters to organize this global initiative. We have a four-hundred-million-dollar vision to complete this headquarters. We are going to build a one hundred thousand seat arena on the ground. Even though we are starting in America, this is a global campaign. God is not going to come on the Earth and do something for just a local place. His purpose is much bigger than just one location or one nation. His vision is world harvest. God is about to do a world harvest. The question is, are you going to be a part of it?

The Lord said to me, *"David, start to share with the army what is about to take place."* As this plan unfolds, God has instructed that I continue to deploy and release the army at our annual August Crusades we hold in Taylor, Michigan. The Lord said in this recent visitation, *"Tell everyone around the world that they must mobilize and get to the Crusade Against Cancer because there I will begin to have you lay out the strategy in detail. The body of Christ needs to hear the orders that have come from me. Share the plan with them so that they can hear what I am saying to the church."*

Church, this is our time. This is the hour to take over the world. Right now, the world does not care about the church. You see them get on TV and disrespect the church and everything that has to do with the church. I am so sick and tired of the heathen and the world disrespecting the church. They do not believe that God is with us and in a way I must say they have the right to think so because we have not demonstrated the power of the living God. But this Joel Army that God is raising up is going to show the world the reality of the living God. God is actually validating Himself and His people in this hour. You must understand that without this validation from God we will not convince the gainsayers and naysayers of our generation. Right now, Jesus and the Father are appearing to millions of people through this face to face movement He told me to start on Earth. You must have heard by now even on secular media how Jesus is appearing to Hindus, Muslims, Buddhists, drug dealers, mafia people, murderers and entire regions all over the world. He is appearing to them and changing their lives. Even ISIS members are being visited by Jesus after I prophesied that that would happen. Many of them have been visited by Jesus and their lives have been changed.

I love the great evangelists of our generation who have done such an awesome work in winning millions of souls like Reinhard Bohnke. I have been greatly blessed by his meetings and crusades, especially in Africa, where he has had huge crusades sometimes with three million people in attendance. But that will be the smallest crusade compared to what God is about to do now. When whole cities, nations, and continents, are about to be saved you will see up to and even more than seventy million people in just one service. Not just three million, but seventy million! There will be millions of people spread out all over the grounds and lands for miles and miles. You need to see how massive the end time harvest is going to be. The harvest that Father is about to bring in now is bigger than anything that has ever taken place upon the planet. And this is in keeping with his nature as the Word says, *"Better is the end of a thing than the beginning thereof"* (Ecclesiastes 7:8). Jehovah Omega has a great end planned for our generation that will far exceed anything our fathers ever witnessed.

Up to this point in time, we have been constructing the weight for the glory that is about to be unleashed on the whole Earth through this strategy God unveiled to me. Isaiah saw this day when he prophesied,

*"And the glory of the LORD shall be revealed, **and all flesh shall see it together:** for the mouth of the LORD hath spoken it"* (Isaiah 40:5).

"For I know their works and their thoughts: it shall come, that I will gather all nations and tongues; and they shall come, and see my glory" (Isaiah 66:18).

For many years, we have been in the presence of the Lord building up the weight of the kabod and doxa and kratos for what God is about to do. God has been amassing an army of harvesters to reap the harvest of the end-time. That is what our Father is. Among many other identities, He is a husbandman. He is a farmer and He has been waiting patiently for many generations and ages for this grand moment to reap the harvest. Are you excited to be part of this? This is going to be a major move of God that will shake the very foundations of this generation. It is going to change our generation and turn it upside down.

If you are not in the ministry to reap the harvest, then I do not know what you are doing. Ministry is not just prophesying, healing the sick, and walking in miracles signs and wonders. That is just a part of it, but the real purpose of ministry is to harvest souls. It is to take the spoils of war from the devil, the souls of men that he took by mind control and mind blinding tactics.

*"But if our gospel be hid, it is hid to them that are lost: In whom **the god of this world hath blinded the minds of them which believe not,** lest the light of the glorious gospel of Christ, who is the image of God, should shine unto them"* (2 Corinthians 4:3-4).

We are breaking his power over their mind the way Jesus did. Matthew records how Jesus broke the mind blinding power of Satan before reaping the harvest. The Bible says, *"The people **which sat in darkness saw great light**; and to them which sat in the region and shadow of death light is sprung up"* (Matthew 4:16). Before Jesus ever preached a message, He first broke the mind blinding power of darkness from off the minds and hearts of the people who were sitting in darkness and in the shadow of death. Once light broke forth on these captives, Jesus began his ministry. *"From that time Jesus began to preach, and to say, Repent: for the kingdom of heaven is at hand"* (Matthew 4:17). That is what is happening right now. We are breaking Satan's power from off the minds of people. We are breaking that mind blinding spirit.

This is not my plan, tis is the Father's plan. This is His biggest roadmap to win the world. He is about to win the world to Himself. We have come to the time of the end when the gospel is about to hit all the four corners of the world. The disciples who are being recruited will be fanning across USA and then across the whole known world with the Gospel of the Kingdom. As the Word says,

*"And **this gospel of the kingdom shall be preached in all the world** for a witness unto all nations; and then shall the end come"* (Matthew 24:14).

They will be preaching a specific message, the Gospel of the Kingdom. Not just the gospel of salvation, nor the gospel of healing, nor the gospel of prosperity. This move of God is not just about bits and pieces or parts of the gospel, but about the all-encompassing message of the Kingdom. This Gospel of the Kingdom will be preached all over the world for a witness. That word witness means that miracles, signs, and wonders will break out everywhere to authenticate the message. That is what will occasion the end and that is why that same scripture says, *"and **then shall the end come"*** (Matthew 24:14). The end is not coming until we bring the Gospel of the Kingdom to all the nations of the world!

Mobilizing the Joel End-Time Army

"And the LORD shall utter his voice before his army: for his camp is very great: for he is strong that executeth his word: for the day of the LORD is great and very terrible; and who can abide it?" (Joel 2:11).

*"For at that time day by day there came to David to help him, **until it was a great host, like the host of God"*** (1 Chronicles 12:22).

I must emphasize that the time has come to harvest the world. And to accomplish this great vision, we are also forming a great dream regiment and division in God's end-time army. In the Davidic army, there was a whole division dedicated to divine intelligence. The Bible says, *"And of the children of Issachar, which were **men that had understanding of the times, to know what Israel ought to do"*** (1 Chronicles 12:32. They provided David with divine intelligence to help him plan more effectively his numerous battles. No wonder King David never lost a battle. We are developing a dream regiment for this purpose. They will be receiving messages from God in the spirit giving us advance notice of what is going to happen in the future. They will be called *The Intelligence* and the *Secret Code*. This end-time battle to bring in the world harvest will need this regiment because as Solomon declared, *"For **by wise counsel thou shalt make thy war**: and in multitude of counsellors there is safety"* (Proverbs 24:6). We will employ the counsel of these dreamers in our battle strategies.

I pray that you will join this glorious end-time army. God has an aggressive army that is going to reap the harvest. This aggressive army will not be passive Christians who just want to sit down on their comfortable seats and do nothing. This will not be an army of preachers who just want to preach to get their limelight and fame and make their name known. That is the wrong focus and the wrong heart for what God is doing in this hour. The heart of the Father is to reap the harvest. His heart is to win the world again. We are in the end-time army. This is all happening now. It is time for you to get involved in this movement to win the world.

I say this with all humility, God has mandated me to teach His people about the Kingdom. God has taken multitudes to Heaven and told them, *"JMMI is not just a ministry on earth among other ministries. I have given David my Kingdom on Earth. I have given him the Keys of the Kingdom under the whole Heaven."* Humility is agreement with the truth as Rick Joyner revealed in his great book *The Final Quest.* I am just telling you the truth. The ministry name for this movement, JMMI (Joshua Media Ministries International) is just to incorporate this movement as a ministry for government purposes. But do not be mistaken or deceived, this is the Kingdom of God on Earth! I do not know of any other ministry that has God the Father and Jesus His Son on Earth working with them like they are working with me.

The Lord told me that I am the Moses of this generation. He came to me in a dream and told me that. I am not just making all this up. He appeared to me face to face and told me what I am telling you. That is why I am bold like this and that is why I can confidently tell you that the whole world is about to be taken over because I have talked with the Lord face to face and there is no way of missing that message. I encourage every pastor and fivefold ministry leader reading this book to be part of this movement to win the world in our generation. Again, nobody has to leave their church, just get in the Kingdom. Seek the Kingdom first. Join us. Join us from all around the world. Enlist in the army and let God use you to bring 10 people to him. Become a harvester. Become a fisher of men.

To enroll in this end-time movement, just visit our website, joshuamediaministries.org. If you have started recruiting disciples for the end-time harvest then turn in those names by email to Godsmovement@joshuamediaministries.org. Aggressively recruit those disciples, send in their information, and we will get every last one of them the information they need to be discipled in the Kingdom. We will also send you CDs and messages on the Kingdom when you enlist and also to everyone you recruit. Once they are discipled in the Kingdom to walk in power, they will turn the world upside down.

To mobilize all the people coming in, we are structuring them into camps of two hundred each and putting captains over them. This is the harvest vision of the Father. The husbandman is on Earth right now to reap the harvest. *"Be patient therefore, brethren, unto the coming of the Lord. Behold, the husbandman waiteth for the precious fruit of the earth, and hath long patience for it, until he receive the early and latter rain"* (James 5:7). Become a part of this movement!

CHAPTER 10
Becoming Sons of God / Little Gods

CHAPTER 10
Becoming Sons of God / Little Gods

I want to prepare you for the next stage of your development in the Empire of God. There is more to who you are! In the first volume of the Kingdom Series, I taught you your identity as a spiritual king and how to manifest the power of that identity. In this second volume, you discovered that you are a king with imperial anointing! You learned that you are not only a king, you have a call to be an emperor!

In the next book in this Kingdom Series, you are going to learn about the sonship office! You will learn that you are not just a king called to be an emperor. You are called to be a son of God! Jesus Christ Himself had to become a Son before the Father started working with Him. As a Son of God, Jesus turned water into wine, stilled the raging seas and waves with just a command, walked on water, multiplied bread and did many other miracles. None of that happened before He came into sonship. God did this because He was going to use Jesus to establish the sonship process as a pattern for us to follow.

A true son is a prince with God. True sons are the ones creation is waiting for. *"For the earnest expectation of the creature waiteth for the manifestation of the sons of God"* (Romans 8:19). You do not hear the church talking about the realm of sonship because they do not have the power to back it up. This is so sad because from the very moment you received Jesus, He gave you the power to start processing you to become sons of God. *"But as many as received him, to them gave he **power to become the sons of God…"*** (John 1:12). You have to receive power to become a Son or a Prince of God. But before you can become a son and a prince with God, you have to understand that a prince with God is first a King with Jesus Christ. I want to share with you why this is so important to your progress in the hierarchy of God's Empire.

You Are a King Under Jesus

"And he hath on his vesture and on his thigh a name written, KING OF KINGS, AND LORD OF LORDS" (Revelations 19:16).

When Jesus rose from the dead, you rose up with him! His resurrection is your resurrection. His promotion is your promotion. As He is so are you! *"… because as he is, so are we in this world."* (1 Joh 4:17) Everything Jesus did He shared with you! You are one of the mighty ones He shared the spoils with! *"Therefore will I divide him a portion with the great, and he shall divide the spoil with the strong…"* (Isaiah 53:12). Let's see just a few of the major blessings you share with the Lord Jesus Christ:

> <u>**You are crucified with Jesus**</u> *"Knowing this, that our old man is **crucified with him,** that the body of sin might be destroyed, that henceforth we should not serve sin." (Romans 6:6). "I am crucified with Christ …"* (Galatians 2:20).

> <u>**You are buried with Jesus**</u> *"Therefore **we are buried with him** by baptism into death …"* (Romans 6:4). ***"Buried with him in baptism,** wherein also ye are risen with him through the faith of the operation of God, who hath raised him from the dead"* (Colossians 2:12).

> <u>**You are quickened together with Jesus**</u> *"Even when we were dead in sins, **hath quickened us together with Christ …"*** (Ephesians 2:5). *"And you, being dead in your sins and the uncircumcision of your flesh,*

hath he quickened together with him, having forgiven you all trespasses" (Colossians 2:13).

You are raised up together with Jesus *"And hath **raised us up together,** and made us sit together in heavenly places in Christ Jesus"* (Ephesians 2:6). *"**If ye then be risen with Christ,** seek those things which are above, where Christ sitteth on the right hand of God"* (Colossians 3:1).

You are seated together with Jesus *"And hath raised us up together, **and made us sit together in heavenly places in Christ Jesus"*** (Ephesians 2:6). *"To him that overcometh will **I grant to sit with me in my throne ...** "* (Revelation 3:21).

You rule and reign together with Jesus *"If we suffer, **we shall also reign with him:** if we deny him, he also will deny us"* (2 Timothy 2:12).

You are glorified with Him *"And if children, then heirs; heirs of God, and joint-heirs with Christ; if so be that we suffer with him, **that we may be also glorified together** (Romans 8:17).

You jointly inherit with him *"And if children, then heirs; heirs of God, and **joint-heirs with Christ...** "* (Romans 8:17).

You were made a king by the Lord Jesus Christ through His death, burial, resurrection, and ascension. You have been made a king according to Revelation 1:6, *"And hath made us kings and priests unto God..."* You are a king up under Jesus which explains why the Bible calls Jesus the King of Kings! You are one of those kings under Jesus! That means that you will also have a kingdom. In this chapter, I want to take you deeper into the imperial realm and prepare you for the next volume in the kingdom series. This is the point I need you to understand, you are a king under Jesus until He can train you long enough to become a prince to God which automatically puts you in the imperial realm in God's Empire.

Becoming a Prince with God

To be a prince with God is greater than being a king unto Jesus. That is what it means when the Bible calls Jesus, *"... the prince of the kings of the earth"* (Revelation 1:5). Jesus is a prince unto God, and it is His job to train us and reconcile us to the Emperor of all Emperors, God the Father. When He fully reconciles you to His Father you become a prince with God! There are men in the Bible who attained this status with God. For example, after twenty years of serving Laban, Jacob became a prince with God! After wrestling with the angel of God all night, Jacob became a prince having power with God!

"And he said, Thy name shall be called no more Jacob, but Israel: for as a prince hast thou power with God and with men, and hast prevailed" (Genesis 32:28).

A prince has power with God! King David also entered this realm with God. God calls David a prince! *"And I the LORD will be their God, and my servant David a prince among them; I the LORD have spoken it"* (Ezekiel 34:24). When David became a prince with God, the Lord of Hosts started working directly with him to consolidate the Kingdom of Israel and to conquer all the enemies of Israel. *"And David went on, and grew great, and the LORD God of hosts was with him"* (2 Samuel 5:10). God also entered into the Sure Mercies of David Covenant of Salt with him because David was a prince with God!

When God made the first Adam, He made him a prince. Adam was the original Prince of the World. That is why when Satan took Adam's crown he then became the Prince of the World. Jesus confirmed this when he called Satan a prince. Although Satan's character is evil, he is still considered a legitimate royal because he lawfully gained the crown when Adam yielded to his authority. Do you notice that Jesus did not call Satan the *King* of the World? He called him the Prince of the World, a prince unto God! Jesus told the disciples,

*"Hereafter I will not talk much with you: **for the prince of this world cometh,** and hath nothing in me"* (John 14:30).

Jesus came to the Earth to reclaim that title from Satan and that is why Daniel calls the Messiah a Prince, *"... from the going forth of the commandment to restore and to build Jerusalem unto **the Messiah the Prince** shall be seven weeks..."* (Daniel 9:25). Right now, Jesus, as the last Adam, has all power in Heaven and in the Earth. He recovered the Adamic crown! Jesus is therefore called the Prince of the Kings of the Earth! Here are some scriptures that refer to Jesus as a Prince:

*"For unto us a child is born, unto us a son is given: and the government shall be upon his shoulder: and his name shall be called Wonderful, Counsellor, The mighty God, The everlasting Father, **The Prince of Peace"*** (Isaiah 9:6).

*"**And killed the Prince of life,** whom God hath raised from the dead; whereof we are witnesses"* (Acts 3:15)

*"Him hath God exalted with his right hand to be **a Prince and a Saviour,** for to give repentance to Israel, and forgiveness of sins"* (Acts 5:31).

*"And from Jesus Christ, who is the faithful witness, and the first begotten of the dead, and the **prince of the kings of the earth.** Unto him that loved us, and washed us from our sins in his own blood, And hath made us kings and priests unto God and his Father; to him be glory and dominion for ever and ever. Amen"* (Revelation 1:5-6).

Spiritual Maturity

You are right now a king with Jesus, but you are also called to be a prince with God. When you complete and fulfill your kingship training with Jesus, you become a prince with God. As a king with Jesus, you can walk in the kingly and imperial anointing and manifest all the powers of your kingship. Your kingship has most of the characteristics of what you manifest when you become a prince with God. Your kingship under Jesus is training you to become a full son with God. That is why baby Christians, from the moment they get saved and receive Jesus they become kings with Jesus and can do amazing signs and wonders. Jesus called the disciples apostles when they were just babes. They were able to cast out devils, heal the sick, cleanse the lepers, and raise the dead even at that stage. Even Jesus was amazed and excited to see the Father allowing the disciples to display so much power in their early stages of growth. After the disciples returned from casting out devils and healing the sick in the name of Jesus, the Bible says,

*"In that hour Jesus rejoiced in spirit, and said, I thank thee, O Father, Lord of heaven and earth, that thou hast hid these things from the wise and prudent, **and hast revealed them unto babes:** even so, Father; for so it seemed good in thy sight"* (Luke 10:21).

Jesus called the apostles "babes" after they walked in so much power as kings. Walking in the power of your kingship has nothing to do with maturity, it simply has to do with who you are! Your identity as a king! That is why you should never judge any person's maturity by the signs and wonders they walk in. This is because the moment you get saved you became a king unto God and Jesus begins to empower you to begin to develop your sonship. As a divine king, you have powers from another world, the Kingdom of Heaven, to rule this one!

When I first got saved at seventeen years old, I walked in powerful signs and wonders just by baby faith. In the first few years of my walk, I was raising the dead, casting out devils and having major revivals in many churches. All this time I was just a baby with Christ! (Matthew 11:25; 1 Corinthians 3:1; 1 Peter 2:2). The early apostles also walked in great power in their first few years with Jesus. *"And they (the Apostles) cast out many devils, and anointed with oil many that were sick, and healed them"* (Mark 6:13). But you must understand that walking in signs and wonders does not constitute maturity. You are a king with Jesus, but you have to become a prince with God through process! Once you become a prince with God, you become a son under God!

When Jehovah Makes You a Little God

That is why at the beginning when you receive Jesus He gives you power to become a son of God or a son under God. It is Jesus' whole objective and assignment to get you into the place of maturity to work with God! When you become a prince unto God, you become a full-grown son or a little god. God looks at you as a son and not just as one of his children. The Bible speaks of babes in Christ, children of God, and sons of God. These are the three categories of growth and maturity. Babes, children, sons! In your walk with the Lord, you are supposed to go through these three dimensions. You have to determine which category best defines you now. You've got to let God show you where you really are in your maturity because it is not your natural age that determines how spiritually mature you have become.

Heirs of God, Joint Heirs with Christ

Now the Bible says that we are heirs of God and joint-heirs with Christ. This is very critical in understanding your growth process from being just a babe in Christ to becoming a child of God and then ultimately maturing into becoming sons of God. We are heirs of God and joint heirs with Christ. This is because it is Christ's objective not just to keep you under him as a king in His Kingdom. Yes, you are one of his kings, but His objective is to take you through a tutorage process to teach you who you really as a joint-heir with Him. As a joint-heir with Christ, He teaches you full sonship. He starts off your training by giving you power to become a son of God (John 1:12).

The word joint means that there are some things that we jointly inherit with Jesus as equals. There are some equal offices that we carry with Jesus and in those offices we are no different from Him. I want you to note this carefully. You must understand this! There is a place in Christ that none of us can ever occupy, but there are some offices that we share with Him, whereby we have the same authority, power, and dominion. When you become a son, you come more fully into that.

Being a joint heir with Jesus deals with you being an heir to the throne. Being a joint heir deals with you being in a Kingdom as a son, as part of a royal family. You are in a royal family! You are the child and son of a king and an emperor! That makes you royal! You are a joint heir because you are seated together with Jesus on the same seat in the heavenly places. Therefore, *"... as he is, so are we in this world"* (1 John 4:17).

So here it is, we are equal with Jesus Christ, but not in every way and not on every level. That is why I always emphasize the need to understand rank. If you do not understand God's ranking system you will not even begin to understand what I am sharing here. You see, an Army general has authority to command troops. Well, a sergeant major does too! They are equal in their ability to command, the general commands on a much higher level because he far outranks the sergeant major. They carry the same properties and characteristic but they operate on different levels because of their rank. So, yes, we may be equal with Jesus in some ways and in some offices, but we do not have the same rank. That is why Jesus said to His disciples,

*"Verily, verily, I say unto you, **The servant is not greater than his lord;** neither he that is sent greater than he that sent him"* (John 13:16).

In other words, whoever is in a submitted position is never greater in rank than those who are in authority. That is what Jesus was saying. You may be able to do greater works than Jesus, (John 14:12) but you are not greater than Him in rank. In the same way, Jesus is equal with the Father on many levels, but God the Father is higher in rank than the Son. Jesus Himself admitted that the Father was greater than Him. It is very wrong and false to teach that Jesus is the same person as the Father. The "Jesus Only" teaching is a false doctrine.

Introduced and Reconciled to The Father

"If children, then heirs; heirs of God, and joint-heirs with Christ; if so be that we suffer with him, that we may be also glorified together" (Romans 8:17).

234

You are not only a joint heir with Christ; you are also an heir of God! As a joint heir, God looks at you and loves you just like He loves Jesus. Joint means *"union; with or together"* (Strong's Concordance G4789 & G4862). You are a king under the authority of Jesus and when Jesus is done training, teaching, and discipling you in your kingship, He then inaugurates you into the realm of becoming a full mature son under God. When that happens, Jesus no longer has to mediate your relationship with the Father. Jesus ultimately wants you to know God for yourself. This is why Jesus told His disciples.

*"**And in that day** ye shall ask me nothing. Verily, verily, I say unto you, Whatsoever ye shall ask **the Father** in my name, **he will give it you**. Hitherto have ye asked nothing in my name: ask, and ye shall receive, that your joy may be full. These things have I spoken **unto you in proverbs:** but the time cometh, when I shall no more speak unto you in proverbs, but **I shall shew you plainly of the Father"** (John 16:23-25).*

But there are some things that you can demand directly from the Father when you come into full mature sonship as a prince with God. This is when you start working directly with the Father as a prince unto God! When you start dealing with the Father you are dealing with maturity. *"And in that day..."* God no longer speaks to you in proverbs or dark sayings. Everything is plain at this point. This is the point in your walk with the Lord when Jesus says, *"ye shall ask the Father in my name, he will give it you."* At this point the Father Himself begins to work with you. When I got to this stage in my walk with God, I asked the Father to come down in our generation and manifest visibly face to face to man, and He did! The Father Himself did it!

"At that day ye shall ask in my name: and I say not unto you, that I will pray the Father for you: For the Father himself loveth you, because ye have loved me, and have believed that I came out from God" (John 16:26-27).

Do you see how Jesus says in verse 26, *"At that day ..."* All these are references to a certain point in time called the *"time appointed of the Father."* There is a time appointed in your walk with the Lord when the

Father will be formally introduced in your life. God wants you to grow and mature from babyhood and childhood to become a Son with Him! This is because as Jesus said in verse 27, *"For the Father himself loveth you..."* The Father Himself wants this but you first have to come through the door of the Lord Jesus Christ. Jesus is the access point to the Father. He is the door hinging you into a relationship with the Father.

When Jesus says, *"For the Father himself loveth you,"* He is saying in other words, *"You will soon be a son in maturity just like I am."* This is the revelation you must grasp, Jesus is not just interested in controlling and monopolizing you as His king. He wants you to become a prince with God. It is His job to prepare you to be a prince with God! And when you become a prince with God you will start doing all the impossible miracles of creation Jesus was able to do in his sonship. You see, a prince with God is also a son of God. This is the realm in which you will not only be able to exercise authority and dominion as a king over principalities and powers and unclean spirits to cast them out and also to heal all manner of sickness and disease. When you become a prince with God you will have power over the five elements, fire, wind, water, earth, time, and space!

When you start breaking into the "Heir of God" realm you start working more directly with the Father. So you see how Jesus starts relinquishing his authority by saying, *"And I say not unto you, that I will pray the Father for you..."* He is revealing to them that now He no longer has to mediate the relationship between you and the Father. Now you can go directly to the Father. Having come into a relationship with Jesus you have come through the door, and now Jesus is pushing you through the doorway into the room to meet with the Father. This is what it means when Paul says, *"God was in Christ reconciling the world to himself."* Jesus at this point reconciles you fully to the Father. The Father Himself begins to develop a relationship with you, *"For the Father himself loveth you!"* Just as God loves Jesus He loves you!

The God Nature in Your DNA

Being a joint heir with Jesus is different from being an heir of God. As a joint heir with Jesus Christ, you are a king under Him. You are one of the many kings under Him in His identity as the King of Kings and Prince of the Kings of the Earth. Jesus disciples, trains, and matures you while you are a king under Him to be a prince under God. For you to be a prince under God is greater than you being a king under Jesus because He is not just a great king, He is the Emperor over all Empires, including the empire Jesus rules over. Jesus teaches you kingship so that you can understand what it takes to be a prince with God. When you become an heir of God, you become a prince with God!

Being a prince with God is a high rank in God's Empire. Jacob became a prince with God after a process of twenty years serving His scheming and deceptive Uncle Laban. You have to learn how to become a prince with God the Father. This is what you need to become to change the world. For some of you, the world is not ready to receive you in this way. You say, *"Hello world, I am coming to you!"* And the world says, *"No, don't come to me."* This is because the Earth does not want to deal with babies, the Earth wants only princes with God. That is the only office the Earth responds to because princes with God are also sons of God.

The Earth does not want to deal with babies. All they respond to are sons. When God made Adam, He made Him a son, a prince with God. Adam was not a baby when he was created. He did not have to grow and become a man. He was a full grown man, a son to God the moment He was created. The Earth does not understand anything else. The Earth and the elements do not respond to babes in Christ or Children of God. All they understand and respond to is sonship. The Earth is groaning and travailing in pain for sons to be birthed again on the Earth.

Ways of Royalty in God's Empire

In an empire, when the son of the emperor goes off into his own kingdom, while he is there in his kingdom he is called a king. But when his father comes to visit the son's kingdom, that son, because he is subject to the father, is no longer called a king, he has to be called a prince. This is a major Kingdom law and part of the divine ways of royalty! This is what it means to be subject to the higher powers. *"Let every soul be subject unto the higher powers. For there is no power but of God: the powers that be are ordained of God"* (Romans 13:1). Do you see this? You may be a king in your own kingdom, but when God comes around you are not a king, you are called a prince. When God leaves, you can then assume your title as a king or an emperor.

Now, this is the point, being a prince with God is higher than being a king with Jesus because as a prince with God you come into imperial power. When you become a prince with God you come into imperial power because you are now dealing with the emperor of all emperors. This is why the soldiers who guarded the Roman emperors were called the imperial guard. They were called the imperial guard because they did not just protect the empire, they protected the emperor. Anytime you are around God, you are around imperial power! So, when you become an heir of God, you walk in imperial power. That is why it is important for you to learn who you are as a king so that you can understand how great the imperial power is. This is what will give you the confidence to walk in and manifest imperial power. You got to have confidence to do what God called you to do. The confidence comes from growing in maturity and knowing who you are.

The Sonship Realm and the God Office

You are called to become a son. This call includes women too. As a woman, although you are a daughter in this realm, in the spirit realm you are called to be a son. The Bible says, *"… there is neither male nor female: for ye are all one in Christ Jesus"* (Galatians 3:28). God is not a woman, He is a male figure, that is why the Bible speaks of Him in masculine terms. The son is not just a person, but an office and both men and women are called to the office of a son. The Earth is waiting for sons to come and command it again. The Bible says,

"For the earnest expectation of the creature waiteth for the manifestation of the sons of God" (Romans 8:19).

The Earth wants sons! You must not stop at being a babe with Christ, or a child of God, you must mature into full sonship with God. The moment you got saved, Jesus gave you the power to become a son of God. Jesus has to give you this power. This power to become a son of God is initiated when you receive Jesus. After you receive Jesus, the power begins to work in you over a period of time until the time appointed of the Father when you are formally inaugurated into full sonship. you must now begin to discern where you are. Are you a baby? Are you a child? Are you a son yet? You must answer these questions.

When Jesus came into full sonship, God acknowledged Him as a son! His sonship was openly validated by the Father Himself. This happened when Jesus came out of the water after being baptized by John the Baptist. As the Bible says, *"And lo a voice from heaven, saying, **This is my beloved Son,** in whom I am well pleased"* (Matthew 3:16-17). He called Jesus His Son. The Father confirmed this on the Mount of Transfiguration when He said, *"... **This is my beloved Son,** in whom I am well pleased; hear ye him"* (Matthew 17:5).

God did not call Jesus a prophet or an apostle, even though He walked in those offices. God called Jesus His son. Adam was not called an apostle or a prophet because there was no need for the church in the beginning. He was called a son. The Bible says, *"... which was the son of Adam, **which was the son of God"*** (Luke 3:38). Adam was a son with God. A son is the highest office that you could ever have with God in these realms. The Earth and the elements could respond to and obey Adam because He was a son. The Earth, the trees, the animals and the plants do not listen to babes or to children, they only respond to the office of sonship because that is what God told the Earth to submit to.

Now, here is the conclusion of the matter. When you come into true sonship, the Earth will obey you! As a babe in Christ, you can try to get the Earth to obey you and nothing will really happen. Now because you are in Christ Jesus, even though you are a baby, some things may happen here and there, on and off but until you become a son you cannot get the Earth to obey you consistently. Until you become a son, you do not have the full reign over the Earth. You do not have the full power to subdue the Earth until you mature into sonship. The Earth only understands the office that God subjected it to in the beginning.

That is why God said at the beginning, *"And God said, Let us make man in our image, after our likeness: **and let them have dominion ... over all the earth"*** (Genesis 1:26). The office of sonship is the only thing that commands the Earth. So being a king with Jesus is still not sonship. In this book, I have taught you the kingly and imperial anointing. You are a king with imperial anointing. The next stage in your kingship is that you got to become a prince with God. Being a king with Jesus gives you the power to become that. Sons of God are princes with God, but they are emperors in this world! That is what I need you to understand.

A prince with God is really an emperor in this world! The world or the Earth is looking for emperors, not kings! They are looking for heirs of God not just joint heirs with Christ. Being a joint-heir with Christ empowers you to deal with certain things such as casting out devils, healing the sick, raising the dead, binding and breaking principalities and powers. But the Earth needs not just joint-heirs with Christ but heirs of God who are sons of God. This is why God was in Christ reconciling you to Himself! Your growth process does not end at the realm of Christ. You are to follow on to know the Lord God Himself, the Father.

Sonship Powers

When you become a son with God, God gives you power over the Earth. This is what the Earth is waiting for! The manifestation of sons of God! Your original domain was to have dominion over the Earth and to rule it! *"And God said, Let us make man in our image, after our likeness: **and let them have dominion ... over all the earth..."*** (Genesis 1:26). The original assignment of a son of God is to have dominion over the Earth itself and everything that pertains to it, including the heavenly bodies that affect the Earth and the elements, wind, fire, water, earth, time, and space.

"Thou madest him to have dominion over the works of thy hands; thou hast put all things under his feet" (Psalm 8:6).

God placed under man's dominion everything he created, the sun, moon, stars, and the Earth! You have therefore been called to have dominion over the five elements of the Earth. Because you are a spiritual king you have power from another world to rule this one. This power is fully activated when you complete the process of sonship. This happens after you complete your training as a king under Jesus and then become an heir of God, a prince having power with God, a son of God!

In this last hour, God is on Earth working with us to have the ability to command fire, wind, water, land, or earth, time and space. *"... And concerning the work of my hands command ye me"* (Isaiah 45:11). As a son, you are to do what God did at the beginning. In the sonship book, I will share with you what the Father Himself taught me, face to face, about exercising dominion and mastery over the elements, as a son of God. After twenty years of walking with my great friend and Lord, Jesus Christ, the Father began coming to me and working directly with me. The Father proclaimed His name over me and formally inaugurated me into the sonship Office.

The Father came to me face to face in a dream and began teaching me more about the sonship office and what powers are inherent in that realm. He taught me how that when you become a full mature son with

Him, you will have power over the elements and over the Earth! You will be able to command the elements and they will obey you! Until you become a full mature son of God you are subject to the elements, but when you become a full son the elements will be subject to you! The son has great power with the Father! You are called to come into that realm!

That is the next dimension! You are to be a son of God! You are to manifest the image and likeness of God as a little god! That is the next frontier!

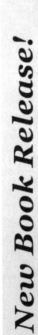

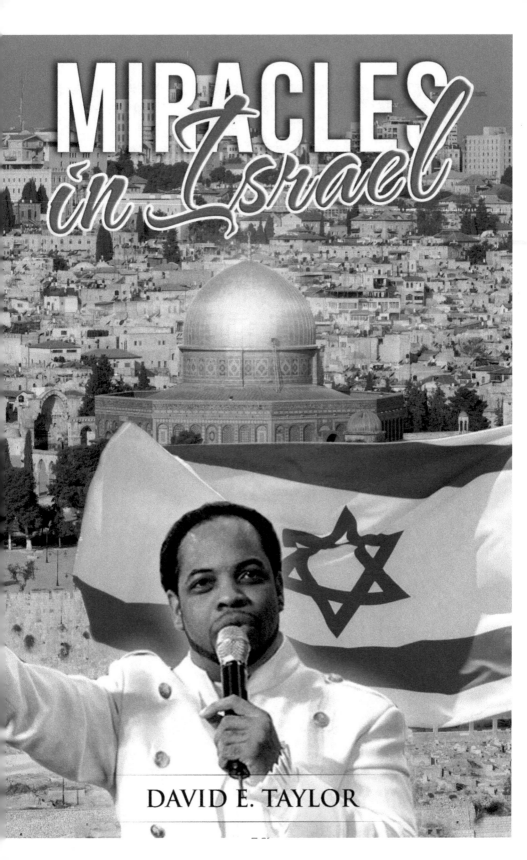

MIRACLES
in Israel

DAVID E. TAYLOR

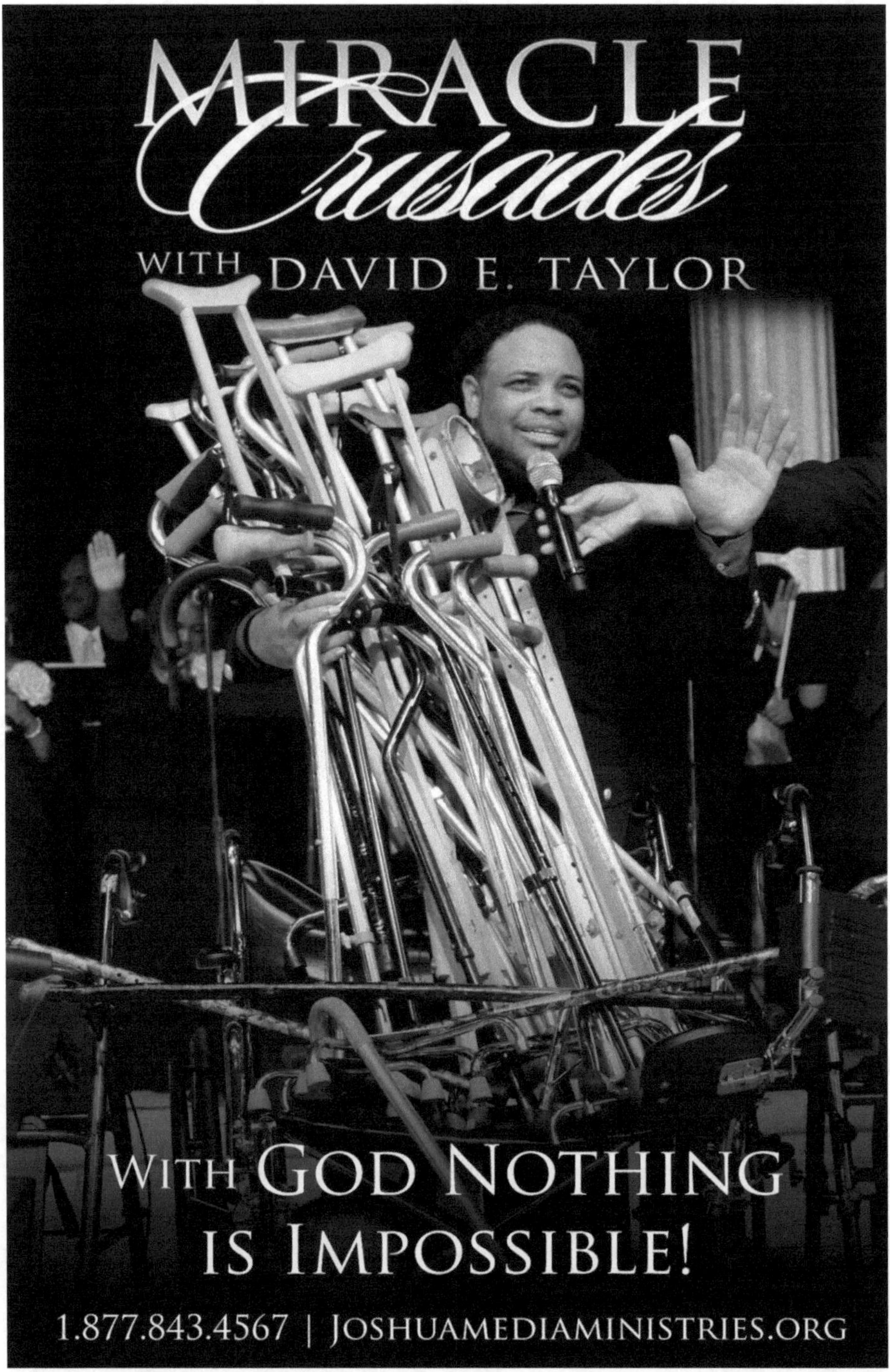
MIRACLE
Crusades
WITH DAVID E. TAYLOR
WITH GOD NOTHING
IS IMPOSSIBLE!
1.877.843.4567 | JOSHUAMEDIAMINISTRIES.ORG

For more information about David E. Taylor, or to contact the author for speaking engagements, and for additional copies of this book and other book titles, as well as a complete list of all products, visit:
www.joshuamediaministries.org
or call 1-877-The-Glory

Send your requests to:
Joshua Media Ministries International
PO BOX 1270.
Florissant, MO 63031

"The Kingdom of God is the Message, Face to Face is the Move!"